Concerning Communication

Epic Quests and Lyric Excursions
Within the Human Lifeworld

Lance Strate

INSTITUTE OF GENERAL SEMANTICS

Published by the Institute of General Semantics
72-11 Austin Street, #233
Forest Hills, New York, 11375
www.generalsemantics.org

Interior Book Design by Scribe Freelance
www.scribefreelance.com

Cover art by Thomas O'Meara

Published in the United States of America
ISBN: 978-1-970164-20-6 (Print)
978-1-970164-21-3 (eBook)

Library of Congress Cataloging-in-Publication Data

Names: Strate, Lance, author.
Title: Concerning communication : epic quests and lyric excursions within the human lifeworld / Lance Strate.
Description: Forest Hills, New York : Institute of General Semantics, [2022] | Includes bibliographical references and index. | Summary: "Concerning Communication: Epic Quests and Lyrical Excursions Within the Human Lifeworld is a collection of essays that range across a variety of topics, including models of communication, language and symbolic communication, sense perception, the self, disability and autism, listening, reading, science, media literacy, ethics, innovation, systems theory, information, communication history, isolation, solipsism, technology, education, media ecology, and general semantics. Lance Strate's unifying theme throughout this volume is the centrality of communication, as a phenomenon, to human life, and the importance of communication, as a field of study, to understanding ourselves and our place in the universe"-- Provided by publisher.
Identifiers: LCCN 2022037059 (print) | LCCN 2022037060 (ebook) | ISBN 9781970164206 (paperback) | ISBN 9781970164213 (ebook)
Subjects: LCSH: Communication. | LCGFT: Essays.
Classification: LCC P91.25 .S87 2022 (print) | LCC P91.25 (ebook) | DDC 302.2--dc23/eng/20220808
LC record available at https://lccn.loc.gov/2022037059
LC ebook record available at https://lccn.loc.gov/2022037060

BOOKS in the IGS Book Series
New Non-Aristotelian Library

Korzybski, Alfred (2010). *Selections from Science and Sanity.* (2nd Ed.). Edited by Lance Strate, with a Foreword by Bruce I. Kodish. Fort Worth, TX: Institute of General Semantics.

Strate, Lance (2011). *On the Binding Biases of Time and Other Essays on General Semantics and Media Ecology.* Fort Worth, TX: Institute of General Semantics.

Anton, Corey (2011). *Communication Uncovered: General Semantics and Media Ecology.* Fort Worth, TX: Institute of General Semantics.

Levinson, Martin H. (2012). *More Sensible Thinking.* New York, NY: Institute of General Semantics.

Anton, Corey & Strate, Lance (2012). *Korzybski and. . .* (Eds.) New York, NY: Institute of General Semantics.

Levinson, Martin H. (2014). *Continuing Education Teaching Guide to General Semantics.* New York, NY: Institute of General Semantics.

Berger, Eva & Berger, Isaac (2014). *The Communication Panacea: Pediatrics and General Semantics.* New York, NY: Institute of General Semantics.

Pace, Wayne R. (2017). *How to Avoid Making A Damn Fool of Yourself: An Introduction to General Semantics.* New York, NY: Institute of General Semantics.

Lahman, Mary P. (2018). *Awareness and Action: A Travel Companion.* New York, NY: Institute of General Semantics.

Levinson, Martin H. (2018). *Practical Fairy Tales For Everyday Living, Revised Second Edition.* New York, NY: Institute of General Semantics.

Levinson, Martin H. (2020). *Sensible Thinking for Turbulent Times: Revised Second Edition.* New York, NY: Institute of General Semantics.

Mayer, Christopher (2021). *How Do You Know?: A Guide to Clear Thinking About Wall Street, Investing, and Life.* New York, NY: Institute of General Semantics.

Levinson, Martin H. (2021). *Practical Fairy Tales For Everyday Living, Revised Second Edition*. New York, NY: Institute of General Semantics. (In Spanish)

Mayer, Christopher (2022). *Dear Fellow Time-Binder*. New York, NY: Institute of General Semantics.

Liñán, Laura T. (2022). *Formal Cause in Marshall McLuhan's Thinking*. New York, NY: Institute of General Semantics.

For Sarah

Table of Contents

Preface

Concerning Communication brings together a set of essays on the theme of communication. That is to say, the essays are concerned with communication as a topic, and they are concerned with the field of communication, or communication studies. Communication is quite naturally a concern for us all, as human beings, insofar as it is a phenomenon and an activity that is central to our species, as social animals. Communication is the basis of all social organization and cultural continuity, the basis of all of our interpersonal relationships, and the basis of that interior landscape that we call the mind. Communication is also, quite literally, commonplace. As a part of everyday life, it is so very ordinary and uneventful, routine and fundamental, that it often escapes our notice, fades from view, is rendered functionally invisible, enveloping us as an invisible environment. Only air, water, and food are of greater necessity to our wellbeing and our very survival, and arguably it is a difference of degree, not kind.

While much of our communication is ignored or forgotten because it is taken for granted, because it is not surprising or unexpected, there are also forms of communication that are, in fact, concerning, or at least ought to concern us. And the essays in this book also relate to aspects of communication that do concern me and perhaps also concern you, that maybe ought to concern all of us, that are concerning in one way or another, that are communication concerns. Along the way, much is said about communication in general, and about general topics in communication, topics that interest as well as concern me. And while the focus in this volume is on communication, the essays are very much informed by general semantics, by systems theory, and by media ecology. For a more comprehensive discussion of the field of media ecology in particular, I would recommend my 2017 book, *Media Ecology: An Approach to Understanding the Human Condition*. That work is not a necessary prerequisite to this one, but if the periodic forays into media ecological territory in this book pique your interest, you may want to turn to that book afterwards for a more structured overview. I also include discussion of media ecology and general semantics in my 2014 book, *Amazing Ourselves to Death: Neil Postman's Brave New World Revisited*, which is very much about concerning developments in 21st century America. In an earlier collection of essays published in 2011, *On the Binding Biases of Time and Other Essays on General Semantics and Media Ecology*, I place special emphasis on general semantics as it relates to both systems theory and media ecology. And a preliminary survey of media ecology can be found in my 2006 book, *Echoes and Reflections: On Media Ecology as a Field of Study*.

While my outlook and interests are fairly consistent across these works, this book places special emphasis on the topic of communication, and for good reason. Keeping in mind the basic general semantics principle of non-identity, I feel obliged to acknowledge that the entirety of my academic and professional identity has been bound up with communication, as a concept, a phenomenon, and a field of study. Back in the 1970s, the most popular major was psychology, and there was a great deal of interest in popular psychology, therapy, and human enlightenment, with much focus on opening the doors of perception, finding yourself, going off in search of your true self, seeking out self-actualization, and the like. Communication was not very well known at that time, unusually interdisciplinary before interdisciplinarity became fashionable, and often involving a strange mix of the practical and the theoretical, the philosophical and the technical. It straddled the border between the humanities and the social sciences, while also extending into the fine arts and the hard sciences, as well as being connected to various forms of professional study. At its worst, as its critics were always ready to point out, it could be extraordinarily superficial. Put downs of that sort go all the way back to Plato. But at its best, which I would argue is how any subject should be evaluated, it is a field that takes all knowledge as its subject matter, that covers the entirety of human behavior and mentation, incorporating it all, all of psychology together with all of sociology and anthropology, with all of the myriad ways of studying the human condition, and our place in the universe. This was the field that grabbed me and held on to me, as an undergraduate. This was what I was looking for, as a graduate student. This was the way that opened up before me, as a researcher and educator. And it was somewhere along the line, sometime after I started teaching and joined the professoriate, that I suddenly discovered that communication had gradually evolved from a bit of an academic backwater into the most popular area of study in the United States. This occurred towards the end of the 20th century, and while it was a development that took me by surprise, it was a development that struck me as entirely understandable. Communication offers clear pathways to careers in the media industries and elsewhere, is eminently useful and practical in any line of work, and at the same time is endlessly fascinating in its emphasis on studying the human condition.

My professional identity, then, is that of a communication scholar, communication researcher, and communication teacher. Having been educated at a time when social science approaches were dominant, I would identify myself as a communication theorist (although I lean towards the philosophical, somehow "communication philosopher" sounds a bit pretentious to me). My formal title, based on the name of my department at Fordham University, is Professor of Communication and Media Studies. And I would note that while I have no objection to the phrase *communication studies*, I find it unnecessary. For decades, *communication* alone was sufficient, along with references to the *field of communication*. It is what I am used to, I suppose, but I do prefer the simplicity of simply calling it, *communication*. It is no different than *history*, *English*, *education*, etc., fields where the same term is used to denote the study and the object of study.

My identity is not confined to communication, however. I am also identified as a general semanticist, a systems thinker, and a media ecologist. Each of these is closely allied with communication, and most certainly with my approach to communication scholarship and pedagogy. I was introduced to general semantics, systems theory, and media ecology in my communication classes as an undergraduate. And this had much to do with my decision to pursue graduate education in communication, leading to a career as a communication professor. As a field, communication easily incorporates general semantics, systems theory, and media ecology. All three fit quite comfortably within communication research and theory, philosophy and pedagogy. All three deepen our understanding of communication in numerous ways. But all three have their own independent existence apart from communication, each one a field, discipline, or approach of its own, not a subset of communication, but one that overlaps with communication in significant ways. But I do believe that communication is at its best when it is informed by all three. And this is reflected in essays collected in this volume. Their origins span several decades worth of work within the field. Some were written relatively early in my career, some more recently. All have undergone a process of revision and updating for inclusion in this collection. Given their separate origins as standalone pieces, there is some overlap among them. Not too much, I believe, but a little bit. I would like to think of it as enrichment, and note that according to information theory, redundancy is needed to avoid the noise that inevitably interferes with communication.

The book's Introduction, "Defining and Modeling Communication," offers some discussion of the process of defining terms and creating models, along with presenting my own definition of communication, and the model of communication I first introduced in *Media Ecology: An Approach to Understanding the Human Condition* (Strate, 2017). Here I provide a new breakdown of the model's components.

The first chapter, "Something from Nothing," has a long history. It began as a keynote address that I delivered, in conjunction with receiving the John F. Wilson Fellow Award, at the 57th annual meeting of the New York State Communication Association in 1999, entitled "Narcissism and Echolalia: Sense and the Struggle for the Self". A further developed version was then published under the same title in NYSCA's *Speech Communication Annual* in 2000, while a shorter version was published under the title, "Something from Nothing," in *ETC: A Review of General Semantics* in 2003 (and subsequently reprinted in several readers). A further revision was incorporated into Part 2 of my book, *Echoes and Reflections* (2006). Some of the discussion from the essay was modified and updated for an article entitled, "The Enigma of Autism," published in *Samyukta: A Journal of Women's Studies* published in 2015 (but cover dated 2011). For this volume, I have significantly expanded the first part of the piece, which is on the subject of communication in general, revising the discussion to provide fuller and more precise explanations of my perspective and approach. The second part, which deals with the concept of self, disability, and autism, has also been revised and updated.

The second chapter, "Sounding Off About Listening," is a revised version of an article entitled, "'I Hear You!' Comments on the Sound Practice of Listening," which was originally published in the Global Listening Centre's online journal, *The Listening Connection*, in 2019, reprinted in *ETC* in 2021. The revised essay also incorporates commentary I provided for the September 2021 issue of the Global Listening Centre's newsletter, the *Global Listener*. The next chapter, "The New Grammarians," with its emphasis on the trivium and its relationship to modern science, as well as the evolution of the concept of grammar, was first published in a special issue (on General Semantics and Media Ecology) of *Anekaant: A Journal of Polysemic Thought* in 2021 (cover dated 2020-2021) and subsequently reprinted in *ETC* later that same year (cover dated 2020).

The fourth chapter, "Media Literacy and General Semantics," is a revised version of an article entitled, "Media Literacy as an Ethical Obligation: A General Semantics Approach," published in *ETC* in 2014. The piece is a modified excerpt of a research report I co-authored with Lewis Freeman, Peter Gutierrez, and Jennifer Lavalle, entitled *The Future of Children's Television Programming: A Study of How Emerging Digital Technologies Can Facilitate Active and Engaged Participation and Contribute to Media Literacy Education*, made possible by a grant from Time Warner Cable Research Program on Digital Communications, and released in 2011. The concern with ethics in that chapter continues into the next one, "Communication and Innovation," with a broader concern towards the consequences of innovations in communication technology, and technology in general. An earlier version of the piece appeared in *ETC* in 2020 under the title, "The Ethics of Innovation".

The sixth chapter, "Communication and Social Systems," emphasizes systems theory as it applies to communication, media, and society. The essay is revised from a book chapter entitled, "Illuminations of Luhmann," originally published in *Nachtflug der Eule: 150 Stimmen zum Werk von Niklas Luhmann*, a festschrift for the sociologist, Niklas Luhmann. The next essay, "Information in the Context of Communication and Mediation," is a substantially reworked version of an article that was published in a special issue (on Information: Its Different Modes and Its Relation to Meaning) of the journal *Information* in 2012, under the title, "Counting Electric Sheep: Understanding Information in the Context of Media Ecology".

The eighth chapter, "Communication and Isolation," is based on a series of three papers that I delivered at New York State Communication Association conferences, published in *New Dimensions in Communications: Proceedings of the Annual New York State Speech Communication Association Convention* in 1991, 1992, and 1994, and entitled, respectively, "Communication and Solipsism: Subjectivity, Self-Reflexiveness, and Media Solipsism," "The Culture of Solipsism," and "Hyperreality and Cultural Solipsism". The pieces were revised and merged into one unified essay, and the original idea for investigating communication and isolation emerged out of a conversation between myself, Thom Gencarelli, and Casey Man Kong Lum. The ninth chapter, "Human Communication and Human Technology," has never been published before. It is based on a keynote address I delivered at the Annual Meeting of the Rocky Mountain Communication Association in 2002, entitled "Human Communication and Human Technology: Coming of Age in the Twenty-First Century". It has been revised and updated in light of the subsequent two decades. Finally, and with the intent of ending on a positive, hopeful note, I include as the last chapter the text of an address presented at the 2016 induction ceremony for Fordham University's chapter of Lambda Pi Eta, the honorary society for communication majors, later published in *ETC* in 2021.

The chapters that make up this book vary in length, which is why I have invoked the twin metaphors of *epic quests* and *lyric excursions* for the subtitle. That they occur *within the human lifeworld* speaks to the universality of human communication, and the universality of its concerns.

All of the thoughts and writings that make up this book owe a profound debt to many more individuals than I can hope to name. But I will proceed to name names, knowing that I can never name them all. First, I would like to acknowledge the educator who inspired me in my first semester of college at Cornell University, when I took, somewhat randomly, an elective called Introduction to Communication Theory: Jack Barwind. The course covered so much of what continues to interest me about the field, and introduced me to general semantics, to systems theory, and to media ecologists such as Marshall McLuhan, Harold Innis, and Jacques Ellul. When my decision to major in biology and go on to medical school turned out to be a mistake, I instead majored in Communication Arts, and that decision made all the difference. I also want to mention my undergraduate advisor, Njoku Awa, who also had a lasting influence on me. I continued my studies in the MA program at Queens College of the City University of New York, studying with and working under Gary Gumpert, who I consider one of my mentors, and also learning from Robert Cathcart, Dan Hahn, Parke Burgess, John C. Pollock, and Peter Dahlgren. It was there that I also met two New York University doctoral students who changed my life, Joshua Meyrowitz and Ed Wachtel. They convinced me to go for my PhD in NYU's Media Ecology Program, where I studied with Joy Boyum, Henry Perkinson, and Terence P. Moran, and two scholars who became extremely important to me as mentors, Neil Postman and Christine Nystrom.

I eventually joined Ed Wachtel as a faculty member at Fordham University, and was also fortunate to work with George Gordon, John Phelan, and Susan B. Barnes for a time. I am privileged to still be working together with Paul Levinson, Lewis Freeman, and so many other outstanding scholars and educators, Amy Aronson, Jessica Baldwin-Philippi, Heidi Bordogna, Hopeton Campbell, Jennifer Clarke, Gregory Donovan, Arthur Hayes, Matthew Hockenberry, James Jennewein, Ron Jacobson, Diana Kamin, Katherine Katsafouros, Mathias Klang, Beth Knobel, Brandy Monk-Payton, Jennifer Moormon, Sharif Mowlabocus, Michele Prettyman, Margaret Schwartz, Ralph Vacca, Kara Van Cleaf, Chris Vicari, Tim Wood, and Qun Wang; thank you too to Michelle O'Dwyer, Marie Trombetta, and Claudia Rivera. I also owe a debt of gratitude to the many undergraduate and graduate students that I have taught over the years, at Fordham and elsewhere.

This book is published by the Institute of General Semantics, and I would like to acknowledge the editor of the book series, Corey Anton, as well as the other IGS colleagues who have contributed to my thoughts and actions, including Eva Berger, Thom Gencarelli, Mike Plugh, Marty Levinson, Jackie Rudig, Dom Heffer, Susan Drucker, Laura Trujillo Liñan, and Nora Bateson, as well as, in the context of the New York Society for General Semantics, Terry Manzella and TC McLuhan. And I want to thank my many friends in the Media Ecology Association, including Paul Soukup, Douglas Rushkoff, Adriana Braga, Robert Albrecht, Jim Morrison, Phil Rose, Karen Lollar, Fernando Gutiérrez, Peggy Cassidy, Jaqueline McLeod Rogers, Julia Hildebrand, Jeff Bogaczyk, Matt Thomas, Bernadette Bowen, Ed Tywoniak, Paolo Granata, Elena Lamberti, Catherine Adams, Ellen Rose, Stephanie Gibson, Mary Ann Allison, Stephanie Bennett, Casey Lum, Ray Gozzi, and so many others. Additionally, I am grateful to Deborah Borisoff, Paul Lippert, Marty Friedman, Perti Hurme, Susan Maushart, Carol Wiebe, Julianne Newton, Bini B.S., Peter Fallon, Brian

Cogan, Heather Crandall, Yong Li, Susan Jasko, and Dale Winslow. And I have benefited from interaction with a great many other scholars and intellectuals, among them Walter Ong, Daniel Boorstin, James W. Carey, Camille Paglia, Frank Dance, Dennis Gallagher, Eric McLuhan, Elizabeth Eisenstein, Denise Schmandt-Besserat, Alan Kay, and David R. Olson.

I think it important to also acknowledge the importance of my spiritual home, Congregation Adas Emuno, to Rabbi Barry Schwartz, and to Cantor Iris Karlin, whose voice buoyed me up as I worked on this collection.

A very special thank you goes to graphic artist Lauren Rowland for making my model of communication a reality, and for recreating the Shannon-Weaver Model for this volume. And I am much obliged to Joshua Clements for his reading and suggestions of the manuscript. Moreover, I must acknowledge Daniel Middleton/Scribe Freelance for the skill and care that went into the design and layout of the interior and cover of this book.

I am deeply grateful to Thomas O'Meara for the donation of the art that graces the cover of this book, and to his mother, Patti O'Meara.

Finally, I want to express my gratitude to my family, especially to my wife Barbara for her patience and understanding, also to my son Benjamin, who has the creativity to make something from nothing, and to my daughter Sarah, to whom I dedicate this book, also acknowledging everyone who has helped her along her path, including the EPIC School, New Bridges High School, and Quest Autism Program.

Introduction
Defining and Modeling Communication

What *is* communication? The question itself is suspect, for as Alfred Korzybski (1933/1993) insists, *whatever we say it is, it is not.* Perhaps then the better question would be, what *is not* communication? And while I find it tempting to say that everything is communication, at least potentially, I would start by saying that communication is not a *thing*. It is not an artifact, not an object, not something tangible or material. While the word takes the form of a noun, it is best understood as a verb. Communication is something we do, not something we have. It is something that happens. Indeed, everything in the universe can be understood as events in spacetime, and communication in particular is the kind of phenomenon that is neither animal, vegetable, or mineral, neither person, place, or thing, but rather best understood as a process.

We refer to communication as *act*, an *act*ivity, a form of *act*ion (for human beings, often symbolic action). Two-way communication involves inter*act*ion, and in establishing a relationship, turns into a trans*act*ion (transactional, in this instance, not connoting a *quid pro quo* exchange, but rather a mutual confirmation of personhood). The root term underlying *communication* is *common*. To communicate is to *make things common*, to share messages and meanings, and thereby establish, maintain, enhance, and enlarge our *common ground*. This all seems very simple and straightforward, but that impression masks some very complex questions. For example, given that dialogue is often seen as the archetype of communication, is it still communication if the communicators fail to reach an agreement? If they fail to reach an understanding, or misunderstand each other? If the meanings are not shared? If the message is not decoded, for example if the communicators do not speak the same language? If one of them is sending a message but the other is unaware of it? What if someone sends a message to someone who is not present? What if someone sends a message but it is never received by its intended recipient? What if it is never received by any-one at all? What if it is a message sent not to anyone in particular, but to anyone who might receive it? To a large group or mass audience? What about when we interact with animals? With computer programs and games? Is prayer a form of communication? What if the person sends a message without realizing it, for example via nonverbal cues? What if a person is silent? Inactive? Is any form of behavior, anything we do or do not do, a form of communication?

We tend to privilege the sender's role in thinking about communication, but what about the receiver? Is it communication if someone takes in information that the sender did not intend to transmit, say by picking up on nonverbal cues? Is it communication when someone receives a message sent for someone else? Is it communication when someone is reading, listening to a recording, watching television or a video, scanning the posts on social media, etc.? Is it communication when someone interprets information about the physical environment, as scientists do? What about when we simply listen to our surroundings? When someone hears voices coming from God or a spirit of supernatural entity? When someone hears voices that are not really there? Is it communication whenever we are making meaning out of our world? Dialogue being the ideal, and allowing for two or more participants, is it communication when we are alone? When we talk to ourselves, when we write ourselves a note, when we think?

I invoke these very basic questions not to suggest that there are *definitive* answers to each one, but rather that there can only be *definitional* answers, answers that will vary depending on how *communication* is defined. Does the definition in use require purpose, intentionality, or are we only concerned with communication as a function, or as an effect? Does the definition in use distinguish between communication and information, or between communication and expression? Does the definition in use require face-to-face copresence, or place a limit on the number of participants, or limit the manner in which messages are conveyed? What all such definitions have in common is the fact that communication is an abstraction (as are most terms, but in this context, communication is the focus), and therefore a category. The question then is what is included in the category and what is excluded, which is to say, what are the criteria being used to determine what is included and excluded. Definitions then are ways of expressing the criteria needed to make such determinations. And rather than saying what, in my opinion, should and should not be included, my concern is with what could and could not be included. In regard to the various questions that I have posed, my answer would be yes. Yes, these instances can be considered communication. I would include them in my category of communication, and many others as well. My criteria are, relatively speaking, open and inclusive. And while my original intent was to resist the temptation to put forth a definition of communication, knowing how easy it is for definitions, however tentative and operational they may be, to become reified and petrified, I will overcome my hesitation. For the sake of readers who require a definition for whatever reason, here is mine: *For the purposes of this introduction to this book, I am defining communication as a category of actions and events that include all forms of meaning-making, message reception, and information transmission, as they occur within a given context, situation, environment, or medium.*

Whether or not you agree with or are satisfied with my definition, what it shares with all other definitions is that it defines a word with other words, and an abstract concept by reference to other abstract concepts. We find ourselves inside of the closed system of language, specifically the English language, more specifically, the English language as it is spoken and written in the United States in the early 21st century. Of course, we are never entirely trapped inside the system, not so long as we have our eyes, ears, and other sensory organs. And as long as we have recourse to forms of representation other than words. Such as images. Communication scholars understand this quite well, and perhaps it is for this reason that we have a longstanding tradition of producing visual models of the communication process. Whether or not visual thinkers have dominated the field, or are overrepresented, I cannot say, but it does seem that communication scholars have felt that written definitions alone are somehow not sufficient to capture the complexity of this basic human activity. Admittedly, the concept of communication is somewhat abstract, and a visual image provides a more concrete way to represent the process by which we communicate. But concepts such as society, history, and art are also quite abstract, maybe even more so, and model making does not occupy the same position in those areas of study and teaching. Moreover, scholars rooted in the ancient discipline of rhetoric, and the allied area of speech, never felt an overwhelming need to produce diagrams of speech acts and rhetor-audience relationships, and the same is true for those studying theatre, elocution and oral performance, or other forms of poetics, philology, and literature. This also applies to the study of journalism, and to mass communication research in its formative years. Not that the impulse was entirely absent, but never so central as it became after the mid-20th century. Arguably, visualization took hold in communication pedagogy and scholarship beginning with the publication of Claude Shannon and Warren Weaver's book, *The Mathematical Theory of Communication*, in 1949, which introduces the Shannon-Weaver Model:

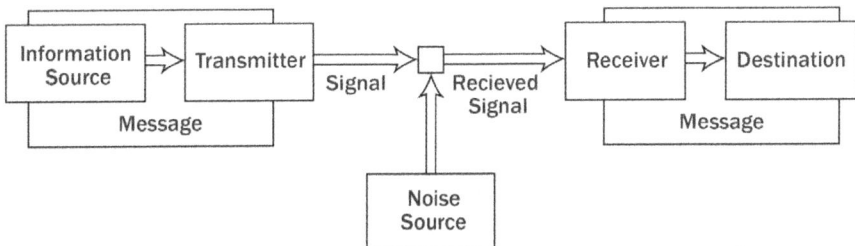

Figure 1 The Shannon-Weaver Model of Communication

Elizabeth Eisenstein (1979) provides extensive evidence and explanation of the decisive role that the printing press with movable type played in the introduction of modern science in early modern Europe. The ability to produce *exactly repeatable pictorial images*, which includes the production of text, numbers, and mathematical tables, as well as diagrams and illustrations, was one of several major characteristics of print technology that contributed to the scientific revolutions of the past six centuries. It is therefore not surprising that Alfred Korzybski (1950, 1993), in devising general semantics as a means of applying empirical methodology to everyday life, and seeking to overcome the ambiguous and potentially misleading qualities of words and language, promoted the use of mathematics for its precision, and images for their concreteness. He introduced his own model back in 1933, known as the *structural differential*, to depict how we relate to and evaluate our environment through the process of abstracting.

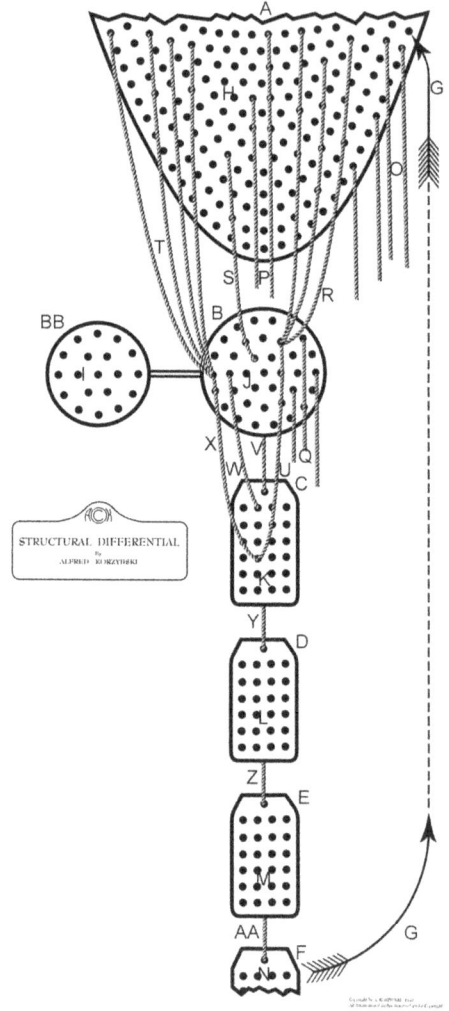

Figure 2 The Structural Differential

In this model,

- the broken parabola represents our external environment, consisting of events in spacetime, of which our knowledge is necessarily limited;
- the strings coming down from the event level represent the process of perception, indicating that we only perceive part of what we are exposed to, as we take information in from our environment;
- the circle represents the object level, as through the process of perception we impose order on the dynamic nature of our environment, and turn events into the stable and predictable objects, the percepts of our familiar reality;
- the next set of strings represent abstracting based on language and

symbol use, as our words and signs only represent part of what we are able to perceive;

- the first tag represents the most concrete level of language use, the naming of individual phenomena and specific descriptions of events and objects;
- the next set of tags represents movement to increasingly higher orders of abstraction through the creation of categories that can be more and more general, and the making of inferences based on our descriptions, leading to other leaps of reasoning and forms of subjective and emotional evaluation;
- the diagram also includes feedback from our abstracting back to the environment, as we act upon and modify our surroundings;
- while the circle on the side represents animal cognition, animals lacking in linguistic ability and symbol use, hence no link downwards, and being unaware that there is more to reality than what they perceive, hence no link upwards to the broken parabola.

While the structural differential influenced many communication scholars during the 1950s, 60s, and 70s, it technically does not qualify as a model of communication. Also, Korzybski's model originally was a three-dimensional object, and he argued that a tactile tracing of its contours would aid in understanding the process. This is in contrast to the purely diagrammatic models used to depict the process of communication.

Purely visual diagrams existed before the printing revolution that began in the mid-15th century, but they were difficult to copy accurately by hand. Walter Ong (1958, 2002) provides the cultural history of the educational revolution initiated by Peter Ramus in the 16th century, which was diagrammatic in nature, as it shifted intellectual discourse away from dialogue and debate, and towards the visual display of knowledge (e.g., outlines, diagrams, and textbooks). Ramist method utilizes a two-valued orientation in which any subject is divided in two, each of the divisions is in turn divided in two, and so on. For example, beginning with science, we can divide the topic into physical and life sciences, divide the physical sciences into physics and chemistry, etc. This method easily lends itself to diagrammatic display, and because it involves a binary approach, has been seen as a forerunner of computer technology, specifically the binary code developed by Shannon. Of course, the technology that formed the basis of Ramism was the mechanical one of the printing press, which included the invention of typography associated with Gutenberg, and also the almost simultaneous invention of engraving, a technology that greatly enhanced our ability to reproduce images.

In considering the origins of the Shannon-Weaver Model and its descendants, we also need to take into account a more recent development: electricity. As one of the many achievements of modern science, electric technology came into its own in the 19th century, and especially given the complexities of wiring (which we still experience today in the tangle of wires that power or charge our devices), electrical diagrams proved to be a useful tool in mapping out the flow of current and the connections among circuits. At the same time, the explosion of mechanical innovation that accompanied the industrial revolution in the 19th century encouraged the creation of all manner of technical diagrams. This culminates in the introduction of the flowchart (note the correspondence here with *flow* as a liquid metaphor for electric power) in the early 20th century as a technique used in engineering (and interestingly coinciding with the development of general semantics by Korzybski, who was trained as an engineer); the flowchart was quickly adopted as a technique by businesses and organization, as an accessory to scientific management.

These developments form the basis of the Shannon-Weaver Model, which is a technical diagram depicting the flow of electronic communications. The information source is the microphone, for example, which picks up the message in the form of sound, the encoder turns it into electronic impulses, the transmitter sends the message in the form of a signal over a channel such as electrical wires or wireless electromagnetic frequencies (overcoming the inevitable signal degradation due to entropy and the interference referred to as noise), the signal is then decoded, turning the electronic impulses back into sound, allowing the message to be played through a speaker or receiver, the message's destination. Claude Shannon's information theory is foundational for the development of the digital computer and binary coding, while computer technology itself was developed by electrical engineers; it is no accident, therefore, that soon after the introduction of computer science, programmers used flowchart diagrams to model their algorithms. Similar models were also used to depict decision-making processes used by human beings in all manner of contexts, a further extension of the flow chart.

The nascent field of communication in the mid 20th century had another connection to electronics that reinforced its connection to Shannon's work on information theory and signal transmission. Broadcasting at that time was almost entirely about radio (early commercial television was known as radio-television, and described as radio with pictures). And radio was seen as an extension of speech and theatre, and as a kind of public address system writ large, so that courses on radio and broadcasting were commonly housed in communication departments.

What I want to emphasize here is that, outside of scientific and technological work, the adoption of visual models to depict a given topic or subject matter is not inevitable, and that there are historical factors at work that led to a model of communication playing a prominent role just as the field itself was taking shape. The problem that soon became apparent, however, is that the Shannon-Weaver Model depicts a technological process, depicts the medium of communication in other words, and does not represent the human beings involved in any act of communication. It is therefore inadequate in a great many ways, and rather than concluding that models are best left to the engineers, communication theorists set about devising new models. Of course, each new model had its own inadequacies, leading to the creation of more models. Introductory communication textbooks came to include a section that displayed a variety of different models. Ultimately, though, every model that anyone comes up with will prove to be inadequate to a greater or lesser degree (including my own).

The saying associated with Korzybski (1993) that is often invoked within general semantics, the *map is not the territory* (p. 58), can be applied to models as well. The similar sentiment is expressed as, *the word is not the thing*, and more generally that the representation is not whatever is being represented. Models are the product of a process of abstracting, which means that they will leave out details regarding whatever they represent. Indeed, it is typically the case that the more detailed and complex a model is made to be, the less useful it is, certainly the less comprehensible; in the case of maps, details that go beyond what we need to know to get to our destination are unnecessary, can be distracting, and at a certain point become dysfunctional by making the map hard to read. That is why models will inevitably oversimplify what they depict; what matters is how useful they may be in helping us to understand a phenomenon, study it, or work with it. A further point about abstracting is that decisions have to be made about what details to include and what to leave out, and there always will be alternative choices that could have been made. In this sense, models have an element of subjectivity to them, which is not to say that they are entirely arbitrary, but rather that choices are made based on preferences, positions and perspectives, and utility.

When it comes to diagrammatic depictions of the process of communication, despite all of the differences among them, all of the ones I have encountered have one thing in common: the presence of lines, sometimes in the form of arrows, but always lines indicating some sort of transfer or flow. Even when other details are added (e.g., shapes representing culture, society, etc.), communication always seems to be depicted in a linear fashion, usually involving straight lines, occasionally alternatives such as the spiral model favored by Frank Dance (1982), but always by lines. Linearity is a bias associated with western cultures

(Lee, 1959), and attributed to the invention of writing (Carpenter, 1960, 1973; McLuhan, 1962, 1964; Schmandt-Besserat, 1978, 1992, 1996). Insofar as western cultures are not typical of human cultures, and writing is a relatively recent development in the history of our species on this planet, a model of communication that does not involve linearity would serve as a useful corrective.

Linearity is also associated with vision. We see lines, often as a function of gestalt perception (for example, we connect the dots and see a line where there is none: ....); by way of contrast, we can hear sequences over time, each segment taking the place of the previous one, but we cannot hear the sequence in its entirety all at once, meaning we cannot listen to the equivalent of a visual line. Tony Schwartz (1974) suggests replacing the typical transportation metaphor for communication, wherein a sender delivers a message to a receiver, to one based on resonance, a rare use of an acoustic rather than a visual metaphor for communication, thought, and learning. His analogy is that of tuning forks made to resonate on the same frequency: strike one, and the sound radiating out as vibrations through the air causes the other to resonate sympathetically. The image this invokes is of circular and spherical ripple effects, which applies to broadcasting, wireless transmission, and even the electromagnetic radiation that surrounds electrical wires.

The circular image also is used in systems theory to depict the boundary that separates the system from its environment; the boundary also holds together the system's parts. And this leads me to media ecology, the study of media as environments (Postman, 1968, 1970; Strate, 2017). In the Shannon-Weaver Model, the medium is not just what is identified as the narrow, linear *channel*; the medium is the model in its entirety, representing the entire mechanism or apparatus. And in media ecology, a medium is not just a form of transmission or connection, it is the entire context or situation or environment in which communication occurs. A message is not some abstract thing that exists independently of a medium, we do not first compose a message and only then decide what medium we should use to communicate it. Rather, the medium comes first, forming the basis of communication, be it language or speech or the body itself; we create messages out of whatever medium we have available to us, and then we may use that same medium or a different one to share our messages with others. This, in part, is what Marshall McLuhan (1964) meant by his famous dictum, "the medium is the message" (p. 7). I have discussed this in greater detail in my 2017 book, *Media Ecology: An Approach to Understanding the Human Condition*. In that book, I introduced a new model of communication, a nonlinear model based on resonance, the systems view, and the idea of formal causality (McLuhan & McLuhan, 2011). Here it is:

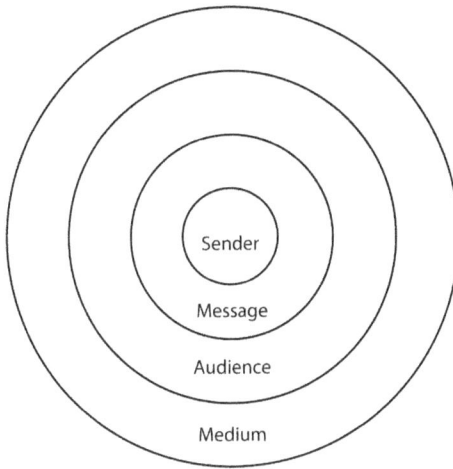

Figure 3 My Model of Communication

At first glance, the model might appear to be fairly conventional, apart from its nonlinear design. We have the four basic elements found in most communication models, The Sender (or Source), the Message, the Audience (or Receiver), and the Medium (or Channel). And the process seems to proceed in the usual manner, beginning with the Sender:

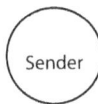

Figure 4 The Sender

The Sender initiates communication by composing and transmitting a Message:

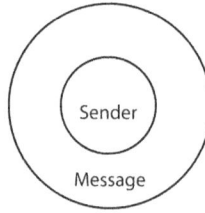

Figure 5 The Sender and the Message

The Message is sent to the Audience, who interprets its meaning:

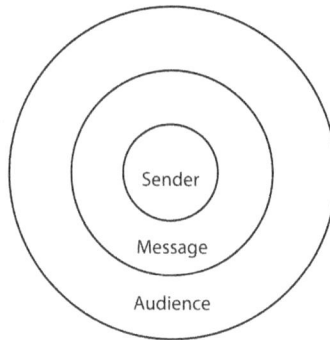

Figure 6 The Sender, Message, and Audience

But then we arrive at the Medium at the outer ring:

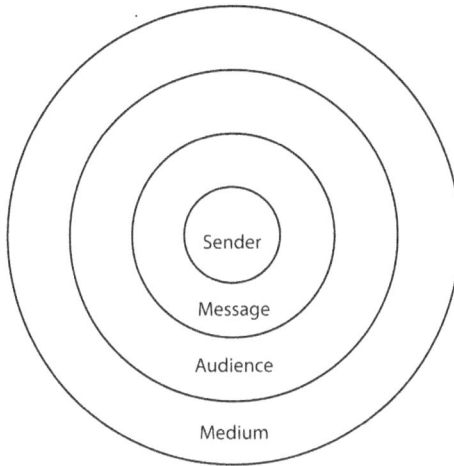

Figure 7 The Sender, Message, Audience and Medium

This violates the standard order in which the medium is interposed between source and receiver. Instead, it coincides with the media ecology approach of understanding media as environments. We exist in biophysical, technological, and symbolic environments, which constitute the media through which we communicate. First there is the medium:

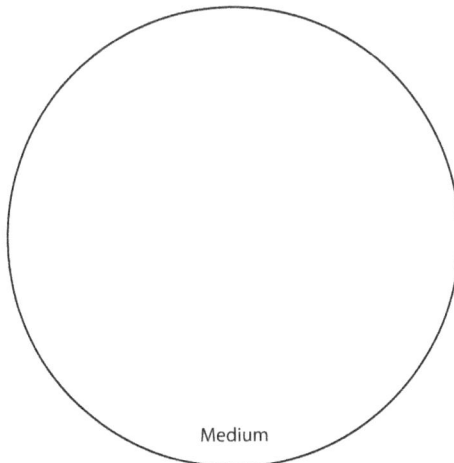

Figure 8 The Medium (or Environment)

More than a channel, the medium is the environment, so that the entirety of the process of communication exists within a given situation and context, within a given biophysical, technological, and (for human beings) symbolic environment; individuals and groups, and societies and cultures, all exist within a given medium or environment. And as all forms of life must in some way take in information about their environment, must be responsive to their environment, as well as in some way modifying their environment, any given population also exists as an audience in relation to their environment:

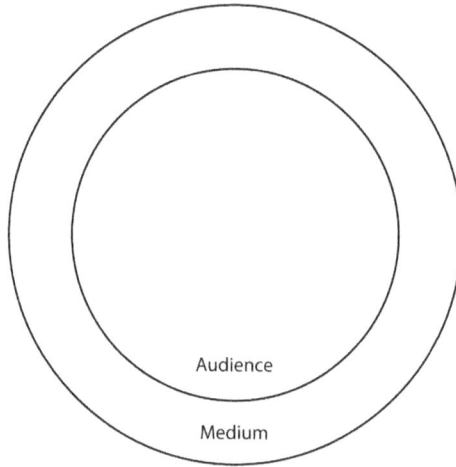

Figure 9 The Medium and Audience

In this sense, the Audience emerges within a Medium, and the Audience is created or caused by the Medium. I use Audience here rather than Receiver to avoid the emphasis on individualism that is another byproduct of literacy, and a bias associated with western culture. Whether we are concerned with the origin of species in biology or of community in sociology, what emerges out of the environment is not the individual, but the group. And it is only an Audience that can receive a Message, that can recognize some change or difference in the environment as having Message value, so that the Message is caused by the Audience:

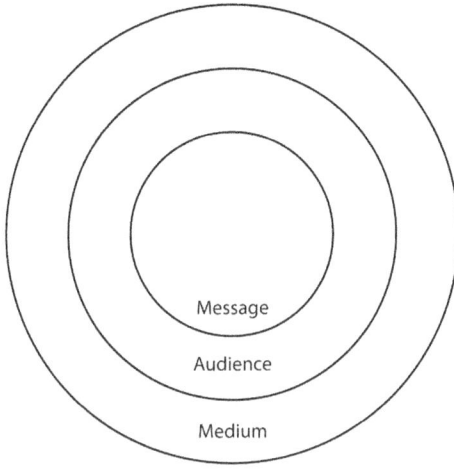

Figure 10 The Medium, Audience, and Message

The Audience not only receives a Message, but develops an interest or appetite for more, creates a demand, or simply requires more communication by virtue of its survival value in sharing intelligence about the outer environment, and in enhancing the connections among members of the Audience. And it is therefore the Audience's need or desire for a Message that causes the emergence of a Sender:

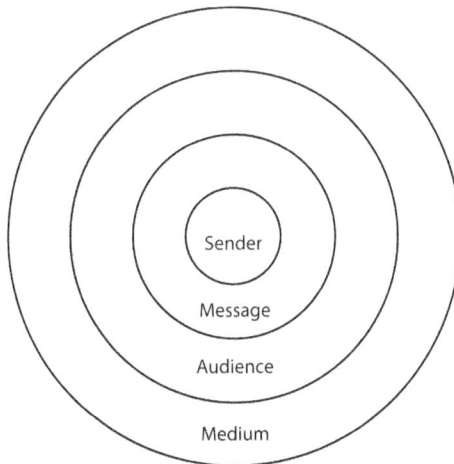

Figure 11 The Medium, Audience, Message, and Sender

Simply put, rather than the start of the process, the Sender does not exist until a Message is sent. Until then, the Sender is part of the Audience, so that it is the Message that causes or creates the Sender. And coming full circle, the Sender composes and transmits the Message out of the available resources in the environment, the biophysical, technological, and symbolic media. This includes the Audience as the basis of the Sender's Message, the Audience, again, having emerged out of the Medium or environment.

Like all models, my model is an oversimplification of what it depicts, as it selects certain details to emphasize while leaving many others out. I put it forth not to argue that this *is* communication, but rather to explain my view in regard to communication, that communication begins with a medium or environment, including the biophysical, technological, and symbolic conditions that we are born into and function within; that within a given medium or environment audiences emerge that are receptive and responsive to the information given off by that environment (which includes other entities within the environment); that audiences, in receiving and recognizing messages, create an interest in and demand for more communication; and that this leads to the emergence of senders who create messages and in doing so create themselves as senders. I have established the general foundation that this understanding is based upon in *Media Ecology: An Approach to Understanding the Human Condition* (Strate, 2017), and this discussion, in providing a new emphasis on communication, serves as a footnote to that book, as well as what I hope stands on its own as an introduction to *Concerning Communication*.

Chapter 1
Something from Nothing

Prologue

Back in the old country, in an older time than now, there lived a tailor. On the day that his grandson was born, he made the newborn a wonderful blanket out of some rare and beautiful material. Joseph, his grandson, loved that blanket, but as time passed and the blanket got worn and frazzled, his mother wanted to throw it out. But Joseph took it to his grandfather, and his grandfather took out his scissors and needle and thread, and said, "There's just enough material here to make a wonderful jacket."

When, in time, Joseph outgrew the jacket and his mother wanted to throw it out, he took it to his grandfather, who again took out his tailor's tools, and said, "There's just enough material here to make a wonderful vest."

When the vest grew old, and his mother wanted to throw it out, he took it to his grandfather, who again went about his trade, and said, "There's just enough material here to make a wonderful tie."

The tie in turn became worn and stained, and Joseph's mother wanted to throw it out, but he again took it to his grandfather, who cut and sewed the material, and said, "There's just enough material here to make a wonderful handkerchief."

But over time the handkerchief grew dirty and tattered, and his mother said, now, finally, it's time to throw it out. But Joseph believed in his grandpa, and brought it to him, and his grandfather once more did his best to salvage what was left, and said, "There's just enough material here to make a wonderful button."

But one day Joseph lost the button. Distraught, he ran to his grandfather's house. His mother, running after him said, "Joseph! Even your grandfather can't make something from nothing," and his grandfather sadly agreed.

The next day Joseph went to school, where he put pen to paper, and said, "There's just enough material here to make a wonderful story."

Material Matters

Material! Such a simple and unassuming word, this key term that our story revolves around. And yet, it is so very central to so much of what we do. Material is a concern for anyone engaged in acts of creation and communication: public speakers need material for their speeches, stand-up comics need material to get their laughs, teachers need material for their classes. We often find ourselves on the hunt for good material, material we can work with, material we can make something out of.

The pun that forms the foundation of this story is based on the double meaning of the word *material*, as both physical stuff and communication content. Of the two, it is the physical stuff that represents the primary meaning, as the word's origin can be traced back to the Latin term *materia*, which refers to the substance from which something is made. The English word *matter* comes from the same root, and here too the basic reference is to something substantial. Something real. Something tangible. Tracing the root meaning back even further, we arrive at the Latin word *mater*, meaning *mother*, hence terms such as *mother lode* and *mother of pearl*. In these instances, we find the meaning of *mother* generalized to indicate an *origin* or *source*, so that a phrase such as *source material*, referring to the underlying basis from which a message is constructed, is the equivalent of the term, *birth mother*. *Mater* is also the root of the word *matrix*, which comes from the Latin term for pregnant animal, as well as womb or uterus. The modern meaning retains the sense of a place, an array, a mold, an enclosure, or more generally a set of conditions—*material conditions*—more recently referring to an imagined future version of the internet, cyberspace, and virtual reality, courtesy of the science fiction writer William Gibson via his 1984 novel *Neuromancer*, and the filmmakers known as the Wachowskis famous for the movie *The Matrix* and its sequels. Put another way, *the medium is the matrix*, in that the two terms are synonyms, both also synonymous with *environment* (the womb being the original environment for us). And, *the material is the maternal*, in the beginning of it all.

When Saddam Hussein referred to *the mother of all battles*, prior to the start of the Gulf War in 1990, he was drawing on a figure of speech used in the Arabic language, *mother of* referring in this instance to the greatest or best. This usage was subsequently adopted in the United States, giving rise to phrases such as, *the mother of all bombs* and *the mother of all budgets*, as well as *the mother of all sandwiches* and *the mother of all yard sales*. Clearly, we are no longer on solid ground, as the earthiness of *mater* has melted away into an airier superlative sensibility. The linkage is discernible, however, between the two meanings, the original vs. the greatest, the first vs. the best.

In a somewhat more modest sense, *material* comes to be used as an adjective to refer to something that is, if not the ultimate or supreme, then certainly significant. For example, we may refer to a *material witness*, meaning a witness whose testimony would be relevant and important; or *information that is material to the investigation*, meaning information that is essential for solving the case; or even a *material change in the situation*, referring to a change that is important enough to have an effect.

In related fashion, we can determine that something *matters*, or that *it doesn't matter*, or at least that it is of *no matter to* the concern at hand. Along similar lines, we hear the rallying cry, *black lives matter*, and the rejoinders that *all lives matter*, or specifically in regard to the police, that *blue lives matter* (both missing the point that the original slogan is a response to the perception that the lives of African-Americans are not as highly valued as individuals categorized as Caucasian, as evidenced by the vastly disproportionate deathrate of African-Americans). As a verb, *to matter* is defined as, *to be of importance or consequence*, which is another way of saying, *to make a difference*. Something that *is material* is something that *makes a difference*. And the phenomenon of difference is central to the concept of information as put forth by Claude Shannon's (1949) information theory, as well as Norbert Wiener's (1950, 1961) cybernetics; Gregory Bateson (1972, 1979) defined *information* most succinctly as a *difference that makes a difference*, in other words, differences that *matter*. *To inform*, then, is *to matter, to be material, to make a difference*. And *information* is a function that is associated with the process of communication, although the term *information* can also refer to the content of communication, something contained within a message.

The connection between material and content is clearest with the new usages that appear as we move from antiquity to the medieval and modern periods, and we come to speak of a topic being the *matter at hand*, meaning that it is the focus of discussion or the priority; or something being *a matter of course*, meaning that it is expected or routine. Similarly, we may say, *for that matter*, in reference to a particular issue, or we may ask someone, *what's the matter?* In these instances, *matter* refers to a subject, as in *subject matter*, or a *question* or *concern*. This dematerialization of *matter*, and *material* itself, parallels the shifting meaning of the term *text*; originally referring to something tangible, which is to say something that has *texture*, notably a physical copy of a book or document, *text* has come to refer to a specific set of words and forms of expression independent of any particular physical artifact. This is one of the effects of the typographic revolution associated with Johann Gutenberg, beginning in the 15th century, which made possible the production of multiple copies of the same document, each copy being, for all intents and purposes, identical to one another; by way of contrast, every copy of a manuscript, written out by hand, is different and unique in clearly discernible ways, often in regards to content, always in regard to at least some aspects of style and appearance. The uniformity of mass produced printed books and documents not only led to the abstract notion of text, but also became the basis of the concept of intellectual property, property that is not material or physical, via the introduction of copyright legislation (later joined by trademarks and patents).

With this in mind, it is important to emphasize that communication content is not something tangible, and messages are not objectively real, insofar as the message sent is never the same as the message received. Rather, we have moved into the subjective realm of individual and collective experience, based on sense perception and cognition, feelings and ideas, memory and imagination, symbolic representations and semantic reactions. In other words, we have moved into the realm of meaning, and as has long been noted, meaning resides not in our words or symbols, but in ourselves as meaning-makers. In senders and receivers. In thinkers and perceivers. In us.

Further, *material* is synonymous with *substance*, referring to something's essential nature. The root traces back to a sense of solidity and presence, of *standing firm*. *Stance* refers to the verb *to stand*, *sub* means *under*, so that *understand* is the equivalent of *substance*. To understand something is to know all about its elemental composition, its inherent properties, its corporeal matter. To put it another way, it is to know (or think you know) all about its essential nature, and we can refer to something essential or otherwise significant as being *substantial*, whether it is tangible, a substantial amount of property, or purely symbolic, a substantial argument—and when proving a claim to be true or supporting a position, we *substantiate* the argument. We also speak of significant individuals as being persons of *substance*, referring to their achievements and inner qualities, and we say, *show them what you're made of*, meaning show them your true nature, your full capabilities, allow them to put you to the test—and when they do, *give it your all!* Following Shakespeare, we may then wish that we were *made of sterner stuff*, after having *the stuffing knocked out of us*. Our response may well draw again from Shakespeare, that *we are such stuff as dreams are made on*. Or such stuff as stories are made of, as the tale of Joseph and his grandfather illustrates.

Form and Substance

But we do not live by material alone. In this instance, even Aristotle would agree with the non-aristotelian principle of non-allness. Substance or matter is not all there is to understand, not all there is to reality. There is also form. Aristotle's mentor, Plato, became so enamored of the concept of form that he argued that it represents the true reality, that the material world was simply a shadow cast on a cave wall, a reflection of the ideal forms that are the only "things" that are real. As Jonathan Sacks (2003) explains in reference to Plato,

> In the world of ideas, difference is resolved into sameness. Particulars give way to universals. The world we see, in which we move and live, he argued in *The Republic* in the famous parable of the cave, is a mere play of shadows. The true essence of things is not matter but form, ideas, not in their concrete embodiment in the world of the senses. That is where trees become Treeness, where men become Man and apparent truths coalesce into Truth.
>
> It is a wondrous dream, that of Plato, and one that has never ceased to appeal to his philosophical and religious heirs: the dream of reason, a world of order set against the chaos of life, an eternity beyond the here and now. Its single most powerful idea is that truth—reality, the essence of things—is universal. (p. 49)

How did Plato arrive at such an extreme and unlikely conclusion? It has much to do with the fact that the alphabet had been adopted in ancient Greece only a few centuries earlier. Literacy was a relatively recent phenomenon, and one of the effects of literacy is to open the door to more abstract kinds of thought than individuals otherwise were accustomed to. In regard to shapes, for example, rather than an abstract term such as *circle*, individuals would resort to concrete language and refer to a circular shaped object or image as a *moon*, or a *plate* (Ong, 1982). Similarly, rather than an abstract notion such as *justice*, the concept might be personified by a deity such as Dike (the Greek goddess of justice), and expressed in the concrete from of narrative, for example in Agamemnon's decision to go to war with Troy over the theft of Helen, as expressed in the *Iliad*. As Eric Havelock (1963, 1978, 1982, 1986) has shown, over the course of the centuries that separate Homer and Plato, the Greeks developed increasingly more abstract language, and the conceptions to go with it.

It follows that Plato was one of the first individuals in his culture to work with highly abstract terminology, terminology of the kind that we associate with the sort of philosophical investigations that we trace back to his dialogues (however much they are attributed to Socrates). And as often happens when we encounter something new and significant, Plato fell in love; he fell in love with abstraction, which is to say that he fell in love with ideas, and with the idea of ideas. And as is often the case when it comes to infatuation, his Platonic love blinded him to all else but the object of his desire: ideas. And so, he came to the revolutionary notion that ideas constitute the only true reality. I use revolution here in the specific sense of turning the world upside down, of making things topsy-turvy, amounting to, in this case, a reversal into absurdity. Moreover, as

Rabbi Sacks (2003) notes, this also leads to universalism, and with it comes a two-valued orientation, either-or thinking. If you believe that you know the truth, and the truth is universal, then every statement is either true of false, and everyone is either wrong or right. Further, knowing what is true gives you the rationale for imposing your views and your will on everything and everyone you can. It is no secret that Plato's philosophy represents an authoritarian, if not proto-fascist perspective. Those who know the truth have the right to rule, and everyone else must obey. This is not only anti-democratic, but sets the stage for great conflict between opposing parties who all claim to possess the one and only universal truth.

As Plato's student, and himself a product of alphabetic literacy, Aristotle also embraced universalism, and the belief that individuals could have access to absolute truth. This, in part, is why Alfred Korzybski (1993) argued that we need non-aristotelian systems, such as general semantics, representing new ways of thinking. Korzybski's intent was not to discard Aristotle altogether, but to build on his work, in the same sense that Albert Einstein's theory of relativity was built on the work of Isaac Newton, resulting in the non-newtonian physics that constitutes our present scientific paradigm. We might even say that Aristotle himself argued for a form of philosophy that could be considered non-platonic, insofar as he did not adopt Plato's theory of ideal forms. Rather, he viewed form and substance as inseparable, together constituting the basis of physical phenomena. Form cannot exist without a physical basis, and matter must always take some kind of form. This non-elementalistic understanding, later referred to as *hylomorphism*, from the Greek words for *matter* and *form*, represents a much more sensible, better grounded view of the world than the madness of Plato.

For Aristotle, matter is the stuff that reality is made of, and form is what gives that stuff its shape. In this, he followed in the footsteps of the pre-Socratic philosophers in his emphasis on matter, and a corresponding materialistic view of the universe was characteristic of natural philosophy and modern science, notably as expressed in Newtonian physics. For Aristotle, all matter was made up of four elements, alone or in combination: earth, water, air, and fire. That fire is not a substance, that it is not matter, that it is instead energy, never occurred to him, for the simple reason that the very concept of energy, as we know it, was unknown to him. Newton arguably was the first to identify energy as a phenomenon distinct from matter, but he still viewed matter as the fundamental stuff that the universe is composed of. It was not until the 19th century and the development of the Laws of Thermodynamics that the paradigm shifted, yielding the understanding that it is energy that is fundamental, and that matter itself merely represents energy in a very stable form. This insight was cemented via Einstein's famous equation, $E=mc^2$, which established that mass can be converted into energy, the amount of energy being equal to amount of mass multiplied by the square of the speed of light, the universal constant. The proof of this came with the splitting of the atom via the Manhattan Project during the Second World War, demonstrating that matter can in fact be destroyed, contrary to Newtonian physics; in contrast to Newton, the first Law of Thermodynamics states that it is energy, not matter, that cannot be created or destroyed, its amount remaining constant within a closed system such as the universe.

With this in mind, the concept of form can still be applied to energy, albeit in a sense that is different from the original connotation of form as shape. Two major forms of energy are kinetic and potential, and other forms include the mechanical, magnetic, electrical, thermal, chemical, gravitational, and nuclear. Substituting energy for matter represents a shift in emphasis to a more dynamic understanding of form, a shift from the relative stability of the concept of structure, to the more fluid sense of relationship and interaction, and from the visual metaphor of shape and frame to the acoustic analogy of rhythm and punctuation. Perhaps the best term in this context is *pattern*, which brings to mind Bateson's (1979) quest for the *pattern which connects*, for the *metapatterns* that connect various forms of matter and energy, as well as Marshall McLuhan's (1964) identification of *pattern recognition* as the essential method for discovering the order that resides within chaotic systems.

Change

In conjunction with the understanding that matter is a form of energy, Einstein's non-newtonian physics established that what we perceive of as *things*, which is to say as discrete and stable *objects*, are in fact dynamic *events* in spacetime, happenings that take place in the context of a specific time and place, *processes* representing, in philosophical terms, *becoming* rather than *being*. All of reality is in flux, constantly in motion, constantly subject to change. This in turn highlights the question of how change occurs.

Newtonian physics and his three Laws of Motion, which are concerned with inertia and force, are built on the basic notion of cause and effect. His third law is famously expressed by the dictum, *for every action there is an equal and opposite reaction*, often illustrated as billiard balls hitting one another. This is consistent with a mechanistic view of the universe, one in which time has no direction, events flow equally forwards and backwards, and knowing the initial conditions within a system would enable you to predict everything that happens from that point on. Non-newtonian physics provides a different understanding, one operating according to the Second Law of Thermodynamics, which indicates that time has a direction, often expressed as *the arrow of time*, which is moving towards a state of greater entropy; moreover, Einstein's theory of relativity indicates that time is not a homogenous sequence of events, while quantum physics replaces certainties with probabilities. These changing concepts of time still work, for the most part, with the same understanding of causality that was associated with Newtonian physics. Otherwise known as *efficient causality*, this particular concept of cause-and-effect relations has held a monopoly position in modern science for centuries, and has dominated most current thinking outside of the sciences. New understandings, however, brought to the fore by systems theory and ecology, by the science and mathematics of chaos and complexity, by the concept of autopoiesis in biology, and the related concept of emergence, all point to alternatives to efficient cause. This includes the causality associated with the interdependence of parts within a system, the ecological effects resulting from changes to the system, the effects of the environment on its contents, and what Terrence Deacon (2012) refers to as the downward causality of the system on its parts.

Clearly, simplistic notions of cause and effect have proven to be inadequate when dealing with chaos and complex systems, and this has led to the introduction of new ideas about causality. But it has also led scholars to retrieve pre-modern conceptions originating with Aristotle's *Metaphysics* (1998), where he identifies four different types of causation, only one of which corresponds to efficient causality. To understand the Aristotelian perspective, however, requires us to embrace a degree of flexibility in our use of the term, *cause*, because it is so strongly associated with Newtonian physics. Instead of thinking of cause as proximate and immediate, based on a particular sequence of acts or events, as in action and reaction, think of cause as the reason why something happens, the explanation regarding the necessary conditions leading to a particular result. With this in mind, the concepts of material and form once again come into play. *Material cause* refers to the substance involved, the material basis for whatever happens. In the case of Joseph's grandfather, the material that he works with as a tailor is, in this sense, a cause or necessary precondition for the blanket, jacket, tie, handkerchief, and button. The material would have been in a certain form prior to the blanket being made, and each subsequent act of tailoring involved a different form. Joseph's grandfather had a particular form in mind each time, the form that a blanket takes, the form that a jacket takes, the form that a vest takes, the form that a tie takes, etc., before actually working on the material. These forms are general patterns that are separate and independent of the specific substance they are allied with in any given instance, as for example different fabrics such as cotton, wool, or silk can be made to take the form of a blanket. This then constitutes a different kind of causality, referred to as *formal cause*. The form guides the action, and the action itself, the cutting and sewing and tailoring that Joseph's grandfather engages in, is the *efficient cause* at work here, which, it should be noted, requires some measure of energy. Aristotle identified a fourth cause as well, *final cause*, which in this case would be the purpose and goal that Joseph's grandfather had in mind, to turn the material into a blanket, or a button.

Efficient cause is the familiar concept of causality, and the material basis of phenomena is also familiar, albeit not so much as a cause in and of itself. Formal cause, on the other hand, is a somewhat mysterious idea, albeit one that has been the subject of significant exploration in recent years. Notably, Marshall McLuhan invoked formal cause as a way to explain how media and technology influence individuals and society, and Eric McLuhan in turn developed this more fully, as expressed in their book, *Media and Formal Cause* (2011); in my Foreword to that book, I note that this represents a decidedly non-aristotelian aspect of Aristotle's philosophy, and that formal cause is the kind of causality associated with the concept of emergence. Jeremy Campbell (1982) similarly connects information theory and linguistics to Aristotle's related idea of final cause, and Deacon (2012) argues that final cause does not require purpose, but rather simply an end state that a system is working toward, e.g., the tendency of closed systems to move toward greater entropy and ultimately a state of complete randomness; Deacon also connects formal cause to emergence and downward causality. These ideas were further explored in the anthology, *Taking Up McLuhan's Cause: Perspective on Media Ecology and Formal Causality* (Anton, Logan, & Strate, 2016; see also Trujillo Liñán, 2022). Simply put, formal cause can be understood as the tendency for phenomena to fall into certain patterns, including the order that emerges out of chaos, and that metapatterns are not just patterns that connect, but patterns that direct (Strate, 2016, 2017).

As previously noted, in reality, form and substance cannot be separated. Just as all matter and all energy must exist in some kind of form, so too all manner of form, pattern, structure, relationship, interaction, etc., must have a physical basis, manifested via matter or energy. Language allows us to separate substance and form conceptually, and consider them apart from one another. Words make it possible for us to tear apart the analogical continuity of our environment into discrete, digital bundles, and the addition of the medium of writing amplifies this ability. We break things up and we break things down, splitting them into their component parts or elements, splitting atoms, splitting etyms, splitting hairs. Our linguistic and grammatological encoding of experience provides us with the powerful tool we call *analysis*, yielding knowledge based on the fragmentation and isolation of phenomena, in contrast to *synthesis*, which requires putting separate pieces together. Analysis is the key that has enabled science to divide and conquer. The irony is that, through science, we have come to understand that conceptually, which is to say linguistically, we are splitting apart phenomena that cannot be subdivided in reality, so that this analytic approach may mislead us about the real nature of the universe. For this reason, in applying a contemporary scientific outlook on the world, general semantics emphasizes the need for a non-elementalistic perspective, i.e., a systems view. The goal is not to eliminate elementalistic procedures and analytic method altogether, but rather to subsume them within a larger, holistic sensibility, just as relativistic and quantum physics did not purge Newtonian physics, instead absorbing it into a larger systematic paradigm.

With this in mind, there is much to be gained from considering each of Aristotle's causes separately, as has already been amply demonstrated via the isolation of efficient causality in the sciences. Formal cause is especially worthy of further exploration as it relates to systems theory and an ecological approach. At the same time, we need to keep in mind that in reality the four causes are part of an interdependent whole. As form and substance are inseparable in reality, formal cause and material cause are as well. Formal cause is also closely linked to final cause, for example as the end product that the tailor has in mind when cutting and sewing, or the final form that the seed is seeking to grow into, or the final form that energy takes when entropy takes hold and we arrive at the heat death of the universe. Formal cause therefore underlies the process represented by efficient causality. Put another way, three of the four causes can be associated with a specific period of time: Material cause is located in the past, being the material that we begin with. Efficient cause represents the present, the moment when the material is being modified. Final cause represents the future, where the process is headed, where it will end up. This leaves formal cause, at first glance as outside of time, but more properly as representing time in its entire range, from past to present to future. Formal cause may seem eternal if we adopt Plato's view of form as permanent and eternal. But why should we, when it is altogether apparent that form is subject to change, that material morphs, from one form in its original state, in the past, via efficient cause to a new form in the future, its final state (until the intervention of another efficient cause). Formal cause is associated with the dynamic environment that we understand the universe to be, according to relativistic and quantum physics. Formal cause is a function of time (Strate, 2016, 2017).

Form and Transformation

Change being the only constant, we can recognize the intimate relationship between *form* and trans*form*ation. Indeed, you might say that the concept of form itself is elementalistic not only because it is inseparable from substance, but also because it represents an ongoing, continual state of transformation. The notion of a singular, stable form is an abstraction, removed from actual reality insofar as our universe is composed of events occurring in spacetime. Form, especially in the common connotation of shape, brings to mind a frozen moment of time, an idea that can be symbolically represented through an image, a painting or drawing, and given a semblance of reality through a photograph. In other words, form tends to be conceived of in visual terms, and this tendency is related to writing and alphabetic literacy, innovations responsible for the visualist biases of western culture. While especially exacerbated by the printing revolution associated with Gutenberg that began in the 15th century, western visualism can be traced back to the literate culture of ancient Greece, the culture that gave us Plato and Aristotle (Havelock, 1963; McLuhan, 1962; Ong, 1967, 1982). That is where and when our visual metaphors for thought originate, metaphors such as *point of view, perspective, reflection, from where I stand, it looks like, it appears that, the way that I see it, foresight, seeing clearly, seeing your way to,* etc. Even words like *in the first place, in the second place,* are visual metaphors, and the sense of place is deeply embedded in the word *topic,* from the Greek *topos,* for place—think of topics as categories sorted out on a page by setting up different lists, and the linkage becomes clear; this also accounts for Aristotle's rule for logic, which make sense as very practical rules for accounting, the law of identity so that you can count the number of similar items, the laws of excluded middle and non-contradiction so that you do not double count the same item in two different lists and thereby give the impression that you have two of an item when you only have one (Strate, 2011a).

As Edmund Carpenter and McLuhan, have noted, in western culture we tend to live in visual space, in particular as associated with Euclidean geometry and its practical applications in architecture, and as further refined via Newtonian mechanistic physics (Carpenter & McLuhan, 1960). In nonliterate, that is to say oral cultures, individuals live in acoustic space, and this is true to a large extent for cultures with writing systems other than the alphabet. In acoustic space, form can never give the impression of permanence and stability. Hearing by its very nature is dynamic. As Ong (1982) puts it, "sound exists only when it is going out of existence. It is not simply perishable but essentially evanescent, and it is sensed as evanescent. When I pronounce the word 'permanence', by the time I get to the 'nence', the 'perma-' is gone, and has to be gone" (p. 32). You can press pause on a video and get a freeze frame, but in place of sound all you get is silence. Just as visual images can give the illusion of permanence, the transcoding of language from speech to writing creates a similar effect, which is why the philosophical concept of permanence originates in the alphabetic culture of ancient Greece.

Put another way, visual space is an environment made up of objects, acoustic space is an environment made up of events, so that, as McLuhan (1962, 1964) noted, Einstein's revolution in physics retrieves the sense of acoustic space associated with oral cultures; this follows the shift from a media environment dominated by alphabetic literacy and typography, to one disrupted by electronic communication, beginning with the telegraph circa 1844. And when we think of form in acoustic terms, we are in the realm of the temporal, the ephemeral, and as Stephen Nachmanovitch (2019) notes, the improvisational. In place of the visual connotation of shape, acoustic form brings to mind musical terms such as *melody*, and especially *rhythm*. We might indeed try substituting *rhythm and energy* for *form and substance*, and to consider rhythm as a form of causality. At the very least, in favoring the term *pattern*, we might register in the sound of that word an echo of the word *patter*.

Still, while *form* can be problematic, there is much that is useful about the term *transformation*. Material, the key term that serves as the foundation of the story of Joseph and his grandfather, is that which is transformed, the subject that is subjected to the process of transformation. Material is the something that dwindles down into nothingness, and also the something that is produced out of seemingly nothing. And we can understand the story to be about a series of transformations, as the rare and beautiful material is transformed into a blanket, the worn and frazzled blanket is transformed into a jacket, the outgrown jacket is transformed into a vest, the old vest is transformed into a tie, the worn and stained tie is transformed into a handkerchief, and the dirty and tattered handkerchief is transformed into a button. And then, the final act is one of symbolic transformation, an ability granted to us, as Susanne Langer (1957) argues, by virtue of our capacity for symbolic communication. Through the medium of language, Joseph's experience is transformed into a story. Symbolic transformation is arguably the most powerful, certainly magical, and quite literally the most transformational form of transformation we engage in. But it occurs within a biophysical environment in which we engage in acts of material transformation (Strate, 2017). Indeed, transformation is a fundamental phenomenon, whether we are talking about how stars turn mass into energy or hydrogen atoms fuse together to make helium, or whether we are talking about chemical reactions or the metabolism that characterizes all living things, by which they transform themselves through growth, their species through evolution, and their environment by ingestion, excretion, and reproduction. Human communication and language are forms of symbolic transformation, as we turn percepts and feelings into words, images, music, and the like.

When it comes to matters material and immaterial alike, transformation is often said to begin with what we refer to as *raw material*. Raw material would be material that is believed to be in its *natural form*, by which we mean that it has not been subject to *human* intervention—it is more or less certain that this material has undergone some sort of transformation independent of human activity, perhaps biological, definitely physical insofar as its origin can be traced back to the big bang. Again, in a universe that is fundamentally dynamic and continually changing, transformation is constant. Still, when raw materials are touched by human hands, or otherwise incorporated into human technological activity, the results are materials that are in some way *processed*, or *manufactured*, otherwise known as *products*, sometimes earning the status of *final product*, but quite possibly only arriving at an intermediate status; such materials are also referred to as *goods*, particularly when they can be bought, sold, or traded, or when they are products to be consumed, hence the phrase, *consumer goods*.

Raw materials are understood to exist in nature, independent of human activity, at least until they are discovered, and then mined or harvested or otherwise collected, procedures that leave their essential nature unchanged. The rare and beautiful material that Joseph's grandfather made into a blanket was not, presumably, raw material, but rather something along the lines of linen, satin, etc., that has been transformed into a bolt or bundle of cloth. In contrast to raw material, manufactured materials are the product of significant forms of human intervention, produced by radical types of procedures that result in dramatic changes, turning them into something essentially different than the raw materials that they are based on, a difference that makes a difference. This helps to demarcate the difference between skilled and unskilled labor, in the sense that the root meaning of *manufacture* is something *made by hand*, *manu* being Latin for *hand*, *factura* for *working*. While in the modern era we tend to associate manufacturing with mechanization and industrialization, traditionally it was synonymous with handicrafts (*hand-crafted*), just as the term *technology* is derived from the ancient Greek word *tékhnē*, which referred to *arts and crafts*. The *manufacturer*, then was an *artisan* or a *crafter* (*craftsman* or *craftswoman* in traditional terminology).

Along similar lines, the Latin words *faber*, referring to an artisan, typically one working with stone or metal, *fabrica* for production or structure, and *fabricare* for build, construct, or make, represent the root of the English term *fabric*, referring to *manufactured material*, the product of a process of *fabrication*. The *material* that tailors like Joseph's grandfather worked with (upholsterers as well) would more specifically be referred to as *fabric*, and like *material*, fabric also takes on added meanings. The slogan of the cotton industry, *the fabric of our lives*, serves as a pun referring to both the material much of our clothing is made of, and the metaphorical basis of our existence. Similarly, a phrase such as the *fabric of the cosmos* refers to the physical structure of the universe. This form of figurative language resonates with a spiritual understanding of the universe, in which a creator or creative force creates the world and its inhabitants, which is to say, *creation* and its *creatures*. This type of metaphor is employed in many different cultures, often personified by a goddess who weaves or spins threads into cloth, for example, the Fates in Greco-Roman mythology, the Norns in Norse mythology, and the goddess Neith in Egyptian mythology. Carole King was following in their footsteps when she sang, "my life is like a tapestry." The metaphor is updated in the 2008 film *Wanted*, in which divine messages are said to be transmitted via a mechanical loom; this likely was inspired by the fact that the technological progenitor of the computer was the Jacquard loom, the first programmable machine, invented at the start of the 19th century. This also underscores the link between creation and communication, which is present in the beginning of the Bible, when God's first creative act is a speech act, *let there be light*, which precedes and causes the actual creation of light. As it does when we are thrust from the dark comfort of the womb into the harsh light of the outer world at the moment of birth, and historically as the spoken word long precedes the invention of writing, sound comes before vision in the story of Genesis.

As for the more modest story of Joseph and his grandfather, the pun at the heart of its conclusion is therefore related to a subtle, pervasive, and deeply embedded metaphor, one that extends to communication being compared to cloth, tale-tellers linked to tailors, and text turned into textile. Across a variety of cultures, stories are *woven*, *yarns* are *spun*, accounts *embroidered*, and false-hoods are *manufactured out of whole cloth*, otherwise referred to as *fabrications*. In ancient Greece, the epic poets who performed the songs of Homer, aka the *Iliad* and the *Odyssey*, were called *rhapsōidos*, rendered in English as *rhapsode* or *rhapsodist*, literally, *a singer of stitched words*, from the Greek word *rhapsōidein*, meaning *to stitch songs together*. This refers to the process of extemporane-ous oral performance, in which composition is improvisational, involving the piecing together of various chunks, such as rhetorical commonplaces and story elements. For the singers of tales of oral cultures, poetry, song, and narrative are constructed by piecing together formulas and formulaic expressions, themes and motifs, characters and plots (Havelock, 1963, 1982, 1986; Lord, 1960; Ong, 1967, 1982; Parry, 1971). And while this is traditionally associated with oral traditional composition, the process of creating a patchwork of pre-existing verbal and narrative formulas also applies to contemporary electronic commu-nications or what Ong (1967, 1982) refers to as secondary orality; for exam-ple, sportscasters knit together various clichés and formulas in calling a game, while rap artists who improvise by drawing on familiar rhythms and rhyming schemes are in effect *rhap* artists, the modern day equivalent of the rhapsodes who sewed together story elements involving familiar characters and themes from myth and legend. This metaphor can also apply to written composition, especially in regard to popular works, but even for what may be construed to be elite literature, in that even the most original forms of expression make use of existing phrases and word combinations.

Stories represent a process of symbolic transformation, of the raw material of experience and imagination, into the finished product based on narrative structure. But they are also subject to additional sorts of transformation, as, for example, when the songs of Homer, oral traditional epics, were turned into canonized literary works. The original singers of tales could only learn the songs by listening and remembering what they heard, and then making the songs their own. Assisted by mnemonic devices and a storehouse of formulas, formulaic expressions, themes and motifs, as well as their improvisational skill, they composed the epics anew with each performance, and each performance would be tailored to the particular occasion and the specific audience that was present (Lord, 1960; Parry, 1971). Variation was unavoidable, verbatim memorization unthinkable in the absence of written records (Ong, 1967, 1982). But shortly after the introduction of the alphabet in ancient Greece, the songs of Homer, aka the *Iliad* and *Odyssey*, were transcribed, creating documents that could be viewed and reviewed. This opened up the possibility of memorizing the epics word for word, and consequently, a new class of performer appeared. They were known as the *Homeridae*, the *Children of Homer*, who relied on written versions of the *Iliad* and *Odyssey*, and who were seen as more authoritative and therefore more legitimate than the traditional singers of tales (Kirk, 1962). In other words, the *Homeridae* obsolesced and to a large extent replaced the original singers of tales in ancient Greece. This is a recurring pattern, that whenever a new medium of communication is introduced, it generates a need for new material (Strate, 2017). And that need is at first satisfied by cannibalizing and absorbing the material of the older medium, in a sense using the older medium as its material, or its content, as McLuhan (1964) observes (see also Bolter & Gromala, 2003; Bolter & Grusin, 1999).

On a more modest scale, the story of Joseph and his grandfather follows a similar pattern. As a Jewish folktale, the origin of the story is lost in the mists of time, a product of an oral tradition in which each telling and retelling of the tale creates or recreates it anew, no two renderings ever quite the same; though the differences may be small or great, they are differences that make a difference. Like much of oral tradition, it also takes musical form, as a Yiddish folk song, "Epes fun Gornisht," which ends with the song itself, in place of the story, as the final product. In written form, the story became the basis of several children's books, combining typography and the printing of illustrations. The one that I am most familiar with is Phoebe Gilman's *Something from Nothing* (1992), a book that I read to my son Benjamin when he was a young boy like Joseph. The book has also been adapted as a video. I should add that the version of the story that I have shared here is my own version, based in large part on Gilman's book. And just as the story has gone though many different transformations, this essay too has gone through a series of revisions over a period of many years.

Communication and Science

The story of Joseph and his grandfather, and the ancient motif it draws upon, the metaphor of material transformation, serves to ground the abstract concept of communication in the concreteness of the human lifeworld. It reminds us that both *form* and in*form*ation do not exist independently of matter and energy. We can separate them conceptually, study them independently, but out there, in the physical environment, they are not isolated entities. Communication, therefore, cannot be fully understood when it is removed from the context of the physical universe. And since science has provided us with our most reliable and accurate means of understanding our environment, communication cannot be fully understood absent a scientific basis. To be clear, I am not arguing for the need for empirical, quantitative sociological and psychological research, which all too often yields trivial or commonsensical results, and is legitimately criticized as scientism, that is, the compulsion to make all discourse appear scientific (see, for example, Burke, 1945; Postman, 1988, 1992; see also Whyte, 1956). We need not adopt a strict behavioral or social scientific approach to knowledge, but neither should we reject that body of work out of hand, nor be ignorant of its conclusions and contributions. Similarly, I am not advocating for a return to positivism, or that we need to be experts in biology, physics, or mathematics. But we ought to understand the key concepts and theories of the hard sciences, and our understanding of communication has to be consistent with established scientific knowledge. This is all the more important in that science in the early part of the 21st century has come under attack in liberal democracies, in conjunction with the rise of authoritarian movements, and in ways paralleling the politicization of science under the communist totalitarian rule of the Soviet Union in the mid-20th century.

Understanding science requires a recognition that it is a human endeavor, and therefore governed by fallibilism. Following Karl Popper (2002), science proceeds by eliminating what is false, rather than determining what is true. All of scientific knowledge is tentative, open to continual testing and revision. Empiricism and scientific method have provided us with our most rigorous means of mapping physical reality, and of continually updating and improving those maps. The fact that we have airplanes that fly overhead, computers and smart phones that put enormous quantities of information at our fingertips, screens that recreate reality and bring long dead persons back to a semblance of life, buildings that stretch up into the clouds, all this and so much more, should make us cognizant of the supreme efficacy of science. Admittedly, it is easy to lose sight of the countless everyday miracles that we enjoy as they become routine, so that they fade into the background and we stop paying attention to them. When you consider the homes that provide us with hot and cold running water, light when it is dark outside, heat when it is cold and cool air when it is hot, and electrical energy to power our devices, we only become cognizant of this invisible environment when things go wrong or stop working, for example when we experience a blackout, hence McLuhan's quip that breakdowns lead to breakthroughs in awareness (McLuhan & Fiore, 1968). For most, however, those breakthroughs are short lived, and the fact that we tend to take the benefits of scientific progress for granted is what has led to the increasing visibility and viability of anti-science fantasy themes and propaganda campaigns, for example in regard to climate change and the public health measures in response to the COVID-19 pandemic. Moreover, that same efficacy of modern science has enabled us to kill one another with the greatest of ease, to develop weapons of mass destruction and delivery systems that bring on destruction from great distances, and other technologies that cause sickness and injury, that pollute the environment and have harmful potentially deadly effects on the ecosystem. What this should instill in us is the realization that, for good or for ill, the power of science is indisputable, and ought not to be up for debate. And that is all the more reason that we need to understand science, and to consciously apply scientific knowledge in ways that maximize benefits and minimize costs, and that allow us to make informed decisions about when to say no to technological innovations.

Understanding science means accepting that we are dealing with probabilities, not absolutes, with an open system subject to change, not a closed system in a fixed state of stasis. It means recognizing the validity of scientific consensus and the preponderance of evidence, as opposed to the impossible demand for perfect proof. It means being guided by reality-testing, not denying facts in favor of belief systems or ideologies. But understanding science also means being aware of how the scientific method works and what its limitations are, not being mystified by science or treating science as an authority never to be questioned. What we might refer to as science literacy requires both a clear knowledge of scientific method and a critical assessment of scientific theory and research. For this reason, there is much to be learned from studies of the sociology of knowledge, and the sociology of science, of the sort associated with Thomas Kuhn's (1996) discussion of paradigm shifts. Similarly, there is much to be gained from considering the social construction of reality, as a psychological and sociocultural phenomenon. Studies that adopt such approaches constitute an important form of reality testing. At the same time, we must not forget that even social construction requires raw materials, and that scientific knowledge and common sense reality alike are rooted in our physical existence; they are not simply a result of socio-political decision-making. If they were not consistent with physical reality, if there was not a degree of structural similarity and structural coupling with the external environment, then they would be entirely dysfunctional, and anyone employing them would not be long for this world. Survival depends on maps that can guide us effectively through the territory, that can get us to where we need to go. It is perhaps an occupational hazard of intellectuals to get lost in the high level abstractions of social construction, in much the same way that Plato became lost in his fantasy world of ideal forms. Anyone with actual experience in construction would be quick to remind you of the obvious necessity of raw materials.

When we think about the idea of social construction in abstract political terms, we exaggerate the ability of human agents to master and control their environment. This is what David Ehrenfeld calls *The Arrogance of Humanism* (1978). When we think about social construction in terms of concrete communication, we become open to the idea that our situational context provides the materials and energy we use to make our reality, and that our environment shapes and limits what we can build. Social construction is a superstructure, to employ Marxian terminology, built on the base of the biophysical environment, and on the technologies with which we modify our environment. I also want to note that science does not preclude religion, however much the two are sometimes at odds with one another. We can be open to the possibility of legitimate spiritual approaches to the study of communication, which after all require acceptance of the limits of human agency, but again such approaches would still need to take materiality and science into account. After all, the theologians tell us that only God creates *ex nihlo*, out of absolutely nothing. All the rest of us must make do with the materials at hand.

Having argued that our understanding of communication must be consistent with science, I also need to emphasize that science, in large part, is based on communication. First, the empirical method emphasizes our reception and interpretation of information we received from our environment. As Paul Watzlawick, Janet Beavin Bavelas, and Don D. Jackson (1967) explain,

> In modern biology it would be unthinkable to study even the most

primitive organism in artificial isolation from its environment. As postulated particularly by General System Theory... organisms are open systems that maintain their steady state (stability) and even evolve toward states of higher complexity by means of a constant exchange of both energy and information with their environment. If we realize that in order to survive any organism must gain not only the substances necessary for its metabolism but adequate information about the world around it, we see that communication and existence are inseparable concepts. The environment, then, is subjectively experienced as a set of instructions about the organism's existence, and in this sense the environmental effects are similar to a computer program; Norbert Wiener once said about the world that it "may be viewed as a myriad of To Whom It May Concern messages." There is, however, the important difference that while the computer program is presented in a language that the machine completely "understands," the impact of the environment on an organism comprises a set of instructions whose meaning is by no means self-evident but rather is left up to the organism to decode as best it can. If to this consideration we add the obvious fact that the organism's reactions in turn affect the environment, it becomes apparent that even on the very primitive levels of life, complex and continuous interactions take place that are nonrandom and are, therefore, governed by a program or, to us an existentialist term, by *meaning*.

Seen in this light, existence is a *function*... of the relationship between the organism and its environment. At the human level this interaction between organism and environment reaches its highest degree of complexity. Although in modern societies problems of biological survival have receded far into the background and the environment, in the ecological sense of the term, is largely controlled by man, the vital messages from the environment that must be correctly decoded have merely undergone a shift from the biological to the more psychological realm. (258-259)

Science, then, represents the most effective means of decoding messages from the biophysical environment, just as many other fields, such as communication, linguistics, literary studies, psychology, anthropology, etc., are devoted to the decoding of messages generated by human beings. Consistent with this understanding is Wendell Johnson's (1946) pithy comments, that "the language of science is the better part of the method of science," and in parallel that "the language of sanity is the better part of sanity" (p. 50). Johnson argued that the two have much in common, following the lead of Korzybski's introduction of general semantics in his 1933 magnum opus, *Science and Sanity* (1993), with its concern with the *organism as a whole in its environment*. By way of adapting scientific method for use in everyday life, general semantics emphasizes the same need for linguistic clarity and precision that is required for scientific investigation. This provides invaluable assistance in the practical need to engage in effective communication, while also enhancing our capacity for understanding communication, and related subjects such as knowledge, thought, perception, and behavior.

Korzybski's (1993) formulation of general semantics begins with the phenomenon of *time-binding*, a term he coined to refer to the distinctly human capability to preserve and pass on what we learn from one generation to the next. Time-binding is made possible by the fact that we have at our disposal the tools of language and symbolic communication, which allow us to store and transmit information from one individual to another, and within groups of individuals. This forms the basis of what we refer to as culture (Hall, 1959; see also Douglas, 1973; Geertz, 1973), and of the cultural evolution that we have at our disposal, supplementing the biological evolution characteristic of all forms of life. Korzybski regarded time-binding as not only uniquely human, but as the defining ability of our species. And because we can transcend the limitations of time and build upon the knowledge of those who came before us, human beings have the capacity to make progress in ways not possible for other forms of life. By encoding experience in the form of language, as Joseph did in writing his story, we seemingly produce something *from* nothing. By communicating that experience to others, and across generations, allowing our ancestors to benefit from our own hard won knowledge, we in effect provide them with something *for* nothing, as James Harvey Robinson explains:

> One cannot but wonder at this constantly recurring phrase "getting something for nothing," as if it were the peculiar and perverse ambition of disturbers of society. Except for our animal outfit, practically all we have is handed to us gratis. Can the most complacent reactionary flatter himself that he invented the art of writing or the printing press, or discovered his religious, economic and moral convictions, or any of the devices which supply him with meat and raiment or any of the sources of such pleasure as he may derive from literature or the fine arts? In short, civilization is little else than getting something for nothing. (quoted in Hayakawa & Hayakawa, 1990, p. 3)

It is important to note that insofar as time-binding enables human progress, it enables progress in time-binding itself. For example, the development of mnemonics, including the memory techniques based on formal elements that we associate with poetry and music, enhanced our ability to preserve knowledge through living memory, individual and especially collective memory, remembering together through acts of commemoration (Havelock, 1963, 1986; Hobart & Schiffman, 1998; Ong, 1967, 1982; Strate, 2012, 2017; Yates, 1966). The invention of writing revolutionized time-binding, making significant progress possible. Oral cultures, by way of contrast, tend to be conservative, resisting novelty so as not to risk losing the hard won knowledge that has already been accumulated and can only be preserved via human memory; their emphasis is on tradition and maintaining the status quo, which is to say, to maintaining homeostasis (Goody, 1977; Ong, 1982). Korzybski (1993) recognized that it was in literate cultures that time-binding resulted in progress being made on a geometric scale; this was especially true following the typographic revolution in early modern Europe which, as Elizabeth Eisenstein (1979) details, led to the introduction of modern science. Language and symbolic communication make time-binding possible, and storage media associated with the written word vastly increase our ability to store knowledge, but this leads to the need to find ways to manage, organize, and especially evaluate the knowledge we accumulate (Hobart & Schiffman, 1998). This was Aristotle's goal in developing his system of logic, and it represented a major achievement in its time, and for centuries after. Other methods of dealing with information overload were added over time, such as calculus, Boolean logic, outlines, indexes, catalogues, a vast variety of reference works, and of course the computer. Notably, modern science itself, characterized as it is by the empirical method, was an especially effective means of evaluating knowledge, although it too has contributed to our present information overload. Still, it provides an essential means of determining what is fact as opposed to opinion, what is testable as opposed to being tautological, what is based on evidence as opposed to what is solely based on inference, or opinion. In short, scientific method, as generalized via general semantics, is an eminently useful way to think and talk and write with clarity and precision, and to think and listen and read critically and analytically.

Communication and Media

The story of Joseph and his grandfather ends, in self-reflexive fashion, with the making of the story, making it, in the end, a story about a story. This is presented not with postmodern irony, but rather with hopeful optimism, indeed with celebration of the human talent for storytelling, based as it is on our capacity for symbolic expression, and our propensity towards symbolic play. It is our linguistic ability, the uniquely human characteristic of language and languaging, that enables us not only to tell stories, but to tell stories about the telling of stories, and, as I am doing in this essay after a fashion, to tell a story about telling a story about the telling of stories. At each step we move further away from the actual material that started off the sequence. Going meta, as it were, is a matter of logical typing (Whitehead & Russell, 1925-1927), of categorization (Johnson, 1946), or pattern recognition (McLuhan, 1964), recognizing the metapatterns (Bateson, 1972, 1979; Volk, 1995) that connect and direct (Strate, 2016, 2017); it is also a matter of metacommunication, instructions that tell us how to interpret messages, relationships established on the basis of communication (Bateson, 1972, 1979; Watzlawick et al, 1967). And it is a matter of media.

For anyone concerned with human communication, or the human condition for that matter, understanding media ecology is essential (Strate, 2017). Defined as the study of media as environments (Postman. 1970), media ecology incorporates general semantics (Postman, 1974; Strate, 2011a, 2017), which is concerned with the *organism as a whole in its environment* (Korzybski, 1993), thereby anticipating systems theory. Korzybski (1993) referred to the *neuro-linguistic* and *neuro-semantic environment*, Johnson (1946) more concisely with the *semantic environment*, and Postman (1970, 1974, 1976, 1979, 1982, 1985, 1988) with the *semantic environment*, *information environment*, and *media environment*. The category of media, as it is used within the field of media ecology, includes language, codes and symbol systems, and all manner of symbolic form, including narrative; it also includes all aspects of the biophysical environment, matter and energy, the body, nervous system, and senses, and all types of technology, including the human environments we create, as well as the situations and contexts we manufacture. Media, in other words, are the observable manifestation of a process of mediation, which encompasses dynamic interaction and relationships, and processes of transformation (Strate, 2017).

It ought to be clear enough, then, that the primary medium of human communication is language, that it is through language and symbols that we relate to our environment, that we abstract information out of our environment, that we mediate with our environment (Strate, 2011a). The contributions of general semantics pioneers, such as Korzybski (1993), Johnson (1946), Hayakawa (Hayakawa & Hayakawa, 1990), and others to the analysis of the social and psychological effects of language and symbolic communication are significant, which is why Postman (1974) referred to media ecology as *general semantics writ large*; Postman himself made important contributions to general semantics (e.g., Postman, 1976; Postman, Weingartner, & Moran, 1969), while also establishing media ecology as a field of inquiry (1968, 1970) and furthering the field's development (e.g., Postman, 1979, 1982, 1985, 1992, 2000, 2006; Postman & Weingartner, 1969, 1971). Scholarship in linguistics also has been influential in the media ecology intellectual tradition, notably the linguistic relativism of Edward Sapir (1921), Benjamin Lee Whorf (1956), and Dorothy Lee (1959), which influenced Edward T. Hall (1959, 1966, 1976, 1983), Carpenter (Carpenter, 1960, 1973; Carpenter & Heyman, 1970; Carpenter & McLuhan, 1956, 1960), McLuhan (1962, 1964) and Walter Ong (1967, 1982). Louis Forsdale (1981) identified the link between the Sapir-Whorf Hypothesis, that language affects the way we view the world, and McLuhan's perspective on media, while Postman and Weingartner (1969) expanded on it, referring to the "Sapir-Whorf-Korzybski-Ames-Einstein-Heisenberg-Wittgenstein-McLuhan-Et Al. Hypothesis . . . that language is not merely a vehicle of expression, it is also the driver; and that what we perceive, and therefore can learn, is a function of our languaging processes" (p. 101).

Lee (1959) also represents a bridge between linguistic relativism and orality-literacy studies associated with Ong (1967, 1982), Havelock (1963, 1978, 1982, 1986), and Goody (1977), as well as Eisenstein's (1979) study of the printing press, and Denise Schmandt-Besserat's (1978, 1992, 1996) groundbreaking research on the origin of writing. The philosophy of symbolic form associated with Alfred North Whitehead and Bertrand Russell (1925-1927), Ludwig Wittgenstein (1961, 1963), Ernst Cassirer (1944, 1953), and Susanne K. Langer (1953, 1957) also has been incorporated within media ecology, and Christine Nystrom (2021) has detailed the relationship between the field and Langer and Whorf. Also of great significance is the symbolic interactionism of George Herbert Mead (1934), Hugh D. Duncan (1962, 1968), and Erving Goffman (1959, 1963, 1967), and Nystrom (2021, 2022) also weaves this tradition together with general semantics and related approaches to achieve an original media ecological synthesis on the nature and origin of symbolic communication.

Additionally, media ecology incorporates the semiotics of Charles Sanders Peirce (1991); the Russian psychological theory of the Vygotsky Circle, associated with Lev Vygotsky (1986) and Alexander Luria (1981; see also Ong, 1982); the English literary theory known as the New Criticism and practical criticism associated with of I.A. Richards (1929, 1936; Ogden & Richards, 1923); and metaphor theory in linguistics as put forth by George Lakoff and Mark Johnson (1980, 1989, 1999), further integrated with general semantics and media ecology by Raymond Gozzi, Jr. (1999). There is also a direct link between contemporary media ecology and the ancient form of study associated with the trivium, especially with the discipline of grammar, which originally referred to the study of language and linguistic expression, as opposed to the modern sense in which it is confined to verb conjugations, parts of speech, and rules for forming sentences (McLuhan, 2006).

Arguably the most famous expression of the media ecology approach, certainly the most concise, is McLuhan's (1964) famous maxim, *the medium is the message*. We can relate this to the story of Joseph and his grandfather by way of the theme of material, which could be considered the common denominator that links the two disparate terms of *medium* and *message*. The material is the message; it is the material that communicators draw upon for their content. And the material is the medium; it is the substance through which we exchange messages, and the environment within which we communicate. We draw upon our environment, including the technological, the biological, and the purely physical, to construct (and deconstruct) our messages and meanings. That is why the medium always precedes the message, just as raw material must be supplied before the finished product can be obtained, just as the physical environment must be in place before life can originate and species evolve, and just as babies must otherwise experiment with making sounds before they can produce meaningful speech. In this context, it is also worth again noting McLuhan's (1964) observation that any given medium can serve as the content of another medium, which is to say that one medium can be taken as raw material to be used and transformed by another medium, for example, the medium of speech as the content of written documents, movies as the content of television, text as the content of hypertext. Ironically, when one medium becomes another medium's material, it is in fact dematerialized, its substance removed, leaving only its form, or style; this process has also been referred to as *remediation* (Bolter & Gromala, 2003; Bolter & Grusin, 1999).

Kenneth Burke's (1950) notion of common ground can also be understood in terms of media and the biophysical environment. Burke argues that communication between two individuals requires a relationship somewhere between absolute difference and absolute commonality. If we were completely the same, identical in all respects, we would have no need to communicate, as one would already know all that the other does. And if we were completely different, with nothing in common, we would be unable to communicate, lacking any basis for shared meaning. Communication can only occur if we begin with some common ground between us, which we can then go on to identify and enlarge. Burke (1945) identifies materialism with the motive of *scene* in his dramatistic pentad, and *scene* is synonymous with *ground*. Thus, our common ground is in fact the shared scene within which we act, beginning as it does with our mutual existence in the material world. In this sense, our common biophysical ground is the fundamental medium through which we communicate. McLuhan (1964), focusing on perception and art, referred to figure-ground relationships, the figure being that which we focus on, the ground being that which recedes, becomes routinized and ignored, rendered effectively invisible. The medium is the background, the figure is the content, and the aim he articulated for media ecology was to reverse the two, to not allow ourselves to always be distracted by the figure, and to instead direct our attention to the ground. This may require stepping outside of the system, if possible, in order to see the system as a system. To accomplish this, McLuhan pointed to the need to find antienvironments or counterenvironments, environments that differ radically from the everyday, routine environments that we inhabit. Much like the experience of visiting other cultures and then returning to our own, experiences that suddenly make us aware of much of what we take for granted and do not pay any attention about our own culture, the same effect could potentially be achieved through experiences involving works of art, or varieties of religious experience and sacred space and time, or through traditional educational environments and good old fashioned printed books, given the ubiquitous quality of our mobile devices and online communication in the 21st century.

Once again, in the folktale that I began this essay with, Joseph's mother and grandfather both explain to the young boy that no one can make something out of nothing, that it is an impossible task. And while Joseph seems to defy that statement, in truth he does not fabricate something out of absolutely nothing. His material is pen and paper, and it is language and experience. He makes this material into something new, and this I would argue is the significance of human communication. Through the magic of sounds and scribbles we alter our environment, and create things that never were. We seem to create something from nothing because, as McLuhan (1964) notes, we tend to focus on the content of our messages and ignore the media that we use to communicate. As an invisible environment, media give us the illusion of a nothing out of which comes a something in the form of a message. I should also point out that McLuhan (1964; see also McLuhan & Zingrone, 1995) specifically argued that media should be understood as agents of transformation, which is fundamental for the field of media ecology; similarly, Burke (1950, 1965) discussed the relationship between rhetoric and change, and Paul Watzlawick (in Watzlawick, Weakland, & Fisch, 1974) wrote about the link between change and communication. I echo these three seminal scholars in our field in emphasizing the point that communication is not so much about creation as it is about mutation, and that the process of representation, signification, symbolization, is in fact a process of transformation.

As long as it is taken with a grain of salt, the phrase *something from nothing* is a wonderful way to express the power of human communication as an agent of change. Of course, taken literally, it sounds too good to be true, like a sham, a cheat, a con. That is the way Plato (1971, 1973) saw it when he condemned rhetoric as a collection of gimmicks and tricks, suggesting that the study of communication is limited to the cosmetic and the counterfeit, that it is a discipline without subject matter, without substance, without material. In effect, he argued that nothing comes from nothing, and that our field is, in fact, a field about nothing. Plato's love for abstract ideas and ideals left no room for the fuzzy logic of rhetoric, let alone the chaos of the human lifeworld. After all, he was part of a philosophical tradition that first invented the concept of permanence as opposed to change, and in this way derived the notion of eternal truth and absolute order. The philosophical tradition that he exemplifies rejected even such untidy mathematical notions as fractions and infinity, viewing them as horribly unwholesome (Logan, 2004). And Plato himself despised the Sophists, the founders of our field, because they saw form as the object of transformation, rather than idealization. The idea of something from nothing would strike him as dangerously irrational, nor would he be open to such contemporary notions as chaos, fractal geometry, and complexity. His logic, however dialectical, would not allow for the eco-logic of self-organizing systems, of a system pulling itself up by its own bootstraps (see, for example, Capra, 1996, 2007; Gleick, 1987; Kauffman, 1995; Luhmann, 1989, 1990, 1995; Maturana & Varela, 1980, 1992; Prigogine & Stengers, 1984; Waldrop, 1992).

I revisit the ancient quarrel between Plato and the Sophists because it shaped and skewed the development of our field. The Sophists understood the centrality of communication, viewing it as the foundation of any worthwhile program of education. Plato all but eliminated communication from his curriculum, and while rhetoric was retrieved by Aristotle, it was relegated to a secondary position where it has remained to this day. Why was Plato's error so powerful? Because all the Sophists could offer were pragmatic approaches to a mundane material reality, while the philosophers were selling an idealism based on which they constructed a beautiful dream world. In other words, it was the ancient philosophers who were actually building something out of nothing.

I am not sure if communication scholars will ever step out of the shadow of the philosophers, but perhaps we might begin with the idea that the study of communication is the study of change, as opposed to permanence. The Sophists were relativists and subjectivists because they recognized the mutability of cultural custom, social organization, and individual perception. They recognized the changing ground of human relationships, and adapted themselves accordingly. And as educators, they promised their students that instruction in symbolic form was the surest path to change and growth. We inheritors of the Sophistic tradition commonly refer to communication as a process and a flow, that is, as characterized by change itself. Communication *is* change, and this, I would suggest, is a tenet that we ought to adopt as a corollary to *one cannot not communicate* (Watzlawick et al, 1967), and a derivative of *the medium is the message* (McLuhan, 1964; McLuhan & Fiore, 1967). Moreover, modern science recognizes the constancy of change, and McLuhan (2006) has persuasively argued that it was not Aristotelian logic or dialectics that formed the basis of modern science, but rather the study of language and linguistic expression, e.g., drama and narrative, otherwise known as *grammar* in the ancient and medieval world (not to be confused with the modern meaning of the word), a discipline closely allied with rhetoric and communication.

Symbolic communication is the most radical form of change that we know, coming as close to giving us *something from nothing* as humanly possible. But the biophysical scene that makes up our common ground allows for modifications only moderately less extreme. For example, in Gilman's book, Joseph's act of communication, his writing of "a wonderful story" is only the last in a series of transformations, as the original piece of cloth goes through periodic alteration at the hands of his grandfather. The story begins with the making of a blanket, but the blanket's cloth was made from raw material, which was the product of living organisms, which arose out of a particular physical environment. The universe is a material environment that is characterized by continuous transformation—it is constantly modifying itself. And somehow, despite the tendency of change to move in the direction of disorder and entropy, some of those changes result in increased organization and complexity, and ultimately life. Organisms not only modify themselves to meet the demands of a changing environment, they also transform their environment to make it more favorable to their own survival and prosperity. This process is called ecology. Sometimes organisms alter their environments through the use of technologies and symbolic forms, and this process in particular is a focus of media ecology scholarship (Nystrom 1973; Postman, 1970; Strate, 2017).

Through communication as information, physical systems defy entropy, organize themselves, and become increasingly more complex. Through communication as social action, social systems maintain themselves in space and modify themselves over time. Through communication as a system of meaning, cultures are established and evolve. Through communication as a system of thought, minds are born and grow. Through communication as a system of symbols, we construct worlds, and we transcend them, just as Joseph transcended the limitations of needle and thread. We may not escape our physical reality, but we are able to change and to improve upon our environment, and ourselves. The media ecology approach to communication focuses on the means and methods, the techniques and technologies that bring about change. It therefore is concerned with the pragmatics of change, in addition to the substance of transformation. In a human context, change may occur as a result of conscious choice and planning, rather than as a product of automatic processes. But our modifications and manipulations often lead to unanticipated and undesirable changes—this is one of media ecology's primary lessons.

Echo and Narcissus

The topic of transformation was very much on the mind of the Roman poet Ovid as he composed his masterpiece, *Metamorphoses* (1955). A literate poet, Ovid imitated the oral epic style of Homer, and drew on oral traditional folktales, much like Gilman (1992) did with her children's book. One of the best known of these myths and legends is the story of Echo and Narcissus. As the tale is no doubt familiar, I will do no more than summarize it here, only touching on the highlights:

Echo was a talkative nymph who used her gift of gab to distract the goddess Juno, allowing her fellow nymphs to escape Juno's wrath. Juno punished Echo by removing her ability to initiate conversation, allowing her only to repeat back whatever she heard. As for Narcissus, he was a young man so beautiful that everyone he met fell in love with him, including Echo. Narcissus was a callous youth, however, and coldly rejected Echo as he did all of his admirers. Broken hearted, the poor nymph faded away until nothing was left of her but her voice. Narcissus was eventually punished by Nemesis, the goddess of vengeance, who caused Narcissus to see his own image in a pool of water. Not recognizing himself, Narcissus was mesmerized by his own beauty. Even after he realized it was only his own reflection, he could not tear himself away, and slowly wasted away until he finally turned into the flower that bears his name, the narcissus, also known as the daffodil.

The story of Echo and Narcissus can be understood in a variety of ways. It is of course a story of metamorphosis, of transformation, of change. And it is a nature myth, providing origins for a species of flower and a sonic phenomenon. Obviously, it is also a story about the perils of vanity, infatuation, and unrequited love. And it can be interpreted as a cautionary tale about gender discrimination, with Narcissus representing patriarchy's false consciousness, and Echo sounding a warning about the self-inflicted wounds of feminine passivity, and the all-too-real danger of anorexia.

McLuhan (1964) saw in Narcissus a parallel to modern individuals who fall in love with their gadgets, their tools, machines, and media. Just as Narcissus failed to realize that the youth he saw was merely his own reflection, McLuhan argues that we by and large bypass the fact that our technologies are extensions of ourselves; we become so totally alienated from their origin that when we fall in our love with our gadgets, we are unable to recognize the fact that we are actually falling in love with devices made in our own image, that in effect we are actually falling in love with ourselves. This certainly seems relevant for the way in which individuals gaze glassy-eyed and mesmerized at television screens, and even more so for the ways in which we become captives of our smart phones and mobile devices, staring lovingly at the images and posts on social media. Noting that Narcissus and narcosis share the same linguistic root, McLuhan wrote of the narcotic effects of technology, of how our inventions function in a manner akin to opioids, dulling our senses and numbing our awareness of our surroundings, and of the cause of our addled state and addiction-like dependencies, our technological extensions themselves. Insofar as we remain comfortably numb, this reinforces the sense that our technologies constitute an invisible environment, through an absence of awareness, a perception of seeming nothingness. Of course, in the ancient myth, it was Echo who actually became an invisible environment in response to the romantic numbness of Narcissus, so invisible that McLuhan himself seemed to have overlooked her in his commentary on the myth.

No one's analysis of Narcissus is better known, however, than that of Sigmund Freud (e.g., 1966). Freud downplayed the case of mistaken identity that triggered the trap set by Nemesis, instead seeing in Narcissus an ego that thinks itself super. Admittedly, Freud did not find Narcissus to be quite so compelling or complex as Oedipus, but he still named a character disorder after him: *narcissism*. One variety, infantile narcissism, is a natural characteristic of early childhood; among adults, however, narcissism is associated with exhibiting self-love and a sense of security and superiority entirely out of line with reality; narcissists devalue others or exhibit disinterest in them, while clinging to a "grandiose conception of the self" (Lasch, 1979, p. 84). In recent popular discourse, discussions of the syndrome have particularly centered on the pathologies of Donald Trump, as he transformed himself from erstwhile celebrity to politician and twice-impeached American president. As for my own treatment of narcissism here, it is necessarily superficial, and does not do justice to the intricacies and debates surrounding this concept. In essence, I wish to follow the lead of Christopher Lasch (1979) and use narcissism to refer in a general way to the problem of too much self.

As narcissism's counterpart, I have enlisted the term *echolalia*, which is not a psychoanalytic disorder like narcissism, only a psychological and neurological symptom. Like McLuhan, Freud acted as if Echo did not exist, and only had eyes for Narcissus. Echo's name only managed to make its way into the psychological literature through its common meaning, as the term echolalia refers to a type of language use in which the speakers repeat back what they have heard. A related term is echopraxia, which refers to the direct imitation of behavior. Echolalia is a normal facet of early language acquisition, and also a symptom of various types of brain disorders and disabilities. Here too, I will not take up all of the specifics of this type of behavior, but rather use it as a metaphor for the problem of too little self.

Narcissism and Echolalia

In writing this essay, putting forth my own thoughts and understandings, and drawing on my own experiences, I run the risk of narcissism. At the same time, most of what I have to say is merely a repetition of what others have said before, so that I also run the risk of echolalia. To be honest, I am not at all certain that I will find a happy medium between the extremes of narcissism and echolalia, a happy medium out of which a balanced sense of self can emerge. But it is very much to the point that it is a struggle to achieve and maintain a sense of self, a struggle that can be lost just as easily as won.

The struggle to find a balance between too much self and too little is, by the same token, a struggle to find a balance between forgetting about others, as narcissists do in their fascination with themselves, and fixating on others, as echolaliacs do as they forfeit their own individuality. The relationship between self and other is essential in the tradition of psychoanalytic commentary practiced by Sigmund Freud (1966), Carl Jung (1969, 1978), Joseph Campbell (1973), Erik Erikson (1950, 1980), Ernest Becker (1971), Norman O. Brown (1985), Francis J. Broucek (1991), and Christopher Lasch (1979); the symbolic interactionist approach used by George Herbert Mead (1934), Kenneth Burke (1945, 1950), Erving Goffman (1959, 1963, 1967), Eric Berne (1964, 1972), Hugh Dalziel Duncan (1962, 1968), Joshua Meyrowitz (1985), and Casey Man Kong Lum (1996); and in the relational perspective associated with Gregory Bateson (Bateson, 1972, 1978; Ruesch & Bateson, 1968), Edward T. Hall (1959, 1966, 1976, 1983), Paul Watzlawick (Watzlawick, Beavin, & Jackson, 1967; Watzlawick, Weakland, & Fisch, 1974), R. D. Laing (1965, 1969) and Kenneth Gergen (1991). Underlying these perspectives is the notion that we are not born with a sense of self, but rather construct one with the raw material of body and brain, and by means of human communication.

As we learn to use our senses and make sense out of our surroundings, we begin to separate ourselves from our environment, and from the individuals that we interact with. We develop a concept of self as we develop a concept of other, a process that is intimately tied to language acquisition. Language gives us a name, and therefore a singular identity. The pronoun "me" provides us with a self that is situated within an environment and is acted upon by that environment. And the pronoun "I" is the perfect expression of the ego acting upon its surroundings. As Ernest Becker (1971) said of "I": "The personal pronoun is the rallying point for self-consciousness, the center of awareness upon which converge all the events in the outside world" (p. 20). First, we learn to speak to others, expressing our selves through words. Then we learn to speak to ourselves, out loud and silently in the form of linguistic thought, the internal monologue. Through such intrapersonal communication we develop self-consciousness (Mead, 1934; Nystrom, 2021, 2022). Symbolic communication gives us the ability to become our own material, allowing us to construct a sense of self. It follows, I would argue, that changes in our mode of communication would change the process of social construction, thereby changing our sense of self.

Echo and Narcissus represent two different extremes in the construction of a sense of self, but they also represent two different modes of sense perception and communication (and as Eric McLuhan, 1998, notes, the two different hemispheres of the brain; see also McLuhan & McLuhan, 1988). As media ecology theorists such as Marshall McLuhan (1962, 1964, 1995), Edmund Carpenter (1960, 1973, Carpenter & McLuhan, 1956, 1960); Harold Innis (1951, 1972), Eric Havelock (1963, 1978, 1982, 1986), and Walter Ong (1967, 1982) have noted, one of the major divisions in modes of perception and cultural formations is that between the ear and the eye. Echo represents the sense of hearing, communication through sound, and the acoustic space that accompanies it. She therefore stands for the sort of media environment that is marked by the absence of literacy and writing, by reliance on speech and song, by emphasis on oral tradition. Such oral cultures lack a storage medium outside of human memory, and therefore rely upon repetition to keep knowledge alive. Just as individual memory acts as a neural echo chamber, the collective memory of an oral society functions as an *echo-system*; it is also noteworthy that within one oral culture, that of the Mayans of Guatemala, their wisest storyteller is called the "echoman" (Sanders, 1994, p. 7). Echolalia, and echopraxia in the form of mimesis, facilitate the storage and preservation of information in an oral culture.

In contrast to Echo, Narcissus represents the sense of sight, communication through visual imagery, and the visual space that it gives rise to. He consequently can be said to stand for the type of media environment characterized by the presence of writing systems, modes of communication that transform language into visual markings and notations, leading to literate habits of mind. Like Narcissus, readers become engrossed in the object of their attention, lured into a life of solitary study, trapped by the process of reflection. Writing freezes language, thereby freeing people from the necessity of memorization. Literacy renders the oral tradition obsolescent, and oral cultures have difficulty surviving when they are thrust into competition with literate cultures, just as Echo fades from view after encountering Narcissus. It is therefore interesting to note that Ovid occupied a peculiar position between the two modes of orality and literacy. That is to say, he was a writer living in a literate society, but that society was a small pocket in a largely nonliterate world; moreover, as a poet Ovid idolized the blind bard Homer, and emulated the oral tradition that supplied the material for the *Iliad* and the *Odyssey*. It is of course impossible to say whether Ovid was fully conscious of the tension between orality and literacy, let alone aware of its allegorical relationship with this particular portion of his *Metamorphoses*, but it is reasonable to assume that the tale of Echo and Narcissus at least unconsciously reflects these tensions.

The interpretations of this myth as being about sense perception and senses of self are quite complementary. Just as Echo represents the extreme of too little self, members of oral cultures have a sublimated sense of self in comparison to literates. Collective, tribal identity dominates, as the preservation of knowledge requires a group effort, and unanimity. The very mode of aural communication is biased towards the group, as audiences listen as a whole, bound together by the simultaneity of sound; this is in contrast to readers reading as isolated individuals. Likewise, group solidarity through conformity and tradition, not novelty and independence, are required for cultural survival; change is only welcome insofar as it maintains balance and homeostasis, as a course correction with the aim of maintaining the status quo.

Of course, from an oral perspective, members of literate cultures, like Narcissus, develop too much self. They are freed from the pressures of conformity and tradition, and encouraged by this mode of visual communication to view themselves as individuals. Writing makes possible, in Havelock's (1963) phrase, "the separation of the knower from the known" (p.197), allowing ideas to be assessed objectively, compared and criticized, and individually evaluated; reading, in turn, encourages both empathy and self-consciousness as we intimately encounter one another's thought-worlds (Olson, 1994, 2016; Wolf, 2007, 2018). Literacy allows us to explore the interior landscape of the mind in a manner heretofore impossible (Ong, 1967, 1982, 1986). Without writing, we would not have the tools to follow the ancient injunction to *know thyself*. In *Metamorphoses*, Ovid (1955) relates that a blind soothsayer, when asked by the mother of Narcissus whether her son would live to a ripe old age, replied, "Yes, if he never knows himself" (p.68). I cannot help but see this as an expression of discontent with literate self-absorption. As we express ourselves through writing, we run the risk of falling in love with our own words, sentences, and thoughts, as they are laid out before us. This type of Platonic love, wherein literacy leads us to adore abstract concepts such as Plato's ideal forms, links to the unattainable ideal of romantic love (potentially resulting in frustration and demoralization, as

Johnson, 1946, explains; see also Postman, 1976). Perhaps, then, Ovid was also registering a critical response to the philosopher who banned poet and sophist alike from his republic? As for literacy and the expanded sense of self (and ego), it set the stage for the cult of individual personality pioneered by Aristotle's student, Alexander the Great (Braudy, 1986). This was further amplified by the typographic revolution in early modern Europe, stemming from the 15th century invention of the printing press with moveable type; typography extended the power of the written word to publicize and immortalize individual names, from the leaders of government, military, and religion, to authors, scholars, artists, and inventors (Eisenstein, 1979).

Now that we have moved into a post-typographic, postliterate, electronic culture, what has happened to our sense of self? There is at once the fear of a return to echolalia in the form of a mass society in which the individual seeks to "escape from freedom" (Fromm, 1965), gives "obedience to authority" (Milgram, 1974), becomes "the organization man [and woman]" (Whyte, 1956), is manipulated by "the mind managers" (Schiller, 1973) who use the media for the purpose of "manufacturing consent" (Herman & Chomsky, 1988), and is integrated into a "technological society" (Ellul, 1964) through the methods of "propaganda" (Ellul, 1965). At the same time, there is the fear that we live in a "culture of narcissism" (Lasch, 1979) in which we are members of "the lonely crowd" (Riesman, Denney, & Glazer, 1950), isolated by our "habits of the heart" (Bellah, Madsen, Sullivan, Swidler, & Tipton, 1985), and reduced to either "bowling alone" (Putnam, 2000), or finding some other way of "amusing ourselves to death" (Postman, 1985) or maybe "amazing ourselves to death" (Strate, 2014). And the truth is that both extremes of narcissism and echolalia seem to coexist today, at the expense of a balanced sense of self.

This crisis of the self has gone by many names: R. D. Laing (1965) wrote about the divided self, and we have all heard about the desperate need to find oneself, and to find self-esteem. Erik Erikson (1950, 1980) identified the identity crisis typically experienced by teenagers, and in recent decades we have heard a great deal about identity politics (Gitlin, 1995), and all too much about identity theft (U. S. Federal Trade Commission, 2002). Media ecologists have noted the blurring of formerly distinct roles such as child and adult (Meyrowitz, 1985; McLuhan, 1964; Postman, 1982), and other forms of identity loss associated with the electronic media (see, for example, Bolter & Grusin, 1999; Carpenter & Heyman, 1970; McLuhan, 1989; Rushing & Frentz, 1995; Sanders, 1994; Turkle, 1995, 2011; Wood, 1996); others see such changes as evolutionary rather than revolutionary, the product of an unfolding modernity (e.g., Giddens, 1991; Romanyshyn, 1989; Tuan, 1982). Postmodernists and poststructuralists refer to the identity crisis as the decentering of the subject, and sometimes the death of the author, celebrating it for its liberating potential (e.g., Barthes, 1977; Jameson, 1991; Poster, 1990). Kenneth Gergen (1991) writes about the saturated self, in which the individual is segmented into an extraordinary number of selves coexisting without integration; he attributes this multiplication of the self to the proliferation of media of interpersonal communication, and finds this form of growth benign, although it certainly can be seen as a variation on the theme of narcissism. Others go so far as to declare us now transhuman (Dewdney, 1998) or posthuman (Hayles, 1999).

Cultural conservatives such as William Bennett (1996) have promoted a notion of character education rooted in nostalgia for the lost sense of a balanced self. They understand as well as anyone that the crisis of the self is a struggle for the self, and that our educational institutions represent one of the principal battlegrounds in this conflict. They also turn to religious traditions for salvation because organized religion has traditionally devoted itself to forging collective identities, regulating social behavior, and molding individual consciousness, even if the self that social conservatives are fighting for is no longer possible in the contemporary media environment, was in many ways illusory, certainly a social construction rather than a natural development, and had its costs that in significant ways outweighed its benefits. The religious experience has been concerned with constructing, reconstructing, and/or deconstructing selves, as it has revolved around the relationship between self and the ultimate Other. In the 20th century philosophers such as Jean Paul Sartre (2010) and Martin Buber (1952) came to speak of the silence of God, which Walter Ong in *The Presence of the Word* (1967) associates with the rise of the mass media and the establishment of the electronic media environment; Ong suggests that all of this secondary orality generates so much noise that the still, small voice of the divine is drowned out. But God's silence can also be seen as another facet of our crisis of identity.

In the end, it is neither Echo nor Narcissus that personifies the electronic media environment, and the contemporary cultures that have emerged within it. Rather it is Nemesis, the goddess who avenges Echo by extending and thereby amputating Narcissus. The numbing effect that McLuhan (1964) refers to also relates to his argument that any given medium or technology, in extending some aspect of the body (or some other attribute), also amputates that organ. Amputation here does not refer to an actual removal of a body part, but rather the idea that it is rendered so insensate that it is effectively absent. The extension does not simply add to the existing individual, or go over the part of the body it is associated with, but rather in effect replaces it, acting much like a prosthetic device; Freud (1961) argues that technology gives us a level of power that previous generations would have thought supernatural, turning us into *prosthetic gods*. The term *cyborg*, short for cybernetic organisms, also has been invoked for the way in which we join together with our tools and machines; the term originates in the mid-20th century in reference to serious efforts to create electronic prosthetics, and was later popularized through science fiction narratives (Gray, 1995; Haraway, 1991; Rushing & Frentz, 1995). The revenge that Nemesis exacts on Narcissus also relates to the laws of media developed by Marshall and Eric McLuhan (1988), which indicate that a new medium or technology will enhance an existing element of the environment, render an existing medium or technology obsolescent, retrieve a previously obsolesced medium or technology from obscurity, and reverse into its opposite when pushed to an extreme. It follows that in electronic culture we see narcissism simultaneously enhanced, the balanced sense of self obsolesced, echolalia retrieved, and both narcissism and echolalia reversed into each other, an oscillation between too much and too little self, with little space in between. Significantly, Nemesis represents something different from either Echo or Narcissus, while in a way connected to both, just as the electronic media retrieves or extends certain qualities of both orality and literacy. Characterizing the electronic era as the Age of Nemesis would surely be consistent with the criticism of media ecologists such as Neil Postman (1982, 1985, 1992) and Jacques Ellul (1964, 1965).

The Enigma of Autism

With this in mind, I now want to turn to an example from my personal life. It is neither a folktale, nor a myth, nor a story with a happy ending. Rather, it is the story of my daughter Sarah, and her disability. In June of 1998, when Sarah was two and a half years old, my wife and I received the diagnosis that Sarah has autism. We had some concerns about her development during her first year, and began to understand that something was seriously wrong during her second year, as she suffered from a series of seizures when she was twenty-one months old. With the aid of medication, the seizures were brought under control, but she often appeared withdrawn, disconnected from the world around her, lost in her own world or focused on things that typical children would not pay attention to. Even more alarming was the fact that she failed to develop language normally. She did exhibit echolalia, repeating back words and phrases like *thank you* and *big* without any regard for their meaning; she also demonstrated a remarkable ability to memorize songs such as Raffi's "Baby Beluga" and Barney's "I Love You" song. As it turns out, this echolalia is a symptom of autism, albeit one that can be, at an early age, a positive indication of the potential for linguistic and cognitive development, at the very least about their chances of not having the most severe form of the developmental disability, and remaining nonverbal.

I do not want to dwell on the devastating impact that the diagnosis of autism had on my wife and myself back when we first received it. I do want to note, however, that despite the fact that seizure disorders are present in one out of four cases of autism (Volkmar, 1989, p. 60), and despite the presence of numerous other symptoms and indicators, the various doctors and therapists that dealt with Sarah kept us in the dark as to this possibility for eight months, and more. Only one brave and charitable occupational therapist gave us a hint a few weeks prior to Sarah's examination and diagnosis by a developmental pediatrician. The experience of an unintended conspiracy of silence is not at all uncommon among parents of children with autism, and ought to be researched further by those in our field who specialize in health communication. The sooner parents are made aware of the situation, the sooner intervention can begin, and time does make a difference.

As you no doubt know, reading is one of the coping mechanisms that we literates employ in times of trouble. And so, after receiving the diagnosis, I immediately set out to read as much as I could about autism. Some of the most helpful sources I came across include Uta Frith's *Autism: Explaining the Enigma* (1989), a classic that is intellectually stimulating and displays a great deal of empathy for individuals with autism. Simon Baron-Cohen and Patrick Bolton's *Autism: The Facts* (1993) proved to be an excellent concise guide. Bryna Siegel's *The World of the Autistic Child* (1996) was one of the most comprehensive general introductions I was able to find, one that offers less optimism and more realism about the condition than most other sources. Shirley Cohen's *Targeting Autism* (1998) was the most balanced I came across, and nearly as complete as Siegel's book. Online, I also consulted the highly informative websites for the Autism Society of America and The New Jersey Center for Outreach and Services for the Autism Community (COSAC), now Autism New Jersey (the best known site, Autism Speaks did not exist at that time). I read about autism as a parent of course, not a scholar. And yet, I could not help but notice the many ways that this disorder intersects with my own intellectual background. As the name of the syndrome implies, autism is a disorder of the self, and it is a disorder profoundly linked to problems in communication and perception. But let me begin with some facts.

Autism was first identified in 1943 by Leo Kanner, while Hans Asperger described a high functioning variation of the condition in 1944, which came to be known as Asperger's Syndrome. It has been firmly established that autism (and Asperger's) are biological, specifically neurological conditions, sometimes described as abnormalities, alternately as simply diverging from the neurotypical. These conditions are generally believed to be present before birth, affecting the development of the brain; speculation that early childhood vaccinations are the cause of autism have not been substantiated and are largely discounted by professionals, but are adhered to by a significant number of parents, resulting in an "anti-vax" movement that mutated following the COVID-19 pandemic and subsequent right-wing conspiracy theories that denied the reality of that disease. As for autism, the failure to identify a specific cause, be it a virus, toxin, or specific genetic flaw, has resulted in much speculation regarding diet, enzymes, chemical additives, etc., an understandable but ultimately dysfunctional response from parents to the extent that this serves as a distraction from providing their children with what they need in the present. Not knowing the specific cause, it follows that no definitive medical tests have yet been developed to identify the presence of autism, so instead, diagnosis depends upon behavioral observation and testing. This means that autism is a fuzzy category, with shifting boundaries.

As a syndrome, autism encompasses a wide variety of traits, some of which may or may not be present in any given case, and which may appear in any number of combinations. Therefore, every individual with autism has a different mix of characteristics, requiring individually tailored intervention, therapy, and learning strategies. For example, unlike many individuals with autism, my daughter can be quite emotional, exhibits a degree of emotional empathy, and can be quite loving, caring, and affectionate (traits that mean a great deal to a parent). Because of the wide degree of variation in the way that the syndrome manifests itself from individual to individual, autism is generalized simply as a *pervasive developmental disorder*, meaning that there are multiple developmental issues. PDD as it is commonly abbreviated, or PDD-NOS (pervasive developmental disorder, not otherwise specified), sometimes appears as an alternative to a diagnosis of autism, or as a euphemism for it. Significantly, autism has come to be understood as a spectrum disorder, meaning that there is a continuum between the severest cases, through the mildest which may go undiagnosed, and perhaps extending to individuals with few, if any, autistic traits.

This also makes it difficult to determine the numbers of individuals with autism within any given population. Still, in the United States it has become commonplace to speak of an epidemic of autism, one that seems to get worse and worse as the years go by. When I first began writing on the subject in 1999 (see Strate, 2000; see also Strate, 2003, 2011b), estimates ranged from 1 in 1,000 individuals with autism in the US, to what seemed back then to be an exaggerated estimate of 1 in 166. According to a study from the CDC issued in 2020, there are an estimated 5,437,988 adults with autism spectrum disorder in the US, representing 2.21% of the population, which translates to 1 in 45 individuals (Centers for Disease Control and Prevention, 2022); a 2016 study estimates that the prevalence among children is 1 in 54 (Centers for Disease Control and Prevention, 2020).

No race, ethnic group, religion, political orientation, or socioeconomic class is exempt from the prevalence of autism, but there is a gender difference, in that the disorder occurs four times more frequently among boys than girls. No wonder then, that autism researcher Simon Baron-Cohen turned his attention to the overall differences in brain structure and function between men and women, in a book entitled *The Essential Difference: The Truth About the Male and Female Brain and the Truth About Autism* (2003). According to Baron-Cohen, autism is an example of the extreme male brain, which excels at analysis and abstract-thinking, and therefore working with complex systems, and is weak in contrast to the female brain in understanding feelings and emotions, in developing a sense of empathy, and in communication and social interaction. I would not dispute the fact that there are biological differences associated with gender, differences that are neurological as well as otherwise being physiological. And as scholars such as Walter Ong (1981) and Deborah Tannen (1990) have established, there are significant differences in the ways that men and women and communicate, and therefore understand each other, and their world. Baron-Cohen's perspective also relates to Leonard Shlain's (1998, 2003) arguments about media ecology and the biology of gender; Shlain follows up on McLuhan's suggestions regarding brain hemispheres and media (McLuhan & McLuhan, 1988), as they specifically relate left hemisphere dominance to alphabetic literacy, right hemisphere dominance to orality. Shlain links this distinction to the tendency for males to be characterized by left hemisphere dominance, and females to be characterized originally by right hemisphere dominance, more recently by a balance between the hemispheres; this leads him to argue that oral cultures, in favoring the right hemisphere, also favor the gender equality associated with the cult of the goddess in antiquity, while the introduction of writing, the alphabet, and literacy resulted in media environments more favorable to the male brain and patriarchal religions and cultures. As for Baron-Cohen's theory regarding the male brain and individuals with autism, it may carry a great deal of weight, but given the fact that over 20% of individuals with autism are female, it would follow that gender is probably not the causative agent, and probably not the main factor associated with its incidence, however much it may be among the most visible—and as the parent of an autistic girl, I find the gender-based argument less than compelling, and certainly not all that relevant.

Autism is diagnosed by three main criteria. The first has to do with impairments in social interaction; Kanner referred to this as "autistic aloneness" (quoted in Frith, 1989, p.10). There are problems developing relationships, reciprocating emotions, and sharing interests with others, as well as a blindness to nonverbal social cues. The individual with autism seems lost in his or her own world, and an alien in our own, lacking in the common ground that typical individuals take for granted. The second impairment is in communication, both verbal and nonverbal, often including delays in language acquisition or sometimes a complete lack of speech. Moreover, the child may not take part in imaginative play, and may lack interest in narrative. There can also be related problems with the processing of sensory information. At times, the individual may seem impervious to sensory stimulation, not reacting to sounds or to physical pain, while at other times he or she may be overly sensitive to certain sensory input. The third criterion is described as "restricted, repetitive, and stereotyped patterns of behavior, interests, or activity" (Siegel, 1996, p. 18). Both simple motions like hand flapping and complex behavioral patterns may be enacted repeatedly. There is a tendency to favor ritual and routine, and to behave obsessively and compulsively. Even in mild cases, interests may be pursued with unusual focus and intensity. These symptoms are related to echopraxia, as the behaviors may be learned by imitation; for example, my daughter was able to pick up and reproduce fairly complex hand maneuvers and dance steps from watching Barney videotapes.

While previously the majority of individuals with autism were also diagnosed with serious intellectual disabilities, the CDC now estimates that just slightly more than half have below average cognitive skills (Centers for Disease Control and Prevention, 2022). Of course, assessing intelligence is highly problematic when dealing with individuals who may be unable or simply unwilling to speak. Famously, some individuals with autism exhibit savant skills, highly developed abilities in one specialized area, such as mathematics, computer science, music, art, architecture, mechanics, biology, or simply memorization, visualization, or manual dexterity. Savants are usually well below normal in other areas, however, and individuals with autism are particularly handicapped in regard to social and emotional intelligence. The unevenness of autistic intelligence is in part what inspired Howard Gardner's (1983, 1993) theory of multiple intelligences. In his book, *Extraordinary Minds* (1997), he writes:

> When planning their political or religious campaigns or creating works of science or art, extraordinary individuals can focus their attention for many hours at a time, screening out even the most dissonant of stimuli. Such attention is desirable, of course, but it may be akin to autism—a pathological condition in which attention is so focused that the individual is unable ever to engage in normal human intercourse. It is not surprising that the incidence of autism is higher in the families of indi-

viduals who perform at a high level in certain academic disciplines, like mathematics, science, and engineering. (p. 134)

Actually, academics of all types seem to have a high incidence of some autistic traits, such as absent-mindedness, intense and single-minded interests, and social deficits. This may well have been the case for Albert Einstein, who did not speak until the age of 5, had a great deal of difficulty with social interaction, and possessed savant skills in mathematics and visualization. The philosopher Ludwig Wittgenstein also exhibited autistic traits; this adds new shades of meaning to his famous quote, "Whereof one cannot speak, thereof one must be silent" (Wittgenstein, 1961, p. 189) given the mutism characteristic of some individuals with autism, and the problems that many of them face in language acquisition. Consider Wittgenstein's quote, for example, in light of the following passages taken from *Through the Eyes of Aliens* by Jasmine Lee O'Neill (1999), a mute autistic savant: "Selective mutism is when the person chooses whom to talk to, and in which situations.... Elective mutism is electing to be silent to everyone. Autistics can have periods of either type which last a lifetime, or several years or weeks" (pp. 45-46). Further, one of the founding fathers of the United States, Thomas Jefferson, may have been mildly autistic (Ledgin, 2000), and the same may be true of America's greatest inventor, Thomas Edison, and his modern-day counterpart, Bill Gates.

Along with intellectuals, artists appear likely to have a better than average incidence of autism, as social impairment would not be a factor in solitary creative pursuits, while visual and musical savant skills would be decidedly advantageous. Thus, Vincent Van Gogh's seizures and psychological difficulties may have been the result of the syndrome, and possibly Andy Warhol's antisocial tendencies and love of repetition; among musicians, Béla Bartók and Glenn Gould both exhibited autistic traits. Religion too, with its elements of repetitive ritual and spiritual isolation, would appeal to high functioning individuals, such as, possibly, the legendary follower of St. Francis, Brother Juniper, as well as the holy fools of Russian Orthodox tradition, and the Buddha. This sort of speculation focuses on extraordinary individuals because of their celebrity, and because history tends to ignore the ordinary and the low-functioning alike. One prominent exception, well known in the field of communication, is the 18th century wild boy of Aveyron, the subject of François Truffaut's 1970 film, *L'Enfant Sauvage* (aka *The Wild Child*). A strong case has been made that the original "wild boy" was not raised by wolves, but rather was an autistic child who had been abandoned or run off (Lane, 1977; Frith, 1989).

Accounts of autistic individuals can also be found in fictional form. Dustin Hoffman's portrayal of an autistic adult in the 1988 film *Rain Man* is particularly well known, and the bestselling novel by Mark Haddon, *The Curious Incident of the Dog in the Night-Time* (2003), takes the reader directly into the interior landscape of the autistic mind. The television series *Parenthood*, which ran on the American television network, NBC, from 2010 to 2015, features an especially realistic depiction of a relatively high-functioning autistic teenager. Another series, *Touch*, that ran for two seasons on the American network Fox from 2012-2013, followed the fantasy trope of the autistic individual with savant skills and near magical powers. *The Good Doctor*, originating as a South Korean medical drama in 2013, adapted for American television and premiering on ABC in 2017, features a young surgical resident who is an autistic savant. These are just a few examples, as overall, the presence in various forms of popular culture of numerous fictional characters characterized by some degree of autism and Asperger's have increased dramatically over the past decade, owing both to growing autism awareness and the epidemic itself. Of no small importance was the fact that the grandson of Bob Wright was diagnosed with autism in 2004; Wright was then CEO of NBC and its parent company, General Electric, prompting the executive to found Autism Speaks the following year, an organization that quickly became the leading voice for autism advocacy in the United States.

It should also be noted that there have been many popular culture characters who exhibit autistic traits but were created before the condition was identified (e.g., Sherlock Holmes), or who are not identified as autistic for other reasons. For example, often unacknowledged is the fact that Tommy, the hero of the 1969 rock opera written by Pete Townsend of The Who, was patterned after autistic children Townsend had observed. Although Tommy's condition is the result of childhood trauma, his symptoms have little to do with repressed memories. Instead, he is unable to hear or see, even though there is nothing wrong with his sensory organs, and he does not speak, even though he is capable of it. Tommy spends his time gazing in the mirror, not out of narcissistic vanity, but because he is lost in his own world; and he displays savant skills of tactile dexterity when placed in front of a pinball machine. Tommy's "amazing journey" actually parallels the delayed development of high functioning individuals, who as adults gain the ability to communicate something about their experiences.

The Struggle for a Sense of Self

Donna Williams has written a number of books about her condition (e.g., Williams, 1992, 1994, 1996, 1998, 1999); the following passage is from *Sensing: The Unlost Instinct* (Williams, 1998):

> Up to the age of four, I sensed according to pattern and shifts in pattern. My ability to interpret what I saw was impaired because I took each fragment in without understanding its meaning in the context of its surroundings. I'd see the nostril but lose the nose, see the nose but lose the face, see the fingernail but lose the finger. My ability to interpret what I heard was equally impaired. I heard the intonation but lost the meaning of the words, got a few of the words but lost the sentences. I couldn't consistently process the meaning of my own body messages if I was focusing in on something with my eyes or ears. I didn't know myself in relation to other people because when I focused on processing information about "other," I lost "self," and when I focused on "self," I lost other. I could either express something in action or make some meaning of some of the information coming in but not both at once. So crossing the room to do something meant I'd probably lose the experience of walking even though my body did it. Speaking, I'd lose the meaning of my own sounds whilst moving. The deaf-blind may have lost their senses; I had my senses but lost the sense. I was meaning deaf, meaning blind. (p. 33)

What Williams describes is a world of fleeting and fragmentary perceptions, an inability to organize sensory data, form gestalts, and construct a meaningful reality. It was only with difficulty that she was able to build a world in which she could understand self and other, but not simultaneously. Either she would shut out her environment and turn inward, or give up her sense of self and become lost in her perceptions. At least in part, this stems from an inability to integrate mind and body. As Williams (1998) later writes (the awkwardness of her prose reflecting the awkwardness of describing the experience):

> Back then, back in the beginning in the time before mind, "I" was not my body nor even considered my selfhood necessarily to exist there. There was me and there was the thing others might have called "my body" but there was no feeling that this thing belonged to me and the concept that it was actually part of me was a very difficult one to grasp in more than just theory. (p. 35)

Lacking a sense of her own body, Williams could not fully separate self from environment, and therefore could not create a coherent and integrated conception of her surroundings. We tend to think of perception as being about the external environment, but in many ways it begins with internal sensation, our ability to perceive and make sense of our bodies, and our boundary with the outside world. Lacking this most basic form of self-awareness, both meaning-making and language acquisition are impaired. While sight and hearing dominate our consciousness, the tactile sense is much more basic to our sense of self, and there are two other body senses we rarely acknowledge. One is the proprioceptive sense, which tells us about the movement and position of our joints and muscles; the other is the vestibular sense, our sense of balance, of gravity, of movement and position in relation to the earth (Kranowitz, 1998). Essential to this sense of balance is the inner ear, which perhaps adds weight to McLuhan's (1964) association of oral cultures with a *balanced* sensorium (see also, Tomatis, 1996). The point here, however, is that both perception and cognition have a common origin in the self-organization of the nervous system. For this reason, sensory integration and auditory integration therapies, which are based on these premises, may be effective supplements to behavioral therapies in improving the cognitive abilities of individuals with autism (see, for example, Kranowitz, 1998; Madaule, 1994; Tomatis, 1996).

The title of Donna Williams's first book, *Nobody, Nowhere* (1992), reflects the difficulty she had in establishing a sense of self, and the consubstantial problem of establishing a meaningful relationship to her environment. What she describes, however, is not a static situation but an ongoing odyssey, a fact that is reflected in the title of her second book, *Somebody, Somewhere* (1994). As psychologist Oliver Sacks (1995) describes it, the brain is:

> dynamic and active, a supremely efficient adaptive system geared for evolution and change, ceaselessly adapting to the needs of the organism—its need, above all, to construct a coherent self and world, whatever defects or disorders of brain function befell it (p. xvii).

The self and world that individuals with autism like Williams tend to construct is extremely concrete. In other words, there is a tendency to get lost in the particulars, the details, as opposed to using abstract, global categories in thought and perception. In mild form, this is an approach associated with a practical, common sense approach to life, but in somewhat different ways, concreteness is a characteristic associated with the mental operations of children (Piaget, 1954), the kind of culture known as "savage" or tribal (Lévi-Strauss, 1966), and individuals with various brain defects and disorders (Sacks, 1987, 1995). Of the latter, Sacks (1987) writes that "their world is vivid, intense, detailed, yet simple, precisely because it is concrete; neither complicated, diluted, nor unified by abstraction" (p. 174). He goes on to argue:

> By a sort of inversion, or subversion, of the natural order of things, concreteness is often seen by neurologists as a wretched thing, beneath con-

sideration, incoherent, regressed. Thus for Kurt Goldstein, the greatest systematiser of his generation, the mind, man's glory, lies wholly in the abstract and categorical, and the effect of brain damage, any and all brain damage, is to cast him out from this high realm into the almost subhuman swamplands of the concrete. If a man loses the 'abstract-categorical attitude' (Goldstein) or 'propositional thought' (Hughlings Jackson), what remains is subhuman, of no moment or interest.

I call this an inversion because the concrete is elemental—it is what makes reality 'real', alive, personal and meaningful. All of this is lost if the concrete is lost. (p. 174)

In other words, the concrete is the basis of human experience—the very term concrete is a material metaphor. Implicit in concrete mental operations is the experience of physical reality, of being "close to the human lifeworld" in Ong's (1982, p. 42) memorable phrase. Sacks (1987) suggests that the quality of concreteness "which characterizes the simple... gives them their poignant innocence, transparency, completeness and dignity" (p. 174). Abstracting, on the other hand, is a process that takes the individual further and further away from reality, a point central to the general semantics of Korzybski (1993), Hayakawa (Hayakawa & Hayakawa, 1990), and Johnson (1946). But the extreme concreteness associated with autism is closely connected to difficulties with language acquisition and language's concomitant capacity for abstraction. Language use for children with autism may be so concrete that a word learned with a particular individual, in a particular place, and during a particular activity, may not be generalized to other people, places, or situations. Among the most difficult words to learn to use appropriately are the highly abstract pronouns *I* and *you*; what could be more confusing than a pronoun that refers at one time to oneself, the next time to another? Of course, this may reflect problems in forming a sense of self and other, as well as difficulty in abstracting.

Even savant skills are based on autistic concreteness. Many do quite well at jigsaw puzzles, because they pay close attention to shape rather than picture—in fact, it is just as easy for them to put the pieces together when they are turned upside down. Memorization, which some autistic individuals excel at, is a concrete activity, as Sacks (1995) explains:

It is characteristic of the savant memory (in whatever sphere—visual, musical, lexical) that it is prodigiously retentive of particulars. The large and the small, the trivial and momentous, may be indifferently mixed, without any sense of salience, of foreground versus background. There is little disposition to generalize from these particulars or to integrate them with each other, causally or historically, or with the self. In such a memory there tends to be an immovable connection of scene and time, of content and context (a so-called concrete-situational or episodic memory)—hence the astounding powers of literal recall so common in autistic savants, along with difficulty extracting the salient features from these particular memories, in order to build a general sense and memory. (p. 200)

Along with memorization, savant skills in visualization also reflect the absence of abstraction. Consider how one such individual with autism describes her thought processes:

I think in pictures. Words are like a second language to me. I translate both spoken and written words into full-color movies, complete with sound, which run like a VCR tape in my head. When somebody speaks to me, his words are instantly translated into pictures. Language-based thinkers often find this phenomenon difficult to understand, but in my job as an equipment designer for the livestock industry, visual thinking is a tremendous advantage. (p.19)

This passage was written by Temple Grandin (1995), who holds a PhD in animal science, and is on the faculty in that area at Colorado State University. In addition to designing livestock facilities, she has written one book on animal science, and two more on her disability (Grandin, 1995; Grandin & Scariano, 1986). I do believe that the Sophists would recognize in Temple Grandin's visual thinking a process akin to the ancient art of memory described by Frances Yates (1966), in which visualization and memorization are closely allied, a set of mnemonic techniques that culminated in the early modern era's memory theater. In comparison to the memory theater as an artificial mnemonic device, Grandin's comparison of her own thought processes to a VCR suggests a more instinctive and intuitive home theater of memory and mental processing. The concreteness of both visualization and memorization are certainly related.

As for visual thinking, it has its inefficiencies in comparison with language-based thought, and does not have the same easy access to abstractions as does thinking with words, but it is probably best understood as a different mode of thought, rather than simply as an inferior, primitive, or undeveloped form of cognition. What Grandin clearly demonstrates is that thoughts are not reducible to words, however close the association between the two for typical individuals. Visual and other forms of nonverbal perception, communication, and mentation are even more basic than language to the making of meaning.

It is in this respect that postmodernists such as Fredric Jameson (1972, 1991) and Jean François Lyotard (1984) fall short, mistakenly viewing language as the only game in town, a closed system that serves as our *prison-house*, to use the phrase from Jameson's (1972) book title. This critique is forcefully made by Alexander Durig in *Autism and the Crisis of Meaning* (1996), where he champions Susanne K. Langer (1957) as an antidote to postmodern nihilism:

> The premises of postmodernism hinge heavily on this conviction that language is the medium of meaning, and that it is not capable of formal logical consistency, or guaranteed communicative success, or purity of transmission of knowledge. This is best summed up in Zeno's paradox. Recall how the Greek philosopher said that perfect communication is impossible because every word has to be explained with other words, which have to be explained with other words, ad infinitum. It is an infinite regress; it is all ends against the middle, and there is therefore no absolute base of knowledge or communication possible. This is one of postmodernism's most powerful arguments.
>
> Langer's response is simple, however. Language is not the medium of meaning; meaning is the medium of language. And the fundamental aspect of meaning is symbolic transformation. (p. 168)

Nondiscursive and nonverbal modes of communication, from the visual and iconic to ritual and significant gesture, are pathways to metamorphosis; parallel to discursive and verbal codes, they are alternate methods of translating our perceptions and experiences of material reality into other forms. More importantly, the nondiscursive and the nonverbal precede language, and serve as the media within which linguistic communication takes form and makes meaning. They constitute the invisible environment that supports linguistic communication, an environment that becomes visible when language acquisition is delayed or disrupted, as is the case for individuals with autism. Typical language development is measured by an increasing ability for abstraction, while the nondiscursive and nonverbal are by nature concrete. Moreover, it goes without saying, or at least ought to, that the concrete and material reality of disability (not to mention disease and death) serves as a better context for understanding the human condition than the abstract and immaterial philosophical musings of postmodernists and Platonists alike. Durig (1996) does suggest, however, that autistic concreteness amounts to a deficit in inductive reasoning, with high functioning individuals maintaining normal to superior deductive abilities, while low functioning autistics may have difficulty reasoning deductively as well as inductively.

Theory of Mind

Difficulties processing sensory input, concreteness, and atypical language acquisition all are interrelated with the distinctive quality of autistic aloneness, social impairment, and what Edgar Schneider in *Discovering My Autism* (1999) calls "the emotional deficit" (p. 94). This is not to deny that individuals with autism have feelings—they most certainly do. As a child, my daughter Sarah was quite capable of throwing temper tantrums, and continues to display anger and frustration on occasion, as well as crying in sadness, demonstrating affection and love, and exhibiting a sense of humor and laughing appropriately (as well as inappropriately). Instead, what is meant by an emotional deficit is a deficit in detecting the subtlety of emotions as a form of social behavior (Duncan, 1962, 1968). As Sacks (1995) relates in his discussion of Temple Grandin: "She said that she could understand 'simple, strong, universal' emotions but was stumped by more complex emotions and the games people play. 'Much of the time,' she said, 'I feel like an anthropologist on Mars'" (p. 259). This sense of distance, and the resultant difficulty forming close relationships, is manifested on the most fundamental of levels. For example, seeing eye to eye is one of the most basic forms of relating to others, but individuals with autism like my daughter tend to avoid making eye contact, not out of shyness, but either because they are not aware of the significance of such nonverbal cues, or avoid them because they experience them as the source of sensory overload.

The simple gesture of pointing at something in one's environment is typically picked up very early in childhood as part of the individual's natural course of development, but for Sarah and many other children with autism, intervention in the form of deliberate instruction is needed or the child may never learn how to point. Pointing implies an awareness of self and other, a shared gaze, a shared attention, a shared meaning. And it is a key step in language acquisition, as we ultimately replace our fingers with words that also "point" to things in our environment. Meaning making is thus linked to empathy, a trait that does not come easily to persons with autism. A lack of empathy does not imply antipathy, however, nor does autistic alienation lead to immoral conduct, as Frith (1989) explains:

> Some of the perceived abnormalities of autistic social behavior can be seen not so much as impairments, but as unusually positive qualities. These qualities can be captured by terms such as innocence, honesty and guilelessness. Autistic people are not adept at deceiving others, nor at impressing others. They are not manipulative or gossipy.... they are not envious and can give to others gladly.... Autistic people may not

empathize in the common sense of the word, but neither do they gloat over other people's misfortune. Indeed they can be profoundly upset by the suffering they see, and they can show righteous indignation. (p.140)

The social, emotional and empathetic deficits of autism all are manifestations of what Frith (1989) believes to be the fundamental impairment of autism: the inability to form a theory of mind, that is, an inability to understand that others have a mind like one's own, and a point of view different from one's own. Typical individuals habitually ascribe emotions and motivations to others, and make inferences about others' knowledge and beliefs. Simon Baron-Cohen (1995), who studied under Frith, refers to what we do as "mindreading" (p. 2). By this he does not mean that we employ extrasensory perception to determine to a certainty what someone else is thinking, although it may appear that way to an autistic individual. Rather, Baron-Cohen points out that we simply employ everyday sense perception to speculate about what others are thinking and planning, with a fair degree of success. Arguing from the perspective of evolutionary psychology, he reasons that, as a species that engages in highly complex social interaction, we have a genetic predisposition towards mindreading.

Along the same lines, Robin Dunbar (1996) argues for the close connection between language and theory of mind, both rooted in the primates' need for social cohesion. Some of the elements of theory of mind are nondiscursive and nonlinguistic, developing during the first two years of normal childhood development; they are also present among individuals with autism and perhaps even among the higher primates (Baron-Cohen, 1995). These elements appear to be a prerequisite for the evolution of language, making possible the nonverbal medium of meaning within which verbal communication takes place. The formation of a complete theory of mind, however, does not occur until the typical individual is already well on the way to language acquisition, sometime after the age of four (Baron-Cohen, 1995). Thus, language and theory of mind appear to be mutually coadaptive systems. From an evolutionary standpoint, apart from the immeasurable value that mindreading would hold for a social species, theory of mind also had tremendous survival value because it is an incredibly efficient way to think about any complex system, be it a human being, organism, or the physical environment. Even if it is inaccurate, looking at a thunderstorm anthropomorphically, as a thinking being that throws lightning bolts, is a more efficient way to understand the threatening quality of this meteorological phenomenon (and subsequently respond appropriately to it) than developing complex scientific explanations.

Rather than thinking in terms of mental states and motivations, individuals with autism tend to view others in the most concrete of terms, as objects and behaviors. They may understand many aspects of volition, desire, and intention in others, but have trouble coordinating understandings of self and other as independent consciousnesses that may or may not share attention, awareness, and belief. For example, a common measure of theory of mind is to test for understanding of false belief. In this sort of test, the subject is presented with a story in which characters A and B together hide money inside a box, which is then closed. A then leaves the room, and while being away, B removes the money from the box and puts it in his pocket. A then returns, obviously not knowing that the money has been taken by B. The subject knows something that the character A does not know, and he or she is asked where A believes the money to be. Typical individuals who are at least four years old correctly identify A as holding the false belief that the money is in the box, as do individuals with other mental handicaps such as Down's syndrome with a mental age of four or greater. Most individuals with autism, even those with highly developed language skills, instead credit A with knowing that the money has been moved to B's pocket. In other words, they cannot distinguish between their own knowledge as outside observers and the more limited perspective that A would hold. Baron-Cohen (1995) refers to this syndrome as "mindblindness" (p. xxiii), and relates it to both social impairment and difficulties in communication, as much of the common ground that we take for granted is not present. Even when verbal skills are well developed and intelligence high, individuals with autism have difficulty picking up the metacommunicational and relational cues (Bateson, 1972, 1979; Watzlawick et al, 1967) that typical individuals take for granted. Nonverbal signals, such as what Baron-Cohen calls (1995) "the language of the eyes" (p. 108), are indecipherable. Consider the following passage from Dorothy Lee's (1959) anthropological analysis of self-image in Greek culture:

> The organs of highest significance are the eyes. They are the seat of the person. With them, lovers and friends communicate, and they are the pre-eminent medium of enjoyment. Love comes through the eyes, and the eyes are mentioned the most frequently in the personal poems. "We have not seen you" means "We missed you."
>
> In the folk songs, a beloved's eyes shoot arrows, strike with a poisoned sword, catch a man in a net, they burn the heart or break it into pieces; they lead astray, they bewitch, they destroy. Glances are rarely sweet, and never soft or gentle, in the love dystichs. Here eyes are always black, perhaps because one is apprehensive if they are blue, the color of the evil eye. It is difficult to overestimate the joy of sheer vision.... When a long-absent loved one is returning, people congratulate, say-

ing: "Light for your eyes." (p. 145)

As Lee describes it, the language of the eyes overflows with meaning in Greek culture, which is a decidedly visual culture. But even in cultures where it is common to avert one's eyes, there is an art to looking away, and a meaningfulness to the averted gaze that is entirely distinct from the failure to fully form a theory of mind, and the related difficulty processing information communicated through facial expressions that is characteristic of autism. At best, high functioning individuals like Temple Grandin can try to learn the rules of mental states and social interaction in a highly self-conscious way, as a formal logic that lacks the flexibility, intuitiveness, and the spontaneity of typical perception and communication. Lacking a theory of mind may also make it difficult to achieve full self-awareness, given that it would be all but impossible to try to see oneself as others do. Thus, Durig (1996) states that the severity of autism is inversely related to the sense of self. He also points to the similarity between autistic perception and meditation, mysticism and spirituality (which generally involve some form of separation and sublimation of the self); similarly, Durig suggests that mental illness might be better understood as the withdrawal, atrophy, and possibly the annihilation of the self.

At the same time, individuals with autism may appear to be all self and no other (as the term *autism* implies), unable to recognize that others have beliefs and understandings that differ from one's own; in this sense, they would seem to exhibit a worldview somewhat akin to infantile narcissism, albeit with significant differences as well. The inability to fully form a theory of mind may result in a failure to fully construct a self, or it may mean that alternate, atypical selves need to be created. For example, typical children engage in role-playing as part of the process of constructing a self, but individuals with autism tend to be impaired in regards to imaginative play. Still, high functioning individuals may appropriate roles without assimilating them fully or properly, or self-consciously acquire and put on personas as "pseudopersonalities" (Sacks, 1995, p. 266; see also Williams, 1992). Thus, autism can sometimes bear a surface resemblance to schizophrenia (for which it was once mistaken), with its surfeit of selves.

Evolutionary Perspectives

Psychiatrist Iain McGilchrist (2009) draws on Baron-Cohen's (1995, 2003) work on autism in his study of the differences between left and right brain hemispheres, noting that the deficits associated with the condition are associated with the right brain, with its emphasis on emotional connections and empathy, and its ability to interpret nonverbal cues such as facial expressions and eye gaze. This is also where the disproportionate incidence of autism relating to gender comes into play, as the female brain is more balanced between the hemispheres than the male brain, which tends to be more fully left-brain dominant (Baron-Cohen, 2003; Shlain, 1998, 2003). The differences are only relative, however, and McGilchrist emphasizes the fact that the division between hemispheres is common to all members of our species, and present as well in other animals. As he explains the basic distinction:

> The left hemisphere yields narrow, focused attention, mainly for the purpose of getting and feeding. The right hemisphere yields a broad, vigilant attention, the purpose of which appears to be awareness of signals from the surroundings, especially of other creatures, who are potential predators or potential mates, foes or friends; and it is involved in bonding in social animals. It might then be that the division of the human brain is also the result of the need to bring to bear incompatible types of attention on the world at the same time, one narrow, focused, and directed by our needs, and the other broad, open, and directed towards whatever else is going on in the world apart from ourselves. (McGilchrist, 2009, p. 27).

McGilchrist argues that the right brain is primary, and the evolutionary development of the left hemisphere was essentially to serve as a tool for the right brain, or to use McGilchrist's metaphor, an emissary of the master. His concern is the ways in which the left brain has become dominant, suppressing right brain function to some degree in human biology, more so in human cultural development, especially in western culture. The dominance may be more apparent in the male brain, but takes its most extreme form in the autistic brain. Along with its emphasis on narrow, focused attention, the left hemisphere is characterized by a concern with what is already known and predictable, as opposed to novelty and the unexpected; with fragmentation and analysis as opposed to synthesis; parts as opposed to the whole; abstraction as opposed to context; categories rather than individual items; differences rather than sameness; an impersonal and objective view rather than a personal approach; disembodied mind as opposed to embodied self; abstract symbols as opposed to the concreteness of nonverbal communication; and interruptions in time as opposed to continuity. The differences might be summed up by characterizing the left brain as digital in its orientation, and the right brain as analogical (for more on the distinction, see Bateson, 1972, 1978; Watzlawick et al, 1967; Wilden, 1980, 1987). Not surprisingly, then, individuals with autism are sometimes compared to, and even identify with computers, robots, and androids as depicted in popular fiction, such as the character Data in *Star Trek: The Next Generation.*

While biological evolution, and cultural evolution, especially in the west, has resulted in an inversion in the relations between right and left hemisphere, Gilchrist's emissary coming to dominate the master, it is also true that there has been clear evolutionary advantage to the ability to construct integrated selves equipped with theory of mind, so it is worthwhile to consider how autism fits into human history. Even though autism has only been recognized for a little over half a century, I think it reasonable to assume that autistic traits are much more ancient. As Gardner (1983, 1993, 1997) makes clear, traits with high survival value such as various forms of intelligence, along with the ability to maintain focus and concentration, are closely connected to many symptoms of autism. It may well be that autism is, to some degree, too much of a good thing, too extreme a combination of otherwise positive traits. This would be consistent with McLuhan's laws of media, (McLuhan & McLuhan, 1988), specifically that a medium, when pushed to extremes, flips or reverses into its opposite. Although the laws of the media were intended to be applied to human inventions alone, with media understood to be extensions of the biological, it is entirely possible to analyze biological phenomena as media in their own right (Strate, 2017); indeed, it may be argued that organisms are themselves the media through which genes modify their environments and perpetuate themselves, an argument put forth by Richard Dawkins (1989). Moreover, all manner of physical phenomena can be viewed as media, which is to say environments, while the laws of media can be understood as identifying the dynamics that apply to any system composed of interdependent parts when change is introduced into that system (Strate, 2017).

As for mindreading, it is also possible that it is a fairly recent evolutionary development (along with language), and that individuals with autism carry traits that were the norm prior to this development. Their repetitive behaviors and echopraxia, for example, are a form of mimesis, a mode of communication that was dominant before language, according to Merlin Donald (1991). Sacks (1995) makes this connection in his case study of Stephen Wiltshire, an individual with savant skills in the visual arts:

> Mimesis—itself a power of mind, a way of representing reality with one's body and senses, [is] a uniquely human capacity no less important than... language. Merlin Donald, in *Origins of the Modern Mind,* has speculated that mimetic powers of modeling, of inner representation, of a wholly nonverbal and nonconceptual type, may have been the dominant mode of cognition for a million years or more in our imme-

diate predecessor, *Homo erectus*, before the advent of abstract thought and language in *Homo sapiens*. As I watched Stephen sing and mime, I wondered if one might not understand at least some aspects of autism and savantism in terms of the normal development, even hypertrophy, of mimesis-based brain systems, this ancient mode of cognition, coupled with a relative failure in the development of more modern, symbol-based ones. (pp. 240-241)

Along the same lines, perhaps the Neanderthals lacked theory of mind, depending instead on autistic traits such as memory and visualization. Maybe they disappeared because their lack of theory of mind made them vulnerable to our own ancestors. Or possibly it was the development of mindreading that led to the creative explosion of art and ritual that occurred circa 30,000 years ago (Pfeiffer, 1982). Julian Jaynes (1976) posits that self-consciousness (and with it, theory of mind) was an even more recent evolutionary development, simply a matter of a few millennia. No doubt, our ancestors could have survived without mindreading, as have other forms of life. But the introduction of theory of mind, whenever it occurred, may have had a revolutionary impact on our species, and was almost certainly associated with the evolution of language and symbolic communication.

Lacking theory of mind, individuals with autism would have been at a decided disadvantage in early human societies, and their social impairment would no doubt collide with oral societies' emphasis on cohesion and conformity. At the same time, the parallels between autism and orality are striking. A concrete mindset is a characteristic shared by members of tribal societies, and as Jack Goody (1977) makes clear, such a mindset is a byproduct of oral tradition and nonliterate culture. Visual thinking has also been associated with oral cultures (Havelock, 1963; Pfeiffer, 1982), albeit not to the degree of individuals like Temple Grandin. Mimesis, too, continues to function as a powerful mode of communication after the evolution of language, in nonliterate and preliterate societies (Havelock, 1963). Certainly, individuals with autism would work well with the structure, formality, and emphasis on ritual found in traditional cultures. The type of language use characteristic of higher functioning individuals, "a tendency to verbosity, empty chatter, cliché-ridden and formulaic speech" (Sacks, 1995, p. 245) bears a certain resemblance to orality's own copiousness and reliance on clichés and formulas (Ong, 1982). And there is no doubt that savant skills, and in particular a strong memory, would be highly valued, and would probably hold enough survival value to overlook individual idiosyncrasies, and to afford individuals with autism special status (i.e., that of a shaman).

David R. Olson (1994, 2016) suggests that theory of mind is not just a product of language, but also of literacy as it encourages the growth of a more self-conscious self than was previously known. It is also true that the literate mindset allows for abstract thinking on a significantly higher level than the oral mindset (Goody, 1977; Ong, 1982). Therefore, autistic modes of cognition and perception may appear even more alien in a literate society than an oral one. And yet, individuals with autism are able to thrive in a literate culture, and often have a certain affinity for reading and writing. Whereas they are usually socially impaired, reading and writing is typically a private, individualized activity (Havelock, 1963, 1986; McLuhan, 1962; Ong, 1967, 1982, 1986). Whereas savant skills are isolated islands of ability, the written and printed word favors specialization in knowledge and roles (Eisenstein, 1979; Goody, 1977; Innis, 1951, 1972; McLuhan, 1962, 1964; Meyrowitz, 1985; Postman, 1982, 1985). Whereas individuals with autism may perceive the world in fragments, literacy tends to foster fragmentation and analysis as methods of understanding phenomena and solving problems (Goody, 1977; Logan, 2004; McLuhan, 1962, 1964). Whereas individuals with autism may have difficulty taking in too much information at any one time, literacy favors linear thinking and the "one thing at a time" approach, as we progress from letter to letter, word to word, sentence to sentence, page to page (Carpenter & Heyman, 1970; McLuhan, 1962, 1964; Ong, 1967, 1982). Literacy is very much associated with the left hemisphere, and has the effect of rewiring the brain, as Maryanne Wolf (2007, 2018) explains, a fact that McGilchrist has not given sufficient attention to (but see McLuhan & McLuhan, 1988; Shlain, 1998, for arguments that literacy significantly increases left hemisphere dominance).

Similarly, whereas individuals with autism have difficulty taking in sensory data from more than one sensory channel at a time, written communication, in contrast to speech, relies solely on the visual stimuli of the printed or written page (Carpenter & Heyman, 1970; McLuhan, 1962, 1964; Ong, 1967, 1982). And whereas some individuals with autism excel at visual thinking, writing and especially print fosters the development of a visual culture and mentality (Eisenstein, 1979; McLuhan, 1962, 1964; Ong, 1967, 1982). In fact, some children with autism can draw in perspective without training, the most remarkable case being that of Nadia, a three and a half year old savant (see Selfe, 1977). McLuhan (1962, 1964) believed that such abilities are purely a product of alphabetic literacy (see also Romanyshyn, 1989; Wachtel, 1995), and it may well be that writing and/or other technologies are needed for the widespread diffusion and adoption of perspective in art. But the basic technique is to draw exactly as one sees, to refrain from any additional processing of sensory data, any additional meaning making. Actually, individuals with autism are naturally capable of a kind of detachment and objectivity that has for long been an ideal of western literate cultures.

Along the same lines, individuals with autism tend to ignore context in their communication and behavior, a condition referred to as *caetextia*, defined as "context blindness" by psychologists Joe Griffin and Ivan Tyrrell (2008; see also Berger, 2022, for an insightful discussion of caetextia as a symptom of contemporary culture), while the act of writing by its very nature takes language out of its context of sound and accompanying nonverbal cues, and out of the context of social interaction, place, and time (Goody, 1977; Ong, 1982; Postman, 1982, 1985). Literate decontextualization is often associated with abstraction (to abstract is to take something out of a more specific and detailed context), but the experience of individuals with autism shows that it may instead involve the removal of an abstract context, leaving behind nothing but the most concrete of elements.

It therefore makes perfect sense that some children with autism are hyperlexic, that is, they learn to read at a much younger age than typical children. (This is not to suggest that their reading comprehension is comparable to typical children, nor even measurable.) Some may find typewriters and keyboards to be a more comfortable communication mode than speech, or possibly the only mode they can use, one example being Jasmine Lee O'Neill, a mute savant who authored *Through the Eyes of Aliens: A Book About Autistic People* (1999). The affinity for the written word is also apparent in one of the more controversial forms of therapy, facilitated communication. Here, adult facilitators assist the individuals with autism in typing on the keyboard, leading them hand over hand in an attempt to overcome difficulties with motor control and coordination. There is a strong possibility that the output might originate with the facilitator, however, which is why facilitated communication has been labeled a pseudoscience and charlatanism by some (see, for example, Maurice, 1993a, 1993b; Siegal, 1996; in contrast, Cohen, 1998, is willing to wait for more evidence before closing the book on facilitated communication). Regardless of the validity and effectiveness of facilitated communication, the literate quality of autism remains.

In our electronic age, individuals with autism encounter an often hostile media environment. From the fluorescent lighting that many find painful, to the sensory bombardment and information overload which disrupt the thought processes of us all, our culture offers neither the routine predictability and slow pace of primary orality, nor the quiet concentration of traditional literacy. As one individual with autism argues, "the way of life of this age is ever more demanding of a certain way of living that is the WORST case of living, for many autistic people, and there are fewer and fewer places to hide, to be sheltered from the media Storms.... and even the 'normal' kid may become mind-fractured into Autism... under all the sense stress and overloads!" (Wilson, 2000, no pagination). This comment was posted on *2worlds*, an electronic discussion list set up by and for high functioning individuals, who object, by the way, to being characterized as disabled, as suffering from a disorder and in need of a cure, rather than simply being different, *neurodivergent* as opposed to *neurotypical.*

Electronic media have allowed for greater affiliation and stronger group identity for all manner of social subgroups (Meyrowitz, 1985), including the disabled, as disability studies scholar Simi Linton makes clear in *Claiming Disability: Knowledge and Identity* (1998). Creating a sense of community is particularly difficult among individuals with autism, and many who are high functioning instead find a niche in the solitary activity of computer programming. But they do feel more comfortable in the company of others who share their mindset than they do with neurotypical individuals, and in fact take comfort in identifying and understanding the nature of their difference (Grandin, 1995; Grandin, & Scariano, 1986; Schneider, 1999; Williams, 1992, 1994, 1999). Indeed, especially through computer-mediated communication, the internet, and social media, high functioning individuals have joined together to argue that theirs is not a disease to be cured, that they are the victims of bias on the part of neurotypicals against neurodiversity, and to form an autism rights movement in support of being recognized as a culture in their own right. This is somewhat controversial, especially as to whether it applies to individuals with severe or moderate autism, and in regard to the parents of children with autism, who want to do whatever they can to improve their children's lives. More generally, Durig (1996) uses the phrase "culture of autism" (p. 11) to refer to the subculture that encompasses individuals with autism, their families, and the professionals who work with them (e.g., physicians, therapists, educators). Both individuals with autism and parents of children with autism have been well-served by the electronic era's information explosion, as it is only in this period that the syndrome has been recognized and facts about it disseminated, resulting in an increasing public awareness of the condition.

I note with some degree of pride that my wife, Barbara Strate, was instrumental in starting up an email discussion list for parents of autistic children in northern New Jersey in 1998. Her MOSAIC group (an acronym for Mothers' Onward Search for Autism Interventions and Causation) has had an enormous impact on the culture of autism in our region, and has served as a model for other communities. Previously, parents had struggled in isolation to obtain needed services, or more often were unaware of the services to which they were entitled. Now, parents are empowered by becoming well informed and organized through an e-mail subscription and more recently, through social media (this is especially significant given that the heavy demands of dealing with an autistic child make physical attendance at support groups all but impossible).

Ongoing Concerns

While members of the autism rights movement would object to references to an epidemic of autism, the phrase and concept has become widespread in mainstream American culture. What remains unclear and somewhat controversial is the reason for the increased incidence of the disability, and even the cause of the syndrome, whether it is due to stresses of our environment, or contaminants and pollutants, or diet and allergies, or infections and vaccinations, or genetic predisposition, or simply improved diagnostic procedures (and it may well be a combination of all of these factors). At present, there is no established medical treatment for the disorder, and in lieu of a method to act upon the brain directly, the only course of action is to work through the interface of behavior and the mind, in other words, through therapy and education. Therapy and education do not undo autism, but they can help individuals with autism cope with their environments (and some who are diagnosed with the disability are later mainstreamed, and on rare occasion declassified). But not all types of therapy are effective.

In the first decades following the identification of the syndrome, psychoanalytic approaches dominated. Bruno Bettelheim, who laid out such a perspective in *The Empty Fortress: Infantile Autism and the Birth of the Self* (1967), was typical of such practitioners: he manufactured a theory out of whole cloth that blamed mothers for their children's disability, and prescribed long-term analysis for both as the way to draw out what he asserted was a normal child hidden behind an autistic shell. Because of this nonsense, parents were consumed by guilt, their life savings were consumed by psychiatrists' fees, and their children's chances for a better life were consumed by inappropriate and ineffectual (and sometimes harmful) therapies. Bettelheim eventually became the bête noir of the autism community, but despite the fact that Bernard Rimland demonstrated the groundlessness of psychoanalytic theories of autism as long ago as 1964, there still are psychoanalysts who continued this sort of practice. And because psychoanalysis is considered a medical procedure, health insurance providers were much more likely to cover this form of fraud than truly effective therapies, as I myself found out to my dismay.

Client-centered approaches of the sort championed by the Rogerian school of psychology proved to be only slightly helpful. It is hard to make the child the center when the child lacks a center. For this reason, such approaches have been criticized as a waste of time and money, however well meaning they may be. Having been educated at a time when humanistic approaches such as championed by Carl Rogers and Abraham Maslow were in vogue, I was surprised to learn that the only approach that had any history of helping children with autism came from the children of Ivan Pavlov and B.F. Skinner, the behavioral school. This approach had been dismissed by the Freudians for relegating the mind to a black box, vilified by humanistic therapists for reducing human beings to inhuman automatons, and delegitimized by Noam Chomsky and his followers for failing to account for the complexities of language acquisition. And yet, as it turns out, operant conditioning and behavior modification, or what is referred to as Applied Behavior Analysis and the discrete trial method, represented the best hope of helping my daughter after she was diagnosed. The specific method was pioneered by UCLA psychologist Ivar Lovaas (1981) and involves breaking down activities into their smallest units. Whereas a complex behavior may be too difficult for the child to grasp, leading the child to give up in frustration, smaller, simpler units can be successfully learned, providing the child with a sense of satisfaction and motivation for further learning. Thus, teaching children to speak would begin with teaching individual phonemes, and teaching children to brush their teeth would involve teaching the child a series of separate behaviors such as turning on the water, picking up the toothbrush, wetting the toothbrush, etc. (Lovaas, 1981, p. 129). Through a process of discrete trials involving drill and rewards, each unit of behavior is taught until mastered.

Scientific research indicates that the Lovaas method is effective (Maurice, 1993b; Smith, Groen, & Wynn, 2000), at least for the high functioning, and for moderately autistic individuals such as my daughter; the method is particularly effective if the program is begun during early childhood, and the intervention is intensive—preferably 30 to 40 hours a week of one-on-one behavioral treatment. This may seem like too much for a young child, but the truth is that individuals with autism work best in a highly structured environment that keeps them engaged with the world. As for the nature of this behavioral approach, some question whether it turns children into robots. Based on my own experience I believe that nothing could be further from the truth. The behavioral units may be learned in a mechanical way, but they accumulate into a human whole greater than the sum of its parts, a self. Given the plasticity of the brain during early childhood, this form of therapy is an attempt to work through the interface of human communication, to reach and teach the brain so that development can proceed in a way more closely approximating that of the typical child. It is not so much an attempt to program children as it is to jump start neural self-organization. Additionally, the fact that Helen Keller's teacher, Anne Sullivan pioneered the technique of discrete trial serves to underscore the humanistic aspect of this approach. I would also add that the discrete trial method can be useful for neurotypical adults, as we all may encounter challenges at one point or another in mastering a given skill.; the approach is very much a function of the basic skill of analysis, breaking phenomena down into components, which is associated with literacy (Goody, 1977; Logan, 2004; McLuhan, 1964). For children with autism, the contemporary Lovaas method focuses on language acquisition, cognitive development, and self-help skills, and therefore is probably best supplemented with therapy focusing on emotional development and social interaction, as practiced by Stanley Greenspan, for example (see Greenspan, Wieder, & Simons, 1998). It is also possible to teach high-functioning individuals how to interpret emotional cues that they might otherwise miss, aka, mindreading (Howlin, Baron-Cohen, & Hadwin, 1999).

In keeping with our capacity for time-binding, progress on various forms of special education and therapy continues, and these methods continue to be modified, refined, and sometimes replaced. I should also note that there are arguments made by high functioning individuals with autism against discrete trial and related methods, insofar as they are thought to be attempts to "cure" autism or force individuals to behave according to neurotypical rules and constraints. While their protests ought to be given serious consideration, from a parent's point of view, the priority is preventing individuals with autism from engaging in self-harm and from behaving in ways that could be harmful to others, also to be able to take care of themselves as much as possible, to master life skills to whatever degree possible, and to be able to communicate.

Given that in the United States we have been experiencing an acknowledged epidemic of autism over the past two decades or more, it is not surprising that considerable time, energy, and resources have been devoted to helping children who are diagnosed with the disability to overcome and/or cope with the syndrome as best they can. What has been overlooked to a large degree is the fact that these children have been growing up, and if there has been an epidemic of childhood autism that first became apparent some 20 years ago, then we are now experiencing a still unacknowledged epidemic of adult autism. For high functioning individuals able to live independently, there is less of a concern, and their needs may be answered through efforts such as the autism rights movement, in advocating for accommodations to be made by the neurotypical majority. For those who have moderate or severe autism, there has been very little planning for arrangements once the individuals turn 21 and are no longer served by our public school system. What can be done to keep them occupied during the day? With assistance, most individuals with autism can contribute to society in some way, be productive, and take pride in their accomplishments, especially because growth, learning, and development continue throughout their (and our) lives. But this requires political will, and economic support, which has become especially problematic following the recession that began in 2008, and then the COVID-19 pandemic that started in 2020 and its consequences. And the need for day programs for adults with autism does not address the need for living accommodations. Many parents may be resigned to the fact that they have children who are not able to leave home, that they will be caring for their adult children as long as they are able, as we will be for my daughter. But what happens to the adults with autism who may become violent on occasion, or who do not realize their own strength and cause injury? And what happens when parents become too old, or too sick, or otherwise are unable to care for these individuals? This is a society-wide time-bomb, and it is going off as I write these words. And this may seem like a problem peculiar to the United States, or the western world, but it would be a mistake to think that other populations are somehow immune and will escape unscathed from what is, after all, a human epidemic.

The enigma of autism, then, begins with understanding a sense of self and a form of consciousness that is extraordinarily alien to the majority. The enigma extends to the question of what is the cause of autism, what is the reason for the current epidemic of autism in the United States, and how much lag will there be until other populations experience a similar explosion in the incidence and diagnosis of the disability. The enigma also includes the question of can there be a cure, should there be a cure, what treatments, therapies, and approaches can be applied in absence of an outright cure, to what extent should we stop trying to force individuals with autism to adjust to society, and instead adjust society to accommodate greater neurodiversity, and ultimately how to deal with the increasing numbers of both children and adults with autism. And more broadly, there is the enigma of what autism tells us about the structure and function of the brain, about consciousness and the sense of self, and about what it means to be human.

As for my daughter, my wife and I continue to fight to provide her with the best possible life chances, and we continue to worry about what the future will hold when we are no longer around to do so, knowing that she will not be able to live independently or fully care for herself. Other parents of children with significant cognitive or physical disabilities understand, but it is difficult if not impossible for anyone else to fully comprehend, let along empathize with this kind of experience.

But what my daughter has taught me is that the self we take for granted is in fact the product of a struggle. It is the most important struggle of our lives, despite the fact that we are largely unaware of it. Through our efforts from early childhood on, we take the raw material we are born with, and we build ourselves. And having done so, we continue to transform ourselves. The self is a product of metamorphosis, not a static entity. There are many kinds of selves we can construct with the materials at hand, but they are not all of equal worth. Some may be too easily overwhelmed by others, some too insensitive. Moreover, different media environments tend to favor or discourage different types of selves. As the materials we work with change, our sense of self may also be altered. Thus, for example, we move from oral cultures' tendency to develop too little self to literate cultures' too much self.

Donna Williams writes of how she moved past the stage of *no self, no other*, but could exist either as *all self, no other*, or as *all other, no self*. It is only with difficulty that she could develop a simultaneous sense of self and other. In a similar way, electronic culture seems to oscillate between the extremes of echolalia and narcissism. The *culture of autism* is arguably a fitting label for our culture as a whole, just as Eva Berger (2022) makes a similar argument based on our general inability to recognize and utilize contextualization. Certainly, the designation I suggested earlier, Nemesis culture, is consistent with our current lack of civility and political polarization. Above all, it is the loss of a balanced sense of self that, I would suggest, is just as much a disability on the cultural level as it is on the individual level, and that our current crisis of the self represents a struggle of the greatest import. It is a struggle over the kinds of selves we want to produce and reproduce.

Ovid's tale of metamorphosis is a tragic one. But the story of Joseph, the tailor's grandson is a human comedy of survival, transformation, and transcendence. It shows us that it is possible to work with the material at hand, and make something that never was. We might begin by retrieving oral culture's selflessness, community-mindedness, and the ability to sacrifice oneself for the sake of others. And we could add to it literate culture's self-fullness, its emphasis on individual rights and responsibilities, and the idea of integrity and moral character. Both narcissism and echolalia can be positive traits if exhibited in moderation and balance. Changes in our media environment may have destabilized our culture's established sense of self, but we have the raw materials and the understanding of media and communication necessary to build a new, integrated sense of self. The struggle now falls to us, as parents and as citizens, as scholars and as communicators, and above all, as teachers, to make something from nothing.

Chapter 2

Sounding Off About Listening

Preamble

We trace the beginnings of scholarship back to ancient Greece, and especially to Plato and Socrates. And we refer to the method they employed as *dialogue*, a form of communication, and we tend to think of dialogue as a form of speaking, albeit in an interactive, turn-taking manner. But, in fact, what we sometimes refer to as the Socratic method, the approach illustrated by Plato's dialogues, is entirely dependent upon listening. Indeed, dialogue only begins in earnest when the participants are willing to listen to each other. Even the counterpart of dialogue, the one-way mode of communication represented by public speaking, can only work when there is an audience to address. Arguably, when considered in the context of formal causality (McLuhan & McLuhan, 2011; Anton et al, 2016), it is the audience that motivates and necessitates the speech, rather than the speaker. But the study of rhetoric, from Aristotle through to the present, has largely been concerned with the speaker, or rhetor, not the auditor, or audience. The appearance and eventual dominance of the electronic media over the past century, much of it incorporating forms of secondary orality (Ong, 1967, 1982), did result in the sudden realization that we need to study and try to understand audiences, which became a major focus of research is mass communication and mediated communication. Not surprisingly, during the 20th century, listening too, in all its myriad manifestations, emerged as a major and highly significant area of inquiry and scholarship. We understand now that understanding listening is vital to our understanding of what it means to be human, and to understanding how we might set about becoming better human beings. With that in mind, I offer a commentary on listening as it relates to and is shaped by the phenomenon of sound, and the sense of hearing.

Hearing and listening are typically listed as synonyms, but it is also quite the commonplace to insist that they are not equivalent phenomena, that hearing does not guarantee listening, that listening requires something more than the simple reception of a message, that it implies paying close attention to what the other person is saying. This idea finds expression, appropriately enough, in the Simon and Garfunkel song, "The Sound of Silence," as Paul Simon's lyrics include the line, "people hearing without listening," following a line about people who are "talking without speaking," and followed by one where they are "writing songs that voices never share". The suggestion that silence is not simply one-sided, but rather the product of a relationship, one that involves individuals unwilling to listen as well as those unwilling to speak, is powerful and insightful. The mournful expression of lost opportunities to make a connection, and to engage in dialogue, is also present, but the specific formula of *hearing without listening* represents a restatement of the old saying, *in one ear and out the other*. And it misses the fundamental fact that listening is a function of hearing, and that the characteristics of hearing informs the process of listening. That it is impossible to fully understand the process of listening without first taking into account our sense of hearing.

Many Varieties of Listenings

The contrast between hearing and listening has become something of a cliché for good reason, because it expresses the idea that listening itself is not a monolithic phenomenon, that there are different kinds of listening, differing in the manner in which messages are attended to, processed, related to, and understood, as well as the contexts in which listening takes place. Within this polar opposition, the term *hearing* represents a less desirable form of listening, one that might be characterized as *bad* in some respect if moral judgment comes into play, or otherwise as *poor*, *weak*, *half-hearted*, *inattentive*, *careless*, and the like. The *hearing vs. listening* dichotomy substitutes, however, for the more complicated notion that there are not just two, but many different types of listening, some better or more effective than others. Consequently, the binary opposition stands as a vast over-simplification, one that ultimately misleads about the relationship between hearing and listening, as I hope to make clear. I do not mean to deny that the contrast between hearing and listening can be used as a heuristic device to introduce the idea that listening is a more complex phenomenon than it might first appear to be. But we need to be wary of reifying the *hearing vs. listening* formula, and to that end it would be useful to follow Wendell Johnson's (1946) extensional device, derived from general semantics, and exchange the singular term, *listening*, for a plural form, *listenings*, to make us mindful that there are a number of different varieties of this activity.

Not only are there different ways of listening, but there are differences in who or what we listen to: to one other person, to several people in a group setting, to a speaker giving a public address or a lecture, to a poet performing, an actor in a play, a singer singing a song, etc. There are differences between listening to other people speaking in our own language, listening to foreign languages being spoken, listening to the nonverbal paralanguage of infants and adults (e.g., crying, yelling, coughing, moaning, etc.), listening to animal vocalizations, listening to song and music, listening to the sounds of nature (e.g., wind, water, etc.), listening to machines, listening to the sounds of the body (e.g., via stethoscope to heart and lungs), listening to ourselves speak and to our inner voice, listening to imaginary voices, listening to some form of the divine or supernatural, etc. There are differences between listening in a home, an office, a classroom, a courtroom, a bar, a church, etc. There are differences between listening in an informal setting, listening to a formal presentation or performance, and listening to recordings, transmissions and broadcasts, computer-synthesized speech and sounds, etc.

Hearing, Listening, Mediating

These all are differences that make a difference, to use Gregory Bateson's (1972) happy phrase. And they are differences that can be studied via the media ecology approach (Strate, 2006, 2011a, 2014, 2017). Defined as the study of media as environments, media ecology is concerned with the way that we do things, and the differences among the means, methods, and modes that we employ, the situations, contexts, and relationships that we act within, the forms, substances, codes, technologies and techniques that we utilize, etc. All of these are aspects of the concept of *medium* and the process of *mediating* as the terms are used within the field of media ecology. Hearing and listening both are types of *mediation*, and therefore can be categorized as types of *media*; both refer to ways that individuals mediate between each other and with their environments. Indeed, the body itself can be understood as a type of medium, as can the individual sensory organs and the nervous system (Strate, 2017).

I should acknowledge that scholars in the field of communication and related disciplines often do not seem to be aware of the distinctions between different sensory modes, or do not concern themselves with those differences. The tendency is to group them together under the heading of *reception* and *decoding*, relegating the senses to a set of more or less interchangeable *channels* of communication. References to *perception* and *perceiving* are often used without acknowledging the different ways in which information can be *perceived*, only that perception may be *selective*. Those utilizing phenomenological approaches study the process of experiencing the world without considering *how* we experience the world. By way of contrast, in the field of media ecology, the question of how we do things is paramount, and the fact that different sensory organs function in entirely different ways becomes quite significant, especially in the work of scholars such as Marshall McLuhan (1962, 1964; McLuhan & McLuhan, 1988, 2011, Edmund Carpenter (1956, 1960, 1973; Carpenter & Heyman, 1970; Carpenter & McLuhan, 1956, 1960), and Walter Ong (1967, 1977, 1982, 2002).

Metaphoric Usage

An emphasis on the significance of sense perception and sensory organs opens up a different way of thinking about the relationship between hearing and listening. Rather than considering hearing to be an inferior kind of listening, we can understand that hearing is the basis and foundation of listening, and that all or most of the key characteristics that we associate with listening are made possible by the sense of hearing. Even when *listening* is used metaphorically, it is essential to understand the basis of that metaphor, which is the sensory organ of the human ear. Linguistics researchers George Lakoff and Mark Johnson (1980, 1999) explain that metaphors are rooted in the human body and bodily, biological experiences, which provide concrete bases against which to compare and experience abstract concepts (see also Gozzi, 1999). Not surprisingly, then, while *hearing* and *listening* are considered synonyms, it is also true that *hearing* can serve as a metaphor for *listening*.

Listening, which implies some form of mentation, is more abstract than the scientifically observable and quantifiable neurological phenomenon of *hearing*. A well known example of the metaphor at work can be heard in the famous Shakespeare quote from *Julius Caesar*: "Friends, Romans, countrymen, lend me your ears." The loan requested by Marc Antony is not of the literal sort associated with Vincent Van Gogh. Rather, a contemporary expression that could substitute for *lend me your ears* would be, *listen up!* Another contemporary utterance, *I hear you*, has become an idiomatic expression in the English language; as such, it does not simply refer to someone speaking with sufficient volume or clarity, but rather goes beyond the openness typically implied by listening, to indicate comprehension and understanding. *I hear you* is a statement not only about my ability to decode your message, but rather indicates an intimate recognition of you as a person, a form of confirmation, albeit not necessarily one accompanied by agreement or approval. This may well be related to the more traditional secondary meaning of *hearing*, which refers to the ability or opportunity to be heard, to express your opinion, tell your story, state your case, as in *receiving a fair hearing*. In this instance, the sense of hearing again serves as a metaphor for listening, one that is deeply embedded and therefore used for the most part unconsciously.

Orality and Hearing

In noting the metaphorical relationship between hearing and listening, I want to stress that there is not a simple hierarchy between hearing as a lower form of physical activity and listening as a higher cognitive function. Rather, my point is that the two are intimately intertwined, and that, as previously noted, in order to understand listening, we also need to understand hearing as a form of sense perception. This essential idea concerning listening has long been made clear in regard to language, that all languages are oral in their origin and essence, that all languages are *tongues*, existing first and foremost as forms of speech. It follows that hearing, and therefore listening, are intimately connected to our capacity for linguistic communication, the characteristic that most clearly distinguishes our species from other forms of life. Language is the basis of our higher mental functions as individuals, and our ability to engage in time-binding (Korzybski, 1993), to accumulate and pass on knowledge over generations, as societies and cultures. The process of language acquisition begins in infancy, and appears to be hardwired into the human brain, while vocalization begins with the first breath drawn after birth, typically when the newborn begins to cry. But hearing takes place prenatally, as the fluid medium of the womb is an excellent conveyer of sound, especially the sound of the mother's voice and heartbeat. Hearing comes before speaking, and also before seeing, because the womb is an environment without light.

The contrast between the eye and the ear has been of particular interest to media ecology scholars, in large part because both are associated with language. In contrast to the organic connection between speech and hearing, however, the association between vision and language is an artificial one, derived from the invention of writing systems, technologies that translate the spoken word into visual markings. Learning how to read is in essence an eye exercise, training the organs to focus on a fixed point of view and follow along a linear path. Consequently, literates place greater stress on vision than nonliterates, and literate cultures come to value vision above all of the other senses. McLuhan (1962, 1964) characterized this extension of the eye as disrupting the delicate balance between the senses, resulting in the dominance of the eye associated with western alphabetic and typographic cultures, otherwise known as *visualism*.

While the written word and literacy made vision increasingly more central to human psyches and societies, the eye has always been an especially important sensory organ for our species. As we have evolved from walking on all fours to walking erect, the process resulted in our head and eyes being elevated, making our visual sense more effective; this also led to the atrophy of our sense of smell, as it brought our nose away from close proximity to the ground, which is a much better medium for conveying odor and scent than the air. Evolutionary change also saw our eyes coming closer together, enabling binocular vision. For these and other reasons, vision paired with hearing as our primary distance receptors. This much they have in common. But consider the differences, which extend beyond the developmental to the structure of the sensory organs.

Eye vs. Ear

One obvious distinction is that we can close our eyes, but not our ears. Our sense of hearing is always on, a constant monitoring of our environment. Seeing is also directional, as we must choose where to look, where to direct our field of vision, which is always a small subset of what we can potentially shift our gaze towards. The choice of what to look at is also a choice of what not to look at, as we can avert our eyes. True, we can cover our ears, but that typically does not completely block out sound. And more importantly, hearing is omnidirectional. No decision is required, our ears pick up sound from all directions. This helps to explain the evolutionary advantage of speech, and why no human society ever encountered has used sign language instead of speech. A hand signal requires visual contact, while a warning cry can be heard from any position.

Vision does have the advantage of precision, specifically our ability to direct our attention and focus, which initially served us well as hunter-gatherers, and was later adapted for the process of reading. Related to this is the ability to close one eye and keep the other open, which appears to be a learned ability associated with literacy (Carpenter, 1973). There is no exact equivalent for directional focus when it comes to the sense of hearing; we can try to concentrate on what is being said, or pick out a particular voice among many, but this is more a mental operation than a particular way of using our ears, apart from turning your head in the act of *cocking your ear*. What this means is that hearing is more of a holistic operation, while seeing is more atomistic; put another way, sight is more favorable to an analytical frame of mind, while sound is more conducive to synthesis. As Ong (1982) put it, "sight isolates, sound incorporates" (p. 72).

Acoustic Space

Edward T. Hall (1966) established that there are different senses of space generated by different sensory organs, and McLuhan, Carpenter, and others have noted the differences between acoustic and visual space. Acoustic space is the experience of space generated by the sense of hearing. Because hearing is omnidirectional, acoustic space is all around us, surrounding us—in this respect, all sound is surround sound. This sense of space is one that is curved rather than straight, Einsteinian rather than Euclidean; it is circular or oval, spiral, spherical or dome-like, just as sound ripples out in all directions, potentially without end. Our position in acoustic space is at the center of it all, surrounded by what we hear. This centering is not so much egocentric as it is ecological, as it places us inside the world, a part of our environment, integrated into our surroundings, requiring us to live in harmony (an acoustic metaphor) with the world. When we are situated at the center of it all, we are in a *subjective* position, which is also *subjectifying*, by which I mean that we treat everything that surrounds us as subjects, as alive and conscious. This may be denigrated as anthropomorphism, but it is also consistent with an ecological understanding, not to mention the Gaia hypothesis. To use Martin Buber's (1970) terminology, in acoustic space we enter into I-You relationships with the world.

The experience of space generated by the sense of vision, on the other hand, is unidirectional, dividing the world into bits and pieces, fragmenting the environment. Whereas acoustic space has no necessary limits, visual space is intrinsically one of boundaries—you might even say it is one that is drawn and quartered. Especially as intensified by the invention of writing, visual space favors the linear, and the quadrilinear. Denise Schmandt-Besserat (1996) has shown how the introduction of writing in ancient Mesopotamia and Egypt altered pictorial art and decoration, as images began to be lined up in rows, following the example of written characters. A similar change can be seen in architecture, as the typical structure of oral cultures is rounded or nonlinear, e.g., the hut, the teepee, the igloo, while following the introduction of writing and the advent of literacy straight lines and right angles increasingly come to dominate on all levels, from furniture and rooms to buildings and streets (Carpenter, 1973; Hall, 1966). Significantly, in visual space, the portion of the world we are attending to is laid out in front of us, and especially as our gaze employs a fixed point of view, we find ourselves distanced and detached from the world, on the outside looking in, alienated from our environment, in the position of being spectators, voyeurs, peeping toms. In this sense, we are outside of the world, not a part of it. This situates us in an *objective* position, giving us the illusion of being completely separate from our environment, uninvolved, and not participants. To be objective is to objectify the world and all that it contains, to treat everything in our environment as objects, as things, or to once again employ Buber's (1970) terms, to enter into an I-It relationship with the world.

It follows that the shift from orality to literacy is accompanied by a shift in emphasis from acoustic to visual space, and this results in a changing view of the world. Whereas in oral cultures, people believed themselves to be part of the world, and endeavored to live in harmony with it, in literate cultures, people came to see themselves as separate and apart from nature, which they came to view as an object to try to own, manipulate, and control. This is particularly characteristic of western culture, defined as it has been by alphabetic literacy. Our many visual and linear metaphors for thought and knowledge originate in ancient Greece, e.g., *point of view*, *perspective*, *regarding*, *clearly*, *line* of inquiry, *train* of thought, *see* what I mean, my *point*, self-*image*, *where I stand*, the way I *see* it, *idea* (same root as *video*), in the first/second/third *place*, *topic* (the root meaning is *place*), to list just a few examples (Lee, 1959; Ong, 1982). Visualism especially comes to the fore with the printing revolution in early modern Europe, which was a necessary prerequisite for modern science, and modernity in general. It becomes commonplace to say *seeing is believing*, whereas in the past it was hearing that was believing (Ong, 1982). The legendary Greek singer of tales Homer was said to be blind because that signified his ability to hear the true story of the Trojan War, as relayed to him by the Muses. The Roman goddess of justice, Justitia, was portrayed as blind or blindfolded, a common sight on courthouse statuary, not because being sightless signifies objectivity, but because it symbolized *hearing* the truth, which to this day is reflected in the fact that oral testimony delivered during the trial has greater value than written statements produced as *exhibits*. Our concepts of truth and justice have changed along with the shift from the acoustic to the visual, just as the saying, *I believe it when I see it in black and white*, a reference to print media, is no longer current, and today a sense of legitimacy is secured through the electronic media, especially television.

In the 20th century, however, according to McLuhan, Carpenter, Ong, and others, the electronic media restored to some extent the experience of acoustic space, accounting for the rise of ecological consciousness and the environmental movement in the mid-20th century. The phenomenon that Ong (1982) refers to as *secondary orality* originates in the latter half of the 19th century with the almost simultaneous invention of the telephone and sound recording, while wireless transmission of voice and music was introduced in the first decade of the twentieth century, with commercial broadcasting beginning in 1920. This brought with it not only the new notion of *mass communication*, but also the concept of the *mass audience*, the root meaning of *audience* being *audio*. This term, *audience*, would also be applied to other forms of mass communication, to moviegoers and television viewers, and even the readership of mass circulation newspapers and magazines. The long tradition in rhetoric and related studies of communication emphasized the study of messages and sources, which is to say texts and their authors or composers; the new research tradition of mass communication gradually motivated new studies of the reception of messages, otherwise known as audience analysis.

Listening and the Electronic Media Environment

I would suggest that it is therefore no accident that listening emerges as a distinct area of interest and subject of investigation over the past half century. Rather, it is a natural response to the secondary orality that characterizes our media environment. In an odd way, while opportunities to listen and choices as to what to listen to have increased over the past century, speech has waned in significant ways. The activity of public speaking has come to be feared more than death, interest in and respect for poetry has gone into steep decline, and the ability to engage in conversation is seen by some, notably Sherry Turkle (2011, 2015), as the equivalent of an endangered species. Listening has moved from the background to the foreground, and we do need to improve our ability to listen to the mediated voices that clamor for our attention, the journalists, opinionists, and propagandists in particular. But there is also cause for concern when it comes to our ability to listen to others in face-to-face situations, in dialogue, in group settings, in audiences at lectures and addresses. While bringing listening to the fore, secondary orality also creates unprecedented challenges to our ability to listen, as we grow habituated to the slick, edited, altered, and amplified electronic voices that lead us to expect a level of stimulation and amusement that cannot be matched in physical situations. Put another way, there is so much noise being generated that as much as we are listening, and forced to listen, it becomes increasingly more difficult to pick out what we really need to listen to, to listen in a deliberate, critical, and conscientious manner. You might say that now people are *listening without hearing*.

Recognizing the auditory nature of listening helps us to understand its significance. Consider what might be the equivalent of listening based on the visual sense. Is *watching* the same experience as *listening*? Is *observing* the same? Is *regarding*? If I say, "I *see* you," is it the same as "I *hear* you"? Or consider one of the most pervasive metaphors in the humanities, originating from modern languages and literary studies, that of *reading*. Carrying a connotation of *interpretation*, scholars produce *readings* of films, television programs, songs and musical compositions. In this usage, *reading* is applied to objects, not subjects. Reading other peoples' nonverbal communication, their so-called body language, is not listening to what they are trying to say or listening to what they mean, but rather trying to detect the unconscious signals they are giving off, signals that they themselves may not be aware of. This is what is meant by *reading someone like a book*; it is an objectifying act. Admittedly, there is another usage that comes to us from wireless voice transmission, as in, *I read you, I read you loud and clear*, and *I read you five by five*. This particular formulation originates as a reference to the technical quality of the transmission, the signal strength and clarity, which is measured by reading display indicators and given a numerical score (hence *five by five*). As a metaphor, it has come to also mean, *I understand what you are saying*, sometimes also indicating agreement as well. I do think it important to note, however, that this is an electronic metaphor for a human activity, using technical terms to express a cognitive connection. Not surprising, its usage outside of technical operations is mainly found in the military, and used in reference to following orders. As Lewis Mumford (1967) explains, the idea of the machine precedes actual mechanical devices, and originates with organized human labor, including ancient military organization. To the extent that this sense of reading is related to a command and control structure, it is a limited and limiting usage, one that remains distinct from the acoustic nature of listening.

Conclusion

On a more personal level, an important insight was delivered by Helen Keller, when she was asked if she would rather be blind or deaf. Her response, to the surprise of many, was that she would rather be blind, because people were kinder to you that way. The sense of sight connects us to the world of objects, and we value it greatly for its utilitarian functions. But the sense of hearing connects us not only to an aspect of our surroundings, but to other people, and while there are ways to compensate, nothing quite substitutes for the intimacy of sound. Hearing is communal, bringing people together as a group. When everyone is hearing the same thing at the same time, there is a sense of unity, whereas if everyone is asked to read the exact same written work at the same time, even then we read as isolated individuals. No wonder that the word *audience* is singular, as opposed to *readers*. This communal quality also contributes to the association between sound and the sense of the sacred and the spiritual (Ong, 1967, 1977, 1982, 2002).

To summarize, the sense of hearing can be characterized as holistic, nonlinear, unbounded, ecological, harmonizing, subjective, relational, communal, and spiritual. Insofar as hearing constitutes the basis of listening, these characteristics also extend to listening, and help to clarify the significance of listening as a sound practice and an area of study.

Chapter 3

The New Grammarians

Introduction

Alfred Korzybski was a grammarian. S.I. Hayakawa was a grammarian. Marshall McLuhan was a grammarian. Neil Postman was a grammarian. Christine Nystrom was a grammarian. I am a grammarian, and maybe you are too. Communication scholars and professionals tend to see themselves as rhetoricians, it is well known, but for some of us, especially those associated with general semantics and media ecology, a better designation would be to refer to us as *the new grammarians*. And for the purposes of disambiguation, let me make it clear that the category of new grammarians that I am concerned with are not individuals who are sometimes referred to as the grammar police, or grammar cops, or sometimes even grammar nazis. Nor am I focusing on the enforcers of political correctness in public and private discourse, sometimes known as the PC police. Neither am I discussing the late 19th century German school of linguistics known as the Neogrammarians. Rather, my interest is in what might be termed *grammar writ large*, an expansive understanding of grammar that reaches back to its origins in antiquity and, in the spirit of time-binding, provides a basis for enhanced understanding of our environment as we move into the future.

The English word *grammar* comes to us from the Latin *grammatica*, which in turn can be traced back to the ancient Greek word, *gramma*, referring to any single letter of the alphabet, or more generally to any written document or record (this forms the basis of the suffix *-gram*, as it appears in words such as *telegram*, *anagram*, *diagram*, etc.). The longer term, *grammatikē*, was used in reference to the art of letters, as was the phrase *tékhnē grammatikē* (the Greek word *tékhnē* being the root of our term *technology*, but originally referring to what we would call *arts and crafts*). *Tékhnē Grammatikē*, typically translated as *The Art of Grammar*, is also the title of a treatise that was traditionally thought to be the first major study of the ancient Greek language, attributed to the Hellenistic scholar, Dionysius Thrax. This would place the origin of the work in the 2nd century BCE, although scholars now believe the work to be of later origin. The important point, however, is that grammar originally referred to the study of language and literature, a form of education encompassing both literacy and literary criticism, poetics and the interpretation of texts. Grammar then is about *reading* both in the restricted sense of the technical skill of being able to decode written messages, and in the elaborated sense of interpretation, evaluation, and meaning making.

It is no accident that the origin of grammar followed the introduction of the alphabet in ancient Greece. Walter Ong (1967, 1982) explained that all forms of study, are made possible by the invention of writing. Indeed, Alfred Korzybski (1993) recognized that the introduction of writing was the basis of exponential growth in the fundamental human function of time-binding, making possible the enormous progress we have made in science and technology, from antiquity to the present day. In contrast to language acquisition in the form of speech, however, learning to read and write does not come naturally to human beings, as Eric Havelock (1982, 1986) has emphasized. Consequently, formal instruction is required, and the first schools were set up following the development of the first writing system, cuneiform, by the Sumerians in Mesopotamia, their purpose being to teach individuals how to decode the characters that make up that logographic writing system (Logan, 2004). In ancient Greece, three competing schools appeared following the adoption of the alphabet (Havelock, 1982). The first, representing the beginnings of the discipline of grammar, was devoted to learning how to read, the focus being on the transcribed versions of the Greek oral tradition, specifically the *Iliad* and the *Odyssey*. The objective was verbatim memorization of the Homeric epics, which only became possible after they were written down; without a text, there would not be anything to check the individual's memory against. The ultimate goal, then, was oral performance. The second type of schooling emphasized the use of writing as an aid to oratory; this was the kind of education associated with the Sophists, and represents the beginnings of rhetoric as the study of the techniques used to influence others in the context of public speaking (and therefore also is typically said to constitute the origin of communication studies). The third school was the one developed by Socrates, Plato, and Aristotle, the form of education we know as philosophy, based on dialogue and dialectic, logic and reasoning, informed by literacy but practiced via oral discussion, debate, and disputation. Each of these schools were rooted in the need to teach individuals how to read and write, each using that ability to enhance language skills, both for externalized speech and internalized thought.

While competition among these three schools was fierce, hence Plato's condemnation of both poetry and rhetoric, all three required the reading and interpretation of texts. And as explained in Plato's *Phaedrus* (1973), writing posed a problem unknown in speech situations, as we cannot ask questions of a text in the same way that we can ask a communicator who is co-present with us. Communicating at a distance poses some difficulty, all the more so with the complete absence of the communicator, particularly as the text survives the death of the author. A teacher may act as surrogate for the author, but this still requires an act of interpretation on the part of the teacher (teachers may role play as the author of a text, but actually are only playing the role of an informed reader). Interpretation also comes into play if the text is written in a language other than the reader's native tongue; the act of translation is inevitably an act of interpretation, and arguably an act of betrayal (as in the Italian saying, *traduttori, traditori*, meaning, [the] *translator* [is a] *traitor*). Vocabulary and the meanings of words shift and change over time, so the older the text is in relation to the reader, the more difficult the process of interpretation. And when the text is written in a language that is no longer spoken, what is sometimes referred to as a dead language, or more charitably as a learned language, interpretation becomes truly challenging. Other barriers also come into play, including variation due to copying by hand and scribal corruption, damage to texts, orthographic differences such as lack of punctuation, and changing writing systems. This all underscores the need to develop forms of exegesis and hermeneutics, especially for sacred texts. That is why interpretative traditions have developed in parallel in all literate cultures, an example being Talmudic scholarship originating in ancient Jewish culture.

In the west during the medieval period, formal education was almost entirely a monopoly of the Church of Rome, and available only to students preparing to join the clergy. Schooling began with learning the ABCs, to become literate or *lettered*, as it were. But most texts were in Latin, a dead language that needed to be learned along with learning how to read and write. This posed additional barriers to gaining access to knowledge, granting the church what Harold Innis (1951) termed a monopoly of knowledge. Consequently, the first order of business was teaching students how to read and write in Latin, and this is how the term *grammar school* originated, grammar here referring to the original meaning of the study of language and literature (the term *grammar school* remains synonymous with elementary school and primary education to this day). The medieval university constituted the equivalent of secondary education, and the core curriculum of the university included three basic subjects, collectively known as the trivium. They were grammar, rhetoric, and logic, the latter otherwise known as dialectic or dialectics. This was followed by four advanced subjects, known as the quadrivium, specifically arithmetic, geometry, music, and astronomy. Together they formed the seven liberal arts, and this constituted the beginnings of liberal arts education.

The War Within the Trivium

This aspect of western intellectual history was of particular significance for Mc-Luhan's early scholarship. He began his undergraduate studies at the University of Manitoba pursuing a degree in engineering, which may have made him especially sympathetic to the work of Korzybski, whose background was in engineering. A voracious reader and lover of literature, McLuhan soon switched his major to English, following in the footsteps of Hayakawa, who received his Bachelor's degree at Manitoba in 1927, the year before McLuhan enrolled; as a teen with a paper route, McLuhan had come into contact with Hayakawa delivering newspapers to the young college student (Haslam & Haslam, 2011). That both would become English professors, and famous ones at that, is quite a coincidence. McLuhan graduated in 1933, the year that Korzybski published *Science and Sanity*, a book that McLuhan encountered while engaged in graduate study. McLuhan completed a Master's degree at Manitoba the following year, and proceeded to enroll in Cambridge University, earning a second Bachelor's and Master's degree, and then his doctorate in 1943. His doctoral dissertation was ostensibly an analysis of the work of Elizabethan satirist Thomas Nashe, a fitting subject for a PhD in English literature. But McLuhan could not be constrained by so narrow a topic, and the scope of his research was hinted at by the title of his thesis, *The Place of Thomas Nashe in the Learning of His Time*. Education in early modern Europe was still grounded in the liberal arts curriculum of the medieval university, and the trivium. This led him to trace the history of that curriculum back through the Middle Ages, back to its roots in antiquity (Gordon, 1997; Marchand, 1989).

After McLuhan produced his influential scholarship on media, technology, and culture in works such as *The Mechanical Bride* (1951), *The Gutenberg Galaxy* (1962), and *Understanding Media* (1964), his dissertation became an object of much curiosity and speculation. And frustration, as plans for its publication did not materialize for many decades. According to William Kuhns (1996), "in 1969, McGraw-Hill announced the upcoming publication in 1970, but it never appeared. Meantime, the sole available public copy, in the library of Trinity College, Cambridge, is reported to be dog-eared and ragged well beyond the normal expiration of a shelf volume" (n.p.). That problem of wear and tear was no doubt alleviated in 2006 with the publication of his thesis in book form, under the title of *The Classical Trivium*, the original thesis title, *The Place of Thomas Nashe in the Learning of His Time*, relegated to subtitle status (McLuhan, 2006). This change provided a more accurate map for the territory that was covered, as most of the thesis is devoted to the history of the trivium, which amounted to a wide-ranging study of the entirety of intellectual history in western culture. McLuhan's analysis suggests that grammar, rhetoric, and logic formed the underlying structure of all western thought and scholarship, with continuing influence on all manner of writing, including poetry, philosophy, theology, history, law, and even medicine and science.

McLuhan (2006) further concludes that the trivium is not a stable and balanced set of subjects, but rather something more akin to informal political parties, religious factions, or nations in competition with one another. From its beginnings within the three competing schools of ancient Greece, grammar, rhetoric, and logic each had their proponents, each group amounting to a school of thought or invisible college, but also functioning as rival factions at war with one another. Kuhns (1996) referred to it as "the war within the word" (np). Western intellectual history could be understood, McLuhan argues, as an ongoing conflict within the trivium, with each subject vying for dominance over the others. In these battles, logic often came out on top, with grammar and rhetoric allied in opposition. And in surveying this intellectual battleground, McLuhan does not hesitate to take sides. He is least sympathetic towards logic, which should come as no surprise to anyone familiar with McLuhan's unique writing style. This meant that McLuhan situates himself in opposition to Aristotelian logic, and therefore embracing what Korzybski (1993) terms a non-Aristotelian perspective. It is important to note in this regard that neither Korzybski nor McLuhan rejects all of Aristotle's philosophical work; McLuhan, notably, makes use of Aristotle's metaphysics, and in particular his notion of formal causality (McLuhan & McLuhan, 2011; Anton et al, 2016; Strate. 2017; Trujillo Liñán, 2022). Rather, Korzybski and McLuhan's mutual opposition is to the logic promulgated by Aristotle and his followers.

The origins of this ongoing conflict can be traced back to Plato's rejection of poetry as providing a false understanding of the world, and his criticism of rhetoric as representing shadows rather than substance, appearances rather than the things themselves; he likened rhetoric to cosmetics in contrast to medicine, and to cooking in contrast to nutrition (see Plato, 1971, 1973). Plato's attack resonates to this day, with *rhetoric* often given a negative connotation, as in *mere rhetoric*, while the term *sophistry*, derived from the teachers of rhetoric in ancient Greece, known as the Sophists, is a pejorative label relating to false and misleading arguments, deception and manipulation. Plato's condemnation also redounds to the term *semantics*, as in *just playing semantics*, and even the more neutral term *words* takes on a negative meaning through phrases like *only words*, or through sayings such as the proverbial *sticks and stones*. Contrasting *words* to *deeds* or *action* ignores the fact that speech acts are a form of behavior and words represent a type of symbolic action (Burke, 1966). And what is also lost in translation is the fact that logic comes from the Greek *logos*, meaning *word*, and the term *dialectic*, which is related to *dialect*, is based on the Latin root *lect*, meaning *to read*. Logic is as much about words, language, and symbols as grammar and rhetoric, and even more so a product of literacy, literate culture, and the literate mindset. Moreover, logic is based on the bias towards linearity inherent in writing systems (Lee, 1959; McLuhan, 1964; Schmandt-Besserat, 1978, 1992, 1996; Strate, *Binding Biases*), and the either-or, two-valued orientation that emerges out of the practice of categorization via written lists (Goody; Strate, 2011a).

The advocates for logic included the medieval Scholastics, who incorporated Aristotelian philosophy with Christian theology, an effort that had its parallels in Jewish and Islamic culture. In early modern Europe, logic found a new champion in Peter Ramus. Walter Ong, who wrote his master's thesis under McLuhan's direction, made Ramus the subject of his Harvard University doctoral dissertation, completed under the guidance of Perry Miller, the founder of the field of American Studies. Ong's study, published under the title of *Ramus, Method, and the Decay of Dialogue* (1958), examines the role that Ramus played in initiating an educational revolution in which the visual display of facts displayed in a linear, logical progression based on a two-valued orientation of either-or binary oppositions, replaced traditional schooling that emphasized discussion, disputation, and debate (see also McLuhan, 1962). It was a shift closely related to the printing revolution in early modern Europe, a shift from education with a strong emphasis on orality to education by the book (e.g., textbook learning); this was the method adopted by the Puritans in England, who went on to settle in the New England colonies of the new world, resulting in that region gaining intellectual leadership in the United States. Ramus's method can also be seen as a forerunner of computer programming, algorithmic flow charts, and binary coding. In this sense, all of our digital technology, software and hardware, our new media and online environments, are built on an Aristotelian foundation. (Korzybski's, 1993, critique of Aristotelian logic, based on the realization that it is a poor representation of the external environment, is consistent with the understanding that virtual environments are artificial realities, and that social media create alternate realities divorced from fact and impervious to falsification.)

The Origin of Modern Science

It is important to emphasize that the problem is not with logic, but rather with the larger context. For Korzybski (1993), Aristotelian logic has its uses in special cases, but not as a general approach to thought and evaluation; his analogy was to Newtonian physics, which is superseded by non-Newtonian physics, but remains useful in limited applications. Along similar lines, McLuhan identified himself as a Thomist (Marchand, 1989; Gordon, 1997), following Thomas Aquinas, who was a great proponent of Aristotelian philosophy, but the particular emphasis was on the epistemology associated with Thomism, which emphasizes external reality and that knowledge is derived from sense perception; notably, Korzybski's general semantics has likewise been linked to Thomism by Margaret Gorman (1962). The problem with logic then stems from the fact that it had often been granted a monopoly on truth, as the sole pathway to accurate knowledge about the world, about the nature of reality. And this no doubt has much to do with its success in the struggle for the hearts and minds of students and scholars. Plato and Aristotle were certain that the truth was knowable, readily obtainable via their philosophical method, and that they were in possession of it. Consequently, they allowed that rhetoric could be useful if and only if it were subordinated to logic, used in service to logic, to promulgate the truth. Of course, the Christian philosophers and theologians who incorporated Aristotelian logic into their own religious systems had somewhat differing notions of what the exact nature of truth might be, as did their Jewish and Islamic counterparts, but they all shared a similar certainty that the truth was either self-evident or could be logicked out of whatever sources of authority they adhered to.

The problem with Aristotelian logic was famously explained by Bertrand Russell (1968):

> To modern educated people, it seems obvious that matters of fact are to be ascertained by observation, not by consulting ancient authorities. But this is an entirely modern conception, which hardly existed before the seventeenth century. Aristotle maintained that women have fewer teeth than men; although he was twice married, it never occurred to him to verify this statement by examining his wives' mouths. (p. 7)

Whether or not this is entirely fair to Aristotle, it is certainly the case that he favored deductive reasoning over induction, referring to inductive reasoning as inartistic; deduction, moving from general premises to specific conclusions, is the basis of logic, while inductive reasoning, starting with specifics and building up to generalizations, is consistent with modern science and empiricism. In a modern sense, following scientific method means basing our theories and hypotheses on the facts that we have gathered by way of observation. And revising them when the facts do not fit our generalizations, rather than forcing facts to fit our preconceived notions. This is fundamental to Korzybski's (1993) non-Aristotelian system, and the extensional orientation that he urged us all to adopt. The question then is how did we make the transition from medieval dialectics to modern science? How did our understanding of how to arrive at truth flip from one extreme to another, that is, from deduction to induction, from internal validity to external verification, from pure reason to observation, from logic to empiricism? The common assumption is a straight continuum between the two, progress in understanding the natural world quite naturally progressing from one to the other. But this view belies the revolutionary nature of the paradigm shift, and McLuhan (2006) provides us with a better explanation.

In his dissertation McLuhan (2006) sought to identify the overlooked but highly significant influence of the grammarians, with special attention to Cicero, who equated encyclopedic knowledge with eloquence and virtue, as well as Cicero's followers, including St. Augustine, Erasmus, the inventor of the essay, and Thomas Nashe, the nominal subject of McLuhan's study. And this also included Francis Bacon, who is credited with introducing empiricism and the scientific method. Why did this innovation come from a grammarian rather than a logician? Because grammarians, as you may recall, were concerned with the reading and interpretation of texts, and reading is an act of observation. It was therefore not too great a leap to go from reading documents to reading environments. As expressed in the theological language of the time, the argument was that God gave us two kinds of books to read and interpret, God's Bible and God's Creation, scripture and nature. Both served as a medium for trying to understand God, for getting closer to God. Setting the connection to the divine aside, the startling conclusion is that it was the grammarians who gave us modern science, not the logicians. And that is why McLuhan (2006) refers to Korzybski (1993) in favorable terms in his dissertation, noting that Korzybski recognized the intimate relationship between language and science, indeed recognized it in a way that no one else had before him. Following Korzybski's lead, Wendell Johnson (1046) put it quite succinctly when he wrote that "the language of science is the better part of the method of science" (p. 50).

Elizabeth Eisenstein (1979) further explained the role of printing in making this paradigm shift possible. When natural philosophers depended on handwritten manuscripts, they typically focused on the interpretation of a single, authoritative text. The printing revolution vastly increased access to texts, allowing scholars to actively compare books side by side with one another, and thereby discover inconsistencies and contradictions that hitherto had gone unnoticed. This created a need to resolve the conflicting accounts and explanations, and the only way to do so was to go out into the world and study the actual environment. In this way, nature became the most authoritative text of all, and the empirical method the most effective way to read and interpret that text. The goal was then to translate the environment as text back into the existing literary tradition, which is why, well into the 20th century, knowledge of Latin was often required of anyone seeking a degree in the sciences. It is also worth noting that the development of scientific instruments and the increasing dependency on them on the part of scientists resulted in empirical data taking the form of *readings*—instruments are extensions of the senses (Ogden & Richards, 1923), for the most part the sense of sight, and their *readouts* on paper and video are encoded in numbers and graphs that need to be *read*. In this mediated form, the environment is not only treated like a text, but translated into a simpler text, via the process of abstracting, a simpler text that is easier to decode and interpret.

Grammar and Schooling

Grammar formed the basis of both modern science and the humanities, and both were revolutionized by the printing revolution in early modern Europe. Print culture gave rise to a new literary form, the novel, as well as a new literary category, fiction (Scholes & Kellogg, 1966). Specialized study in English literature was still a relatively new discipline in the early 20th century, drawing on both grammar and rhetoric. This was true when McLuhan was a student, and one of his Cambridge University mentors, I.A. Richards, was a leading scholar in this area of study. The book Richards co-authored with Charles K. Ogden, *The Meaning of Meaning* (Ogden & Richards, 1923), introduced the famous model known as the semantic triangle, and emphasized the importance of understanding how symbols generate meaning. This is a concern associated with grammar, and Richards maintained a grammarian approach, even in his monograph entitled *The Philosophy of Rhetoric* (1936). The approach to symbols, metaphor, and the close reading of texts pioneered by Richards parallels and precedes Korzybski (1993); whatever differences might exist between the two, their approaches are mainly complementary and allied in their resistance to the dominance of the dialecticians. Of particular importance is the fact that the semantic triangle highlights the role of the referent in the process of signification, which is to say that it stresses the existence of an observable reality outside of language and symbol systems. This is in contrast to the semiology of Ferdinand de Saussure (1983), who views meaning as generated within systems of symbols and signs, between signifier and signified and via binary oppositions, rather than in relation to an outer world available via sense perception. For this reason, I would suggest that McLuhan biographer Terrence Gordon (1997) is mistaken in his claim that McLuhan was a follower of Saussure, a claim no other McLuhan scholar makes, I might add.

For McLuhan at Cambridge in the mid-20th century, the study of English literature would have been understood to be part of a larger discipline known as *philology* (the term is also derived from the Greek, meaning the love of words, the counterpart to *philosophy*, meaning the love of knowledge). A direct descendant of the medieval discipline of grammar, philology represents the humanistic study of language; by way of contrast, the field of linguistics, which is also devoted to the study of language, is based on the social and behavioral sciences. Philology is also concerned with the study of texts, of literature, significantly including historical studies of texts and languages. This encompasses not only what we refer to as modern languages and literature, and comparative literature, but also the discipline of classics, which focuses on ancient Greek and Latin texts, as well as biblical studies, and the study of all ancient and archaic languages and texts, including Old English and Middle English, i.e., *Beowulf*, Chaucer's *Canterbury Tales*, etc. Perhaps the most famous philologist of the 20th century was on the faculty at nearby Oxford University, J.R.R. Tolkien, author of *The Hobbit* and *The Lord of the Rings*. I have elsewhere argued that Tolkien, who first created fictional languages and then the stories to go with them, viewed language along similar lines as McLuhan and other media ecologists and general semanticists (Strate, 2011a). I would also note that Tom Shippey (2000), who at one time held the Walter Ong Chair in English at Saint Louis University, explained that Tolkien was one of three 20th century novelists whose works were grounded in a conscious concern with language. The other two are George Orwell, whose concept of Newspeak in *1984* is based on linguistic relativism otherwise known as the Sapir-Whorf Hypothesis, which in turn had a significant influence on McLuhan and other media ecologists, and James Joyce, whose linguistic invention and wordplay was of great significance for McLuhan.

As previously noted, the printing revolution in early modern Europe was a great boon to grammarians, automating the handicraft of writing, and through mass production making a wide variety of texts available. This made literacy all the more valuable, leading to the proliferation of schooling, and specifically of grammar schools. With that in mind, consider, for example, the following quote written by one of Thomas Nashe's better known contemporaries from Elizabethan England:

> Thou hast most traitorously corrupted the youth of the realm in erecting a grammar school; and whereas, before, our forefathers had no other books but the score and the tally, thou hast caused printing to be used, and, contrary to the king, his crown and dignity, thou hast built a paper-mill. It will be proved to thy face that thou hast men about thee that usually talk of a noun and a verb, and such abominable words as

no Christian ear can endure to hear. Thou hast appointed justices of peace, to call poor men before them about matters they were not able to answer. Moreover, thou hast put them in prison; and because they could not read, thou hast hanged them; when, indeed, only for that cause they have been most worthy to live.

These lines are taken from William Shakespeare's historical play, *Henry VI, Part 2* (4.7.31-46), and they reflect an awareness on the part of the Bard of the transformative power of the printing press with movable type, an awareness discussed by Marshall McLuhan in *The Gutenberg Galaxy* (1962). They also reflect mixed emotions regarding the innovation, a reception not uncommon in early modern Europe (Eisenstein, 2011). The lines are uttered by Jack Cade, the leader of a populist rebellion, his anti-elitist stance coinciding with the anti-intellectual sentiments expressed here. Cade's claim that grammar schools are guilty of corrupting the youth echo the trial of Socrates, in which the philosopher was accused and convicted of corrupting the youth of Athens. Corrupting the youth remains synonymous with teaching to this day, which is why we strive to make classrooms teacher-proof through the use of assigned textbooks and standardized testing. As for the quote, it is in grammar schools that children learn about nouns and verbs and the parts of speech, distinctions that never come up in everyday discourse. In schooling, the pragmatics of communication are set aside in favor of the syntactics of language, as well as its semantics, including the expansion of vocabulary, or the learning of *abominable words*. This is reminiscent of the contemporary phenomenon of first generation college students, returning home and angering the parents who paid their tuition by references to philosophical positions and sociological theories that prove alienating to their elders. In this sense, corrupting the youth is not only about filling their heads with ideas, but also giving them new means of expression. And this can indeed be divisive, and potentially dangerous to the status quo. As for hanging the illiterate, the reference is to the Benefit of Clergy, a provision that originally exempted clergy from being tried in secular courts in Britain. To prove their clerical status, individuals would be required to read a passage from the Latin Bible, and this benefit was eventually extended to lay persons, so that it was not so much that individuals were hanged because they could not read, but rather that those who could read were spared.

The sentiments expressed by Shakespeare are something of an anachronism. The invention of the printing press with movable type coincided with Henry VI's troubled reign, although it was not until a few years after his death that the invention was brought to England by William Caxton. And with it came numerous social and cultural mutations, as scholars such as Elizabeth Eisenstein (1979) and S.H. Steinberg (1996) have documented. The mechanization of writing made it possible to mass produce written works, and increased access to reading materials, resulting in rising literacy rates. By creating a market for the selling of books, printing encouraged the writing and publication of works in the vernacular as well as in Latin, and Shakespeare was instrumental in establishing English as a legitimate literary language. The effect was also to reduce if not eliminate local linguistic differences, standardizing and homogenizing vernacular languages within national boundaries (McLuhan, 1962; Steinberg, 1996). And as the status and utility of literacy increased, so did schooling. Neil Postman (1982) noted that, "in a relatively short time the English transformed their society into an island of schools" (p. 39), and that:

> There were, in fact, three kinds of schools that developed: the elementary or "petty" schools, which taught the three R's; the free schools, which taught mathematics, English composition, and rhetoric; and grammar schools, which trained the young for universities and Inns of Court by teaching them English grammar and classical linguistics. Shakespeare attended a grammar school in Stratford, and his experience there inspired him to express a famous complaint (for he had probably been required to read Lyly's *Latin Grammar*). (p. 40)

Today this part of the primary curriculum is sometimes referred to as language arts, which incorporates rhetoric in the form of composition and public speaking, and largely forgoes the teaching of Latin. And yet, the shadow of Latin lingers, having altered how English grammar is taught. In this regard, the 18th century was pivotal. It was at this time that members of a burgeoning middle class, the result of urbanization, democratization, capitalism, and industrialism, as well as typographic literacy, were looking for ways to increase their social standing to match their wealth. As Postman and Weingartner (1966) explain:

> In their desire to attain a status to which their new-found affluence and freedom entitled them, these people assumed an almost compulsive interest in English grammar. To them, language became a medium of social prestige, or, to use a modern term, a medium of upward social mobility. Toward this end, wealthy merchants and their wives employed tutors to inform them of the elegant modes of speech. The tutors responded to the demand by producing "latinized" English-grammar books, which is to say, books attempting to describe the structure of English in terms of the structure of Latin. (p. 47)

For English speaking populations, the bias of print media towards the homogenization and standardization of language not only designated one particular dialect as proper and correct, as in the phrase, the *King's* (or *Queen's*) *English*; it also led to the adoption of arbitrary rules foreign to the language, originating from Latin. For example, in Latin infinitives are one word, whereas in English they always begin with the word "to", as in "to walk," "to talk", and "to chew gum". It is therefore quite possible in English to split an infinitive, and thereby to boldly go where others have gone before, and there is nothing inherently wrong or confusing about doing so. Similarly, in Latin it is impossible to end a sentence with a preposition, but in English we are perfectly capable of doing so, and again, there is nothing necessarily wrong about it, neither does it create any difficulties in conveying meaning. (E.B. White famously provided an example of ending a sentence with five prepositions: "A father of a little boy goes upstairs after supper to read to his son, but he brings the wrong book. The boy says, 'why did you bring that book that I don't want to be read to out of up for?'") The rationale for imposing these Latin-derived rules onto English was almost theological in its origin, and based on a desire for linguistic purity, in the face of linguistic pollution. According to Postman and Weingartner (1966),

> It was typical of the grammarians of the eighteenth century to assume (1) that language was a divine inspiration, originally perfect, but debased by man; (2) that, consequently, language possessed a natural logic that could not be violated even by common consent; which is to say, common usage; (3) that the consummate expression of linguistic purity and perfection was to be found in Latin and Greek, especially Latin, and that the grammar and inherent logic of Latin were criteria by which the excellence or depravity of language could be judged; (4) that English could be improved by the application of rules of Latin and by the insistence on a strict adherence to these rules; and (5) that the function of a grammarian is to preserve, protect, and otherwise defend the language from "decay." (p. 49)

This approach to the teaching of grammar is referred to as *prescriptive*, and it gave rise to the notion that some people have good grammar and some have bad grammar, or worse yet, that some people do not have grammar at all. Prior to this innovation, notably in oral cultures and traditional cultures, the concept of a grammatical error simply does not exist. The prescriptive approach to education has much to do with changing the meaning of the term *grammar*, from its original, expansive sense, to its reduced, restricted association with rote learning of linguistic rules, and no doubt is responsible for the negative connotations that the term often evokes. It can also be viewed, however, as the beginnings of linguistics as a field of study distinct from philology. In linguistics, language is studied in isolation from the larger context of literature, or for that matter of oral tradition or folklore.

An alternative to the prescriptive approach in linguistics emerged during the 19th century. *Descriptive* grammarians were not interested in making value judgments about what style of speech should be considered wrong or right. Rather, embracing a social and behavioral science perspective, they aimed for an objective study of different languages, viewing differences in a neutral manner, and noting that variations are neither good nor bad, but simply different. From a descriptive approach, every dialect has a grammar, all grammars are equally valid, and the aim is simply to understand the unique properties of a language. For scholars associated with descriptive linguistics, "grammar is the study of the ways in which a language achieves structural sense" (Postman & Weingartner, 1966, p. 55).

Language, Culture, and Media

Descriptive linguistics forms the basis of linguistic relativism, also known as the Sapir-Whorf Hypothesis, associated with Edward Sapir (1921) and Benjamin Lee Whorf (1956), as well as Dorothy Lee (1959), and more recently Lera Boroditsky (2011); the basic concept was in circulation prior to the 20th century, possibly introduced by Wilhelm von Humboldt in the early 19th century. Linguistic relativism is often expressed as the idea that the language we speak affects or determines the way we view the world; put another way, different languages give us different tools for thought, and also guide our perception in different ways. This view influences and parallels general semantics, and is an important foundation for the media ecology of McLuhan and others who followed. The best known examples of linguistic relativism have to do with differences in vocabulary, the cliché being the idea that the Eskimo have a dozen words for *snow* while we have only the one, as well as pointing to words that are unique to a particular language and more or less untranslatable (Rheingold, 1988). The more significant factor in influencing perception, thought, and behavior, however, is the grammar of the language, that is, its structure and syntax; in recognizing the greater impact of grammar over vocabulary, we can discern a parallel and precursor to McLuhan's (1964) emphasis on medium over message.

The descriptive approach was to a large degree pushed aside by the *generative* approach championed by Noam Chomsky (1972) and his followers. While they share an interest in grammar as the structure of language, their primary concern is with a posited deep structure that underlies all human languages. This universal grammar is believed to be hardwired into our species, a genetic inheritance and inborn language instinct. It is certainly the case that our biology includes the capacity to make a wide variety of sounds, due to the structure and positioning of our larynx and the entire vocal tract. It is also true that the human brain has evolved to enable speech and symbolic communication, through structures such as Broca's Area and Wernicke's Area. The generative approach goes further than this, with the argument that our genes also encode a basic set of rules that make up this universal grammar, a deep structure out of which the surface structure of different languages with their different syntactical formulations are manifested. It is worth noting that Chomsky's approach is dialectical rather than grammarian, based on deductive logic rather than the empirical study of languages (he even referred to his perspective as Cartesian linguistics at one point). Most importantly, his generalizations have not stood up to empirical testing (Wolfe, 2016). The idea of a universal grammar in some ways retrieves the prescriptive view that language has a natural logic, and that there is a pure version of language, not Latin in this case, but the generative grammar out of which all specific forms arise. Chomsky and his followers dismissed linguistic differences as insignificant, and were opposed to linguistic relativism, even though it would be perfectly possible for both views to coexist. The grammarian view, however, would maintain that differences between different languages are differences that make a difference, that different languages do influence thought and perception differently, and that structural differences on all levels are significant.

Within linguistics generally, study focuses on topics such as the *parts of speech*, and that phrase serves to underline the fact that the word *tongue* is synonymous with the term *language*, the root being the Latin *lingua*, meaning exactly that, *tongue*. This helps to remind us that the written word is merely a means of recording language, not language itself. Writing does make it possible to study language, and is the foundation of grammar, rhetoric, and logic, of philology and linguistics, and indeed of all forms of study (Havelock, 1982; Ong, 1982). But the distinction between speech and writing has not always been made clear within linguistics, and when it has, the study of writing has been more or less an afterthought. For this reason, I.J. Gelb, in his book, *A Study of Writing* (1963), introduced the term *grammatology* to refer to the study of writing systems, including the logographic, syllabic, and alphabetic. Derrida (1976) adopted the term in reference to his own method of deconstruction, which in an odd turn made writing primary, and speech a function of writing (see Ong, 1982, for a critique). However problematic that may be, it does serve to isolate writing as a separate symbol system from speech, which indicates that there is a distinct grammar of the written word that can be differentiated from the grammar of a tongue, and therefore isolated and studied in its own right. Consistent with linguistic relativism, neurological research indicates that literacy actually alters brain structure and function (Wolf, 2007, 2018), and that different writing systems are associated with different ways of thinking, perceiving, and communicating (Havelock, 1982; Logan, 2004).

That writing systems are inventions, tools, and therefore technologies (Ong, 1982) would be fairly obvious. That languages and other symbol systems are also inventions, tools, and therefore technologies, is often obscured by the fact that they are made possible by our biology, and based on our genetic predisposition. This overlooks the fact that all of our tools, technologies, and media are extensions of our bodies, an observation made by Ralph Waldo Emerson (1883), Ogden and Richards (1923), Edward T. Hall (1959), and famously, McLuhan (1964). Moreover, we clearly have an innate capacity for tool use, as evidenced by the fact that other animals also make and utilize tools. We typically refer to symbols as arbitrary and conventional, which indicates that they do not spring fully formed from our DNA, but rather are arbitrary because they are human inventions, and conventional because they are subject to widespread adoption. That language is an invention is most clearly evident in regard to naming; recall the story related in the Book of Genesis of how Adam named all of the animals, the process of naming coinciding with his being granted dominion over nature. Parents assign names to their offspring, and people name various significant parts of their environment, both natural and artificial. Naming is also a tool of perception, relating to figure-ground relationships: whatever has a name can be seen as a figure in the foreground of our awareness; whatever is nameless is part of the background and generally not consciously focused on or attended to. We understand that words can be invented, the process of neologism also expands to include the invention of phrases and expressions, and the idea of rhetorical invention in addition to linguistic invention. Poetry involves the creative use of language, while professionals develop jargon to facilitate communication within a group and helping to maintain its boundaries. Importantly, general semantics is predicated on the idea that language is a tool, one that can be modified and refined (Johnson, 1946). And this includes not only vocabularies, but grammar and syntax as well, for example through changing the ways in which we use the verb *to be* (Korzybski, 1993, argues for avoiding the *is* of identification and related usages).

Understanding language to be a human invention is consistent with linguistic relativism, and indeed helps to explain the existence of entirely different languages and language families, and why those differences are truly significant. The extreme version of the Sapir-Whorf Hypothesis, that language determines worldview, has opened up the entirety of linguistic relativism to unwarranted criticism (Nystrom, 2021). Without a doubt it is more accurate to say that language influences thought and perception, and to eschew determinism, which is an unfortunate carryover from the Aristotelian and Newtonian perspective. Rather, we can understand that our linguistic, semantic, and media environments allow for differing and unique worldviews and modes of thought to emerge (Strate, 2011a, 2017). The extreme version of the Sapir-Whorf Hypothesis includes a reductionist view of culture as completely derived from language, and this too is inaccurate, but again that does not require us to abandon linguistic relativism altogether. Quite the contrary, Edward T. Hall (1959) extended the Sapir-Whorf Hypothesis by suggesting that all of culture can be understood as a kind of language writ large, influencing the way we think and perceive. This applies to the differences between different cultures taken as a whole, Hall's definition of culture being, simply, that *culture is communication*; it also applies to specific subsets of a culture, such as clothing, architecture, food, etc., including language, all of which can be understood as individual, specific codes or symbol systems. Of course, cultural artifacts and cultures in their entirety are also human inventions, which is why we often place culture in binary opposition to nature. Along similar lines, the concept of art, whether seen as a product of culture or a separate phenomenon, is often described as a species of language, or a set of languages, but perhaps more properly as symbolic form, following the highly significant work of Susanne Langer (1953, 1957; see also Nystrom, 2021).

Paralleling Hall, Edmund Carpenter (1960) explained that all languages are types of media, and all other types of media are languages:

> English is a mass medium. All languages are mass media. The new mass media—film, radio, TV—are new languages, their grammars as yet unknown.... each codifies reality differently; each conceals a unique metaphysics (p. 162).

The idea of media as languages can be traced back to the Soviet filmmaker and film theorist Sergei Eisenstein (1942, 1949), who argued that film can be understood as a language, with shots as the vocabulary, and film editing or *montage* as the grammar or syntax. The idea of media as languages was significant to McLuhan's understanding of media, and this includes viewing all technologies, not just communication technologies, as languages. In *Understanding Media* (1964), he refers to media as translators, translating experience into representations, sense perception into vocalizations, and nature into art; this is similar to the idea in physics that the lever is a machine that *translates* force. I would also point to the example of learning how to drive, and how at a certain point we stop thinking consciously about what we are doing as the activity becomes a kind of second nature; at that point, it could be said that we have become fluent in *car*, by which I mean the language of the automobile. The idea of technology as a kind of tongue is emphasized in McLuhan's posthumously published *Laws of Media*, co-authored by Eric McLuhan, where they introduce the tetrad or four laws of media (enhance, obsolesce, retrieve, and reverse) as the grammar of technology (McLuhan & McLuhan, 1988). Neil Postman, whose background was in English education, was instrumental in bringing these threads together, initially in his first book, *Television and the Teaching of English* (1961), in his first collaboration with Charles Weingartner, *Linguistics: A Revolution in Teaching* (1966), and notably in their second work, *Teaching as a Subversive Activity* (1969), where they introduced, "the Sapir-Whorf-Korzybski-Ames-Einstein-Heisenberg-Wittgenstein-McLuhan-Et Al. Hypothesis ... that language is not merely a vehicle of expression, it is also the driver; and that what we perceive, and therefore can learn, is a function of our languaging processes" (p. 101). This coincides with Postman's (1970) formal introduction of media ecology as a field of inquiry he defined as, "the study of media as environments" (p. 161) a field he later described as "general semantics writ large" (Postman, 1974, p. 76).

Ecology and Systems

To the extent that general semantics is concerned with language, it builds upon the descriptive approach to grammar, and is closely connected to linguistic relativism. But it also represents a new kind of prescriptive approach, substituting non-Aristotelian principles, such as consciousness of abstracting and an inductive, empirical, and extensional orientation, for the original prescriptivists obsession with Latin grammar. Korzybski's (1993) concern was with structure (and structural differentials), and the relationship between the structure of reality, which is to say the structure of our environment, and the structure of our language and worldview, the structure of our thought, and perception. For example, he explained,

> A language, any language, has at its bottom certain metaphysics, which ascribe, consciously or unconsciously, some sort of structure to this world. Our old mythologies ascribed an anthropomorphic structure to the world, and, of course, under such a delusion, the primitives built up a language to picture such a world and gave it a subject-predicate form.... Neither Aristotle nor his immediate followers realized or could

realize what has been said here. They took the structure of the primitive-made language for granted, and went ahead formulating a philosophical grammar of this primitive language, which grammar—to our great semantic detriment—they called 'logic', defining it as the 'laws of thought'. Because of this formulation in a general theory, we are accustomed even today to inflict this 'philosophical grammar' of primitive language upon our children, and so from childhood up imprison them unconsciously by *the structure* of the language and the so-called 'logic', in an anthropomorphic, structurally primitive universe. (Korzybski, 1993, p. 89)

Holding aside Korzybski's use of the term *primitive*, a term that is typically avoided in contemporary discussion due to its pejorative connotations, his equation of structure with grammar, both linguistic and philosophical grammar, is significant. Korzybski's (1993) often invoked metaphor that the *map is not the territory* (p. 58) refers then not just to representation, but to the difference between the grammar of maps as distinct from the grammar of territories, both of which are read—we read maps and we read our surroundings. The prescriptive goal, then, is to create a mapmaking grammar that is consistent with the grammar of the territory, so as to produce maps that are as structurally similar to the territory as possible, general semantics providing the method for doing so. Media ecology provides a further prescriptive component in the concern regarding media and environment, and the ways in which our media and technology affect our environment, and ourselves (Strate, 2017). This is particularly apparent in the approach taken by Postman and others, including Lewis Mumford (1943, 1967, 1970) and Jacques Ellul (1964), and subdued but still discernible in McLuhan (1964) and Ong (1982). The inclusion of both prescriptive and descriptive elements parallels the double meaning of ecology itself, as both a subdivision of biological science, and an activist approach that embraces conservation and environmentalism. In this context, we can frame ecology as the study of the grammar of the biosphere, and specific natural environments. Jeremy Campbell moves in that direction in his popular work, *Grammatical Man* (1982):

Information theory shows that there are good reasons why the forces of antichance are as universal as the forces of chance, even though entropy has been presented as the overwhelmingly more powerful principle. The proper metaphor for the life process may not be a pair of rolling dice or a spinning roulette wheel, but the sentences of a language, conveying information that is partly predictable and partly unpredictable.

These sentences are generated by rules which make much out of little, producing a boundless wealth of meaning from a finite store of words; they enable language to be familiar yet surprising, constrained yet unpredictable within its constraints.

Sense and order, the theory says, can prevail against nonsense and chaos. The world need not regress toward the simple, the uniform, and the banal, but may advance in the direction of richer and more complex structures, physical and mental. Life, like language, remains "grammatical." The classical view of entropy implied that structure is the exception and confusion the rule. The theory of information suggests instead that order is entirely natural; grammatical man inhabits a grammatical universe. (p. 12)

Extending the concept of grammar beyond speech and symbols, communication and culture, media and technology, and connecting language to information theory is a step in the right direction. More significant than the connection Campbell forges between Claude Shannon and Noam Chomsky, however, is the fact that Korzybski's (1993) general semantics was also a precursor of systems theory, as elaborated upon by Gregory Bateson (1972, 1979) and others, which in turn informs the work of media ecology scholars such as McLuhan and Postman. Whereas the systems view emphasizes the structure of systems, the relationship of the parts as they join together to form a whole, we can understand that that structure is the grammar of the system, a grammar that may be made up of a stable and unchanging set of rules, or a grammar composed of a dynamic and interactive set of relationships. Moreover, there is the relationship between the system and its environment (Watzlawick, Bavelas, & Jackson, 1967), and this systems, relational, or ecological view is not that far removed from the older grammarian idea of reading the environment as we would read a book. Simply put, Korzybski began with science, which led him to the idea of relationship and structure, and from the idea of the structure of the environment to its relationship to the structure of language. McLuhan began with grammar as it relates to language and literature, and from there to the idea of the grammar of the environment as it relates to the grammar of language, studied via texts.

Even more basic would be the idea of the environment as a form of speech, or more accurately, events as speech acts, which we can listen to. In the words of Martin Buber (2014), "this speech has no alphabet, each of its sounds is a new creation, and only to be grasped as such... the sounds of which the speech consists... are the events of the personal everyday life" (p. 16). This is consistent with the idea that God speaks the world into being, beginning in the Book of

Genesis with the command, "Let there be light." This also relates to the concept of divine logos, originating in ancient Greece, and significant in Christian theology (Ong, 1967, 1982). Holding religion aside, the idea of listening to the environment, in contrast to reading the environment, suggests a more intimate relationship, one of immersion rather than voyeurism, participation rather than passive spectatorship. Listening situates us in acoustic space, and in a subjective, I-You relationship with others and our environment; reading places us in visual space, and in an objective, I-It relationship with others and our environment (Carpenter & McLuhan, 1960). In this sense, visual space is consistent with modern science and the view that we are separate and in opposition to nature, whereas acoustic space is consistent with an ecological understanding that we are inside and a part of our environment. And acoustic space was dominant in oral cultures, while visual space is a product of literacy. In our contemporary electronic culture, acoustic space has returned from being repressed (McLuhan, 1964; McLuhan & McLuhan, 1988). Visual space is still available to us, however, and we desperately need to find a balance between the two.

McLuhan (2006) characterized the grammarian as interested in connections, as opposed to the dialectician's focus on divisions; likewise the grammarian is interested in concrete observations, in answering the question general semanticists are known to pose, *what is going on?*, whereas dialecticians tend to get lost in high level abstractions. Dialecticians focus on analysis to the exclusion of all else, whereas grammarians are interested in synthesis, in putting the pieces together to form a whole greater than the sum of its parts, and above all with *understanding*. The new grammarians are concerned with the grammar of the word and the world, the grammar of language and media, the grammar of culture and consciousness, the grammar of our symbolic, technological, and biophysical environments. This does not mean that logic and rhetoric must be excluded and exiled from the grammarian republic of letters, but instead that grammar needs to be restored to its rightful place, as the foundation of a curriculum, a methodology, and a body of knowledge that is anything but trivial, but rather, one that is vital for our survival.

Chapter 4
Media Literacy and General Semantics

C an there be professional media ethics without media literacy? That is
to say, can media professionals truly function in an ethical manner un-
less they have taken steps to promote and encourage media literacy? I
would suggest that there is a moral obligation on the part of media organizations to ensure that media audiences can decode their messages accurately, interpret them appropriately, and most important of all, evaluate them critically.

When all of a society's business is conducted via word of mouth, that is, in
oral cultures, the only prerequisite for participation in the culture is the ability
to speak the language, that is to say, fluency. Since language acquisition comes
quite naturally to our species, decoding messages and interpreting meanings
would not be much of an issue, although critical evaluation has always been a
major challenge for us humans, as Alfred Korzybski (1950, 1993) famously explained. The invention of writing added a new wrinkle to the problem, as more
and more of a culture became encoded in written form, including its religious,
legal, economic, and political communications. The eventual result was that
schooling, based on the traditional literacy associated with reading and writing
(and the numeracy of arithmetic and mathematics), became a moral imperative. And as the printing revolution in Europe gave rise to the Enlightenment,
it came to be understood that education based on the book is necessary for
the maximization of the individual's freedom and autonomy in a democratic
society. Now that we live in a world where public discourse is dominated by
telecommunications technologies, it follows that media education is likewise
an ethical necessity for participation in contemporary technological societies.

It is easy enough to say, yes, media education is an ethical obligation, and
ought to be taught in the schools. In the United States, there is a long standing
tradition of trying to address social problems through public education, for example in the addition of curricula and courses addressing sex education, drug
use, and racial prejudice. And while such efforts are certainly laudable, they do
not speak to the question of what ethical obligations might fall to other institutions, apart from the schools, such as the family. In regard to media education,
it would surely be reasonable to ask whether there is anything that media organizations and industries can do to promote media literacy. Certainly, funding

school programs on media education might be one answer, although there are problems related to conflict of interest when an industry funds programs whose aim is the critical evaluation of that industry, as for example when companies that produce snack foods provide educational materials about nutrition. But given the special case of the media industries, would it be possible for media organizations to include and incorporate media literacy-oriented messages and functions as part of their content? And assuming it is possible, would media organizations not then be under an ethical obligation to do so?

Of all of the types of programming that media professionals produce, content directed towards children and youth would be the most in need of media literacy messages. Children are presumably less experienced than adults in receiving media messages, less sophisticated in their ability to interpret those messages, and less able to engage in critical evaluation. At the same time, children are eminently educable, and it is our obligation to prepare them to take their place as responsible and participating members of a democratic society. To this end, media literacy ought to be incorporated as one of the primary objectives of children's media, and this idea became the basis of a research report entitled *The Future of Children's Television Programming: A Study of How Emerging Digital Technologies Can Facilitate Active and Engaged Participation and Contribute to Media Literacy Education* (Strate, Freeman, Gutierrez, & Lavalle, 2010). The focus of our research was to investigate how digital technologies might be used to incorporate media education into children's programming, but to do so, there first must be some way to operationalize media literacy as a goal, and general semantics provides a good place to start. Although Korzybski did not have much to say about media per se, he offered a system for critical evaluation of messages and information, and others such as Neil Postman (1976, 1979, 1985, 1988), John C. Merrill (1997), Greg Hoffman and Paul Dennithorne Johnston (1997), and Renee Hobbs (2004) have applied general semantics to the study of media in various ways (as have I on previous occasions, e.g., Strate, 2011a, 2004, 2017). In this instance, Korzybski's three non-Aristotelian principles of thought might serve as a useful basis for incorporating media literacy into children's media.

The first non-Aristotelian principle is that of non-identity, that our representations and understandings of our environment should not be mistaken for the environment itself, or as Korzybski (1993) was fond of saying, the *map is not the territory* (p. 58). Fictional narratives depend upon the audience's willing suspension of disbelief, but a media literacy program would require reminders of their unreality. Nonfictional reports about the world strive for the authenticity and accuracy, but need to remind audiences that they are necessarily inaccurate in some ways, that mediated reports, depictions, and monitoring of situations are not identical to direct experience and unmediated assessments. The principle of non-identity points to the need to delay reactions, carefully evaluate mediated messages, and consider all conclusions drawn to be tentative, subject to change, and in need of further testing. Such testing could take the form of comparison of messages coming from different sources, and better yet of engaging in reality testing through unmediated experience if possible. At minimum, the incorporation of the principle of non-identity into media content could be accomplished by statements made before, during, and after the program, the equivalent of a kind of warning label. A more sophisticated approach would incorporate messages concerning non-identity into the very narrative or report itself.

The second non-Aristotelian principle is that of non-allness, that our representations and understandings of our environment are necessarily incomplete, abstractions of reality, selections taken from all that makes up our environment. This means that media producers make decisions about what to describe or present, who to speak to, in what order to arrange things, and in the case of audiovisual media, where to point the camera, what lighting to use, what type of shot to employ, and how to select and edit the footage that is shot. Again, including statements about the inevitability of selection, the many ways in which gatekeeping and editing play a role in the finished product, and the subjective element present in the process, could serve as a beginning, but a more in-depth approach would present alternative selections and combinations for comparison, and perhaps even allow viewers to make their own choices about what to include and exclude, and how to arrange the material.

The third principle is that of self-reflexiveness, that our representations and understandings can extend not only to our environment, but back towards themselves, so that we can also have representations of our representations, and representations of our representations of our representations, etc. In this sense, there is media content that refers to the world in some way, and media content that refers back to itself or to media content in general, and there can also be content about content about content, etc. In regard to media literacy, it would follow that a goal would be to distinguish between reporting and depicting events in the world, and media organizations reporting and depicting, and celebrating themselves. At the same time, self-reflexiveness is exactly what is required in order to incorporate media literacy into media messages. A form of *metacontent* informed by media literacy objectives would certainly have the potential for increasing awareness and self-consciousness of mediation, and to encourage audiences to evaluate their own activities as consumers of media messages. Fundamental to this effort would be the recognition of the difference between content that asks the audience to step back and critically evaluate messages as mediated content, and content that promotes uncritical acceptance of messages as if they were unmediated experience. Moreover, self-reflexiveness would also include recognition of the source or communicator, awareness of the authors, directors, and actors that create the narrative rather than only fostering the suspension of disbelief, and identification of the reporters and editors and camera operators in the case of news, documentary, and nonfiction, with an acknowledgement of their role in constructing the presentation.

The three non-Aristotelian principles of general semantics do not constitute a media literacy program or curriculum in its entirety, but do provide a good starting point and foundation for such efforts. As such, it is worthwhile to recall that Alfred Korzybski first put forth these principles out of concern to improve individual freedom and autonomy, and to alleviate the personal and social problems that give rise to conflict, prejudice, and a failure to live up to our full human potential. In applying the principles to media production, it becomes clear that there is much that media organizations can do to incorporate media literacy into media messages, especially for children's media, and that to do so would be to fulfill an ethical obligation on their part.

Chapter 5
Communication and Innovation

In his book, *Computer Power and Human Reason,* Joseph Weizenbaum (1976) argues that, just because we can do something does not mean that we ought to do it. The word *ought* is one that we seldom hear nowadays, and perhaps this says a great deal about who we are. Weizenbaum argues that *ought* ought to be restored to our professional and personal vocabularies. This means making choices, and basing our decisions on rational and ethical criteria. Given limited time and resources, he suggests that our efforts should be directed not at technological wizardry, but at solving real, human problems. And that human standards ought to be employed in evaluating technical activities.

Alan Kay was one of the first computer scientists to think about computers as media of communication, and this led him to develop the graphical user interface or GUI, popularized as the Macintosh and Windows operating systems, and the Mac and Android iOS. Kay took inspiration from Marshall McLuhan (1964), who expanded the category of media to include language and symbolic form, and all forms of technology. McLuhan followed the line of thinking originated by Ralph Waldo Emerson (1883) that every invention is an extension of ourselves. It follows that our extensions are ways that we *mediate* between ourselves and some part of our environment. And what comes between us and our environment becomes our environment.

McLuhan's (1964) famous aphorism, *the medium is the message* (p. 7), is meant to convey the idea that the most significant impact of a medium is not in the way that it is used, but rather in the fact that it is used. Any given television program matters less than the fact that we can watch television. Any particular set of passengers or cargo on an airplane matters less than the fact that we have airplanes flying overhead, transporting people and goods all across the globe. Any one use of electric lighting matters less than the fact that its very existence turns night into day and makes possible a 24/7/365 society. The different specific ways that guns are used are of less significance than the fact that firearms are present and readily available (with devastating results in the United States). And any specific application of social media, mobile communications, data processing, etc., pales in comparison to the fact that we have adopted these innovations with scarcely a thought as to the consequences of doing so, and are experiencing the myriad ways that they are mutating our political and economic systems, our relationships, and our senses of self.

Norbert Wiener (1950, 1961), in his cybernetic formulations, characterized the environment as a complex message system. In other words, the environment is a medium. We understand that fish swim in the medium of water, just as we move through the medium of air, and our eyes depend on the medium of light. Agar is a medium that microbiologists use to grow bacteria, and the batch of bacteria they grow is called a culture. Cultures are produced within media, by microbes, and by humans as well. The environments we inhabit include the biophysical environment, which we associate with physics, chemistry, and biology; the technological environment, the many ways that we add to and modify our environment through our inventions, our tools, implements, weapons, machines, containers, buildings, settlements, forms of organization, procedures and techniques, etc.; and the symbolic environment, our languages, codes and modes of communication, art forms, etc., which provide us with ways of perceiving and understanding our world, finding meaning and guiding our actions.

From a systems perspective, it ought to be clear that when you have a set of interdependent parts together forming a whole, a change to one small part of the system can reverberate throughout the entire system, leading to systemic change. The eventual result of disrupting a system may be a reconfiguration of the system at a higher level of complexity, or it may be the collapse of the system. From a human point of view, every innovation constitutes a change within the system, and therefore an outright gamble that the outcome will not do more harm than good. Every innovation will have its unavoidable costs in addition to whatever benefits it confers. There is no such thing as a free lunch, not in physics, not in technology, and not in human life. Ideally, we would have the opportunity to weigh the costs and benefits, and determine if the innovation is worth adopting, or not. But instead, unable to predict future events, we are trapped in a situation that is the equivalent of *buy-now, pay-later*.

The effects of any innovation will also include what in medicine is euphemistically called *side effects*, but after all the side effects are real effects, sometimes more powerful than the intended effects, and sometimes worse than the disease being treated. Medical testing is used to try to gauge the desirable and undesirable effects of any drug or procedure, but we all know that the results often fail to take into account long term effects, or the effects of widespread use, as in the case of opioids or antibiotics. For every innovation, there will always be consequences that are unforeseen and unpredictable. When you add something new to a system, the change does not stop there, but changes other parts of the system, and those changes change other parts of the system, and so on, with all of these changes interacting with one another. The result is not the same system that we had before with some small addition to it, but a system that has been transformed, essentially a brand new system.

The automobile has had its costs and its benefits. Who could have foreseen how it would empower women and minorities? Alter courtship rituals among the youth? Lead to the growth of suburbs and exurbs? Result in the paving over of much of our terrain? Further our dependency on fossil fuels and play a significant role in climate change? Become a major cause of fatalities, especially for teens and young adults? And consequently, make organ transplants a commonplace medical procedure? (What other supply of healthy organs do you imagine there might be, apart from the victims of automobile accidents?) Are we better off, then, with cars, or would we better off without them? How do we even begin to assess the consequences of a technology that has been with us since the late 19th century, let alone weigh the costs and benefits of microcomputers, social networking, mobile devices, robotics, VR, AR, AI, etc.? At the very least, understanding the consequences of innovation should serve as a check on the tech industry's boundless optimism and boosterism. It should, at minimum, instill in all of us a modicum of caution in regard to innovation.

The tech industry, it seems, is governed by one and only one guiding principle: *more. More* speed. *More* information. *More* memory. *More* processing power. *More* users. *More* eyeballs. *More* dependency. *More* profits. And yes, sometimes *more* is a good thing, but we know that there can be too much of a good thing as well. Too much of the medicine that cures us can make us sick. Too much of the food that nourishes us leads to obesity. Too much exercise can cause permanent damage to bone and muscle. Too much information leaves us overloaded, unable to make sense of it all. What we need is balance, the fundamental ecological value. What we wind up with are systems that are woefully out of balance.

Weizenbaum (1976) was inspired by the social critic Jacques Ellul (1964), who argued that the only value that exists within technological systems is efficiency. The technological imperative always seeks out the most efficient means to any given end. The overriding *more* is *more* efficiency. *More* efficiency with no other end than, *more* efficiency. To counter this prevailing value system, or what Lewis Mumford (1934, 1967, 1970) called machine ideology, we need something beyond ordinary media ethics. Building on McLuhan's (1964) broad understanding of media, and Neil Postman's (1970) introduction of media ecology as a field of inquiry defined as the study of media as environments, we need *media ecology ethics*. And we can start with the words of Aldous Huxley (1937/2012): "The ends cannot justify the means, for the simple and obvious reason that the means employed determine the nature of the ends produced" (p. 10).

A media ecology ethics would insist that we must always pay attention to *how* we do things, because how we do things will have much to do with what we end up doing, and what we end up with, and who we ultimately become. A media ecology ethics would insist that the phrase, *by any means necessary*, is inherently unethical, if not utterly abhorrent. A media ecology ethics would require the ends to determine the means, and would demand that, before a new medium or technology is adopted, there must be an answer to the question, *to what end?* And if the answer is that it will increase efficiency in any area, a media ecology ethics would deem that insufficient as an end, because efficiency is not a human purpose, it is simply the logic of the means applied to the means itself.

Postman (2000) offered the following four questions to guide us in evaluating any innovation: "To what extent does a medium contribute to the uses and development of rational thought?" (p. 13). "To what extent does a medium contribute to the development of democratic processes?" (p. 13). "To what extent do new media give greater access to meaningful information?" (p. 14). "To what extent do new media enhance or diminish our moral sense, our capacity for goodness?" (p. 15). And beyond the specific questions posed, the basis of a media ecology ethics would be, simply, to question, to encourage the asking of questions, and to promote the asking of good questions. Especially questions about what we *ought* to be doing, questions about the means we employ, and our ultimate ends. This would be a beginning.

Chapter 6

Communication and Social Systems

Many scholars have addressed the relationship between communication and society, some specifically understanding that a society is a social system, one of the most prominent being Niklas Luhmann (1982, 1989, 1990, 1995, 2000). Systems, generally speaking, are understood to be composed of interdependent parts, such that the whole that they create are other than the sum of its parts, and typically greater than the sum of its parts. At first glance, we might assume that the parts that make up a social system are people, individuals, or in the case of other species, organisms. A more sophisticated sociological view would instead think of the parts that make up a society as institutions, perhaps also values. But in Luhmann's theoretical formulation, they are something somewhat different: Acts of communication are the parts that join together to form the whole that we call a social system.

I have previously situated Niklas Luhmann's work within the field of media ecology (Strate, 2006, 2010, 2011a), a field of inquiry formally introduced by Neil Postman in an address delivered to the National Council of Teachers of English in Milwaukee, Minnesota, in 1968. In doing so, Postman explained that he was not inventing the field, only naming it, which is why media ecology is not viewed as a discipline with a distinct founder, in the sense that Auguste Comte is viewed as the founder of sociology, for example, or Karl Marx is considered the founder of the school of thought that bears his name. Indeed, Postman established the practice of retroactively identifying individuals as media ecology scholars based on their perspective and approach, regardless of whether they identified themselves as such, or even were aware of the field's existence. Along these lines, I would suggest that media ecology is best understood as an open system, one that is not contained within hardened boundaries, but rather functions as a network of scholars and intellectuals, and their publications.

Postman (1970) defines media ecology as "the study of media as environments" (p. 161), and in taking an ecological approach to understanding media, the field naturally incorporates the systems view as articulated early on by scholars such as Gregory Bateson (1972, 1979), Kenneth Boulding (1956), Buckminster Fuller (Fuller & Applewhite, 1975), Ervin Laszlo (1972), and Ludwig von Bertalanffy (1969). Bertalanffy used the phrase *general system theory* following the example of Alfred Korzybski, who introduced the discipline of *general semantics* in 1933 in *Science and Sanity* (1993), anticipating much of systems theory, and influencing a number of media ecology scholars, including Luhmann. A systems orientation is reflected in the work of Marshall McLuhan (1964), Walter Ong (1967, 1977), and Neil Postman (1976, 1979, 2006); in the first doctoral dissertation on media ecology completed by Christine Nystrom (1973) under Postman's direction; in Joshua Meyrowitz's magnum opus, *No Sense of Place* (1985), based on his dissertation directed by Postman and Nystrom; in Kenneth Gergen's *The Saturated Self* (1991), which builds on Meyrowitz and incorporates the study of relational communication based in large part on Bateson's work and associated with Paul Watzlawick and his colleagues (Watzlawick, Bavelas, & Jackson, 1967; Watzlawick, Weakland, & Fisch, 1974); Watzlawick's scholarship can also be seen in Postman's writings on language and communication (e.g., Postman, 1976). Fritjof Capra's *The Web of Life* (1996) is noteworthy for its synthesis of systems theory and ecology, and more recently, systems concepts relating to chaos and complexity can be found in the work of McLuhan associates Robert Logan (2007, 2010) and Frank Zingrone (2001). And the systems concept of autopoiesis introduced by Humberto Maturana & Francisco Varela (1980, 1992) has been incorporated in Katherine Hayles's *How We Became Posthuman* (1999), as well as being foundational for Luhmann's (1982, 1985, 1990, 1995, 2000) social theory.

As noted, one of the most basic ideas in systems theory is that the whole is other than and often greater than the sum of its parts, which is to say that there is a difference between the parts that make up the system and the system itself. This parallels the distinction between members of a group, class, or category, and the category itself, as expressed in Alfred North Whitehead and Bertrand Russell's (1925-1927) theory of logical types (see also Korzybski, 1993), and which also can be expressed as the difference between communication and metacommunication, or between the content and relationship levels of communication (Watzlawick et al, 1967; Watzlawick et al, 1974). This also mirrors the distinction between content and medium as expressed in McLuhan's (1964) fundamental statement regarding the media ecology approach, "the medium is the message" (p. 7). Luhmann's sociology is consistent with this view, and deepens our understanding, as he argues that society can be regarded as a social system whose parts are not individuals or institutions, but acts of communication. The act of communication is the content inside of the system, while the medium exists on the level of the system itself. To further distinguish between the media environment and the social system, we might turn to Postman's (2000) discussion of the beginnings of the formalization of the field of media ecology for elaboration:

our first thinking about the subject was guided by a biological metaphor. You will remember from the time when you first became ac-
quainted with a Petri dish, that a medium was defined as a substance
within which a culture grows. If you replace the word "substance" with
the word "technology," the definition would stand as a fundamental
principle of media ecology: A medium is a technology within which
a culture grows; that is to say, it gives form to a culture's politics, social
organization, and habitual ways of thinking. Beginning with that idea,
we invoked still another biological metaphor, that of ecology.... We put
the word "media" in the front of the word "ecology" to suggest that we
were not simply interested in media, but in the ways in which the interaction between media and human beings give a culture its character
and, one might say, help a culture to maintain symbolic balance. (pp.
10-11)

In this instance, we can substitute Luhmann's *social system* for Postman's
culture to arrive at the understanding that our media, technology, and codes
and modes of communication constitute the environment that surrounds our
social systems, or put another way, the membrane or boundary between the
social system and the natural environment. And as Luhmann explains, following the lead of Maturana and Varela, the formation of a boundary closes off
the system from its outer environment to a large extent; this is essential for
the system's formation, and especially in the case of autopoietic systems, for
their self-organization. The relative closure of the boundary constitutes another way to understand McLuhan's notion that the medium is the message, which
emphasizes the self-reference inherent in all acts of communication. This also
illustrates how incorporating Luhmann into the media ecology intellectual tradition can provide added illumination for Luhmann's sociology.

All forms of life respond in some way to stimuli originating from the environment, or as Korzybski (1993) explains, all forms of life engage in some
form of *abstracting*, taking information in from the outer world. Organisms
with nervous systems engage in the form of abstracting that we call sense perception. And the human organism, which Korzybski identifies as unique as a
time-binding species, also engages in the form of abstracting that we call symbolic communication, employing language and other symbol systems to generate and accumulate knowledge. Korzybski was not alone in this linking of
perception and language. For example, Susanne Langer (1957) argues that perception is a symbolic activity, a form of metonymy where the fraction of the
environment that we take in stands for the environment as a whole. McLuhan
(1964) argues that language is a form of perception, indeed, that languages are

organs of perception.

In other words, we relate to our environments through a process of *mediating*, of *interfacing*, of *abstracting*. Through this process, we build up an internal model of the outside world, or to use Korzybski's (1993) favored metaphor, an internal *map* to represent an external *territory*. Like Korzybski, Luhmann stresses that the map is not the territory, but it is also important to recall that the whole point of Korzybski's general semantics is the understanding that all maps are not constructed equally, that some correspond better to their territories than others, that maps are ideally structural reflections of the territory they represent, or as Maturana and Varela (1992) put it, are *structurally coupled* with their territory. Korzybski stresses the fact that scientific method has had the greatest success in creating maps that are structurally coupled to their territory, that are the most effective in allowing us to navigate our environments, and predict the future results of present actions and events. Similarly, while Luhmann (2000) notes the lack of connection between mass media and outside world, the maps that our media provide can be (and ought to be) evaluated pertaining to their relative accuracy as reflections of the external environment of society in regard to geopolitics, economics, the natural environment, etc.

While the universe is the only system that is, in theory, completely closed, all systems require some degree of closure simply to exist and maintain their identity, and especially if they are engaged in self-organization. And as living systems, we can only take in part of our environment through abstracting, because its totality would overwhelm us. We create barriers for our own protection, biologically, psychologically, and sociologically. And we do so technologically as well, or as Max Frisch observes in his cybernetics-inspired novel *Homo Faber* (1959), "technology is the art of never having to experience the world" (p. 178). McLuhan (1964) regards media and technology as extensions of the human organism, following a tradition that can be traced back to Edward T. Hall (1959), C. K. Ogden and I. A. Richards (1923), and Ralph Waldo Emerson. (1883). But McLuhan insists that every extension is also an amputation. The medium that extends our reach into the world does so by situating itself between ourselves and the world, so that it also becomes a barrier between ourselves and the world. And as a barrier, the medium becomes part of our world, part of our environment, the boundary that separates system from environment, which becomes in effect our environment.

Luhmann also draws upon media ecology scholars Eric Havelock (1963, 1986), Walter Ong (1967, 1977, 1982), and Elizabeth Eisenstein (1979) to argue that innovations in communication technology such as the introduction of writing in the ancient world, and the printing revolution in early modern Europe, vastly increased the volume of information circulating within social systems, in turn allowing social systems to increase in complexity. Complexity is not simply a matter of a system growing larger; rather, it involves the development of specialized subsystems (see also Goody, 1986), each of which has its own boundary, maintained by a specialized language, and often involving a binary system or as Korzybski (1993) would put it, a two-valued orientation. So, for example, the legal system's boundary is based on guilt or innocence, the political system's boundary is based on winning or losing elections, and the educational system's boundary is based on passing or failing. Each subsystem closes itself off from the larger system that constitutes its environment, becoming relatively autonomous. This understanding of the growing complexity of social systems supports and supplements the arguments made by Jacques Ellul (1964) about the technological society, and the autonomy and growth of technical systems. The mass media also function as a subsystem, and their main function according to Luhmann is to create an inner map of the outer reality, essentially constructing a simplified and self-reflexive conception of the environment. This too has its counterpart in Ellul's (1965) thought, in the form of the propaganda function required for technological societies to maintain their existence, whose main emphasis is sociological rather than political, and whose main goal is to integrate individuals into society rather than spur them on to action.

The bias of written communication and print media is towards increased specialization (McLuhan, 1964). And newer forms of information technology, based as they are on the alphanumeric code, seem to amplify that bias, thereby supporting Luhmann's arguments. But systems theory does not allow for qualitative differences in the form that information takes, for example the distinction between the acoustic and visual senses that McLuhan (1964) and Ong (1976, 1977, 1982) emphasize, or between words and images as discussed by Langer (1957), Postman (1979, 1982, 1985), and Meyrowitz (1985). Whereas literacy enforces certain boundaries between groups and subsystems through the differentiation of levels of education and reading skills, and the extended vocabularies and jargon peculiar to each individual field and sector, the electronic and audiovisual media break down the barriers between groups and subsystems, and among social systems insofar as they are defined by national boundaries, vastly increasing the general accessibility of information. Here we can see how media ecology can provide an important complement to Luhmann's approach, and why Luhmann needs to be situated within media ecology as field of inquiry. The shared information environment that the audiovisual and electronic media have created is unprecedented in human history, prompting McLuhan (1962) to construct the oxymoronic phrase, *the global village*.

And this also leaves us with the question of whether the breaking of boundaries is ultimately a positive development for humanity? Has the increasingly complexity of modern society been a dysfunctional development, and does the change in media environment allow for the creation of a more organic way of life? Or given the parallel between the differentiation of society and the differentiation that the embryo undergoes to develop into an independently functioning organism, is this new form of undifferentiated communication tantamount to tumors within an otherwise healthy body, in effect a form of media cancer that threatens to turn into a terminal disease for human civilization? If we are to have any hope to grasp what is happening to our world, and to discover what if anything can be done about it, we need to begin with the approach provided by Luhmann and other media ecology scholars to understanding our media environment and the kinds of social systems that it has been and continues to be giving rise to.

Chapter 7

Information in the Context of Communication and Mediation

Introduction

We commonly speak of information as something that is sent by a sender and received by a receiver, or otherwise as something that is shared through the process of communication. In this sense, information is either the message that is being communicated, or a component of that message, typically thought to be the most significant portion of the message, if not its entire raison d' être. The implication is that information is a *thing*, some*thing* that has physical existence, some*thing* that can be contained within a message or a signal, some*thing* that can be moved from one location to another. This view of information therefore is consistent with views of communication based on metaphors of transportation or transmission, or of a flow through a pipeline, a stream, or channel, or of a football that is run or thrown or kicked from the line of scrimmage to the goal line or posts, or of a ping pong ball hit back and forth between two players. And insofar as it is conceived of as a *thing*, information is seen as a some*thing* that we can *have*, that we can *own* or that we can *obtain*. Of course, information is no*thing* like that, which is to say that information is not a *thing* at all. But even though Claude Shannon's information theory (Shannon & Weaver, 1949) introduced a different understanding of information from our everyday usage, it too is often interpreted to mean that, rather than some*thing* that we already have, information is some*thing* that we do not already have, some*thing* that we *need* (see, for example, Nystrom, 2021). While eminently useful, this also introduces the seeming paradox that the moment that we actually receive information, that some*thing* that we now *have* ceases to *be* information (and all that we are left with is mere *data*).

What kind of *thing*, then, could information possibly be? In his popular book, *Being Digital*, published in 1995, Nicholas Negroponte, former head of the Media Lab at the Massachusetts Institute of Technology, famously set up a polar opposition between atoms and bits to illustrate the transition from print media and other material products (e.g., film, records, tapes, disks) to digital media. In doing so, he implied that the two are comparable as aspects of our material reality, that matter and information are both different types of *substances*. To be more precise, he implied that the two types of "particles" are in some way comparable as components of our physical reality. But are they really the same kinds of phenomena, or might they be apples and oranges (or shall we say, atoms and oranges?). After all, atoms are the building blocks of matter, whereas bits are not a component of material reality, which is why the shift from atoms to bits that Negroponte points to is in fact a form of dematerialization. The term *bit* was coined by Shannon to represent the basic unit of information, a shortened form of the phrase *binary unit*. A bit then is a mathematical concept, derived from a base 2 numeral system, the basis of the binary code of computers and digital technology, and subject to logarithmic calculation. Bits have no physical form, neither as matter nor as energy.

From the perspective of the physical sciences, the counterpart of matter is energy, so that it would make more sense to contrast atoms with subatomic particles such as electrons and photons, and with forms of energy such as electricity and the electromagnetic spectrum. With this understanding, it becomes clear that media ecology scholars such as Marshall McLuhan (1962, 1964) and Lewis Mumford (1934) were correct in identifying electrical energy, electric technology, and the electronic media as the key turning points in technological evolution, with digital technology simply being a further elaboration of the main shift. Understanding that energy is the appropriate equivalent to matter helps to clarify the fact that information represents another type of phenomenon altogether. A more nuanced approach would be to define information not as a substance, but as a *property* of a substance, i.e., a property of a signal or message, or a property of a stimulus (which presupposes an organism that responds to it) or a property of energy. Like other properties, such as weight and size, information can be measured, so this view is consistent with information theory, within which Shannon placed information into direct relationship with the measurement of entropy (Shannon & Weaver, 1949; see also Wiener, 1950, 1961). Simply put, information is what is needed to reduce and ultimately eliminate uncertainty. Whenever there are a certain number of possibilities, information reduces that number, and continues to do so until all that we are left with is certainty.

Imagine a well-shuffled deck of cards. I ask you to guess what the top card is, and your chances of being correct are 1 in 52. I turn that card over and it provides you with information, not only about the card itself, but about the remainder of the deck. The task of guessing the next card just became slightly easier, as the chances of being correct are 1 in 51. Turning that card over, it supplies slightly less information than the first card, as it reduces slightly less uncertainty. Proceeding in this manner through the deck, each card I turn over provides a little less information, as each time the chances of guessing correctly are more and more in your favor. Now imagine we are down to our last two cards, all the rest have been turned over. Your chances of guessing are 1 out of 2, 50-50. Whether you guess correctly or not, the final card left face down has no information whatsoever, because based on the 51 cards that have already been exposed, you can determine what that last card is to a certainty. Alternately, if we were to open a brand new deck that has never been shuffled, so that the cards remain in order (not counting jokers, new decks typically start with the ace of spades, followed by the two of spades, and so on in ascending order, followed by diamonds in the same arrangement, then clubs, then hearts), then even the first card up would provide zero information, in that there would be no uncertainty as to its identity. In this way, information can be measured in terms of probability, which is to say randomness, chaos, entropy.

As for those nasty bits that Negroponte refers to, they refer to the information that is needed to reduce possibilities by half. One bit, then would be whether the card is red or black. If you were to guess one or the other, either way the answer would eliminate half of the deck. Another bit would be which of the two suits left is the correct one, and again the answer would eliminate the remaining half, leaving only 13 cards. Continuing on (and rounding up), we could ask questions to cut the number down to 7, then to 4, then to 2, and finally down to certainty. This would represent 5 bits of information as the maximum amount needed to reduce 52 possibilities down to a single certainty, which constitutes the most efficient way to reduce uncertainty. It is also sobering to consider that, from the perspective of information theory, information is a means of reducing or eliminating possibilities, of potential choices, and therefore of freedom. Coming to a fork in a road, I have two choices before me, uncertainty about which one to pick, and the freedom to decide between them. Making a decision, I take one of the two paths, the choice is made, the uncertainty is gone, and so is the freedom of that moment. Alternately, while still at the fork, if I gain information about one of the roads leading to a dead end, forcing me to take the other one as the only way to reach my destination, the uncertainty is gone, but so is my freedom of choice.

Information as News

From a communication theory perspective, information is best understood as a *function*, as a function of form (in*form*ation), and therefore as one of various different functions of communication (e.g., to inform, to persuade, to educate, to entertain, *etc*. (Lasswell, 1948; Wright, 1959). As a function, information also relates to purpose (the intent to inform, whether successful or not), and to effects (the effect of having been informed, whether that was intended or not). This process, then, is nested within the process of communication, which itself can be understood a function of a larger process, which can be referred to as *mediation*, which is the function carried out by *media*, in other words, by environments (Strate, 2017). In sum, the general function of mediation (which can occur among individuals and between individuals and their environments) includes the more specific but still general function of communication, which in turn includes the specific function of information. In this way, understanding information helps us to frame communication and mediation as kindred concepts. Information, communication, and mediation represent three orders or levels of functions, corresponding to content, relationship, and environment, each one a subset of the next.

Gregory Bateson (1972) emphasizes the fact that information is essentially about *differences*, including and especially second order differences, that is, *differences that make a difference*. The function of information constitutes an alert about changes or differences in the environment of an organism, or in its own internal workings. As he puts it:

> When I strike the head of a nail with a hammer, an impulse is transmitted to its point. But it is a semantic error, a misleading metaphor, to say that what travels in an axon is an "impulse". It could correctly be called *news* of a difference [emphasis added]. (Bateson, 1973, p. 454)

The discernment of difference can be seen as a form of cognition, or information processing, and it is a function that can be carried out by a variety of different systems, be they biological, technological, or sociological. Systems at the very least must maintain a boundary against their environment, in order to maintain their integrity and identity, their very existence as systems separate from their environment. This closing off from the environment is associated with the process termed *autopoiesis* by Humberto Maturana and Francisco Varela (1980, 1992), which allows for the self-organization of the system; while their focus is biology, the concept can be generalized to other types of systems, including social systems (Luhmann, 1989, 1990, 1995, 2000). Establishing a boundary between system and environment, self and not-self, is essential, but that boundary must, to some degree, be permeable, open enough to allow the system to absorb whatever materials and energy it needs to maintain and renew itself. And the ability to differentiate between what in the environment is safe and nourishing to absorb and what is not, also involves information processing, and therefore a form of cognition. In other words, in being open to evaluating substances in its environment, first and foremost the organism is open to evaluating information about the environment, or as Bateson (1972, 1979) would put it, *news* about the environment (for this reason, I like to say, as a variation on McLuhan, that *the medium is the membrane*; see Strate, 2018). From a functional perspective, gathering and processing news about the environment is one of the main tasks of the system's boundary, along with maintaining the integrity of the system itself.

The sociological function of surveillance of the environment (Lasswell, 1948) is considered universal to the human species (and to other social species as well), and the internal dissemination of information about the environment, and about other parts of the system, is what we commonly refer to as *news*. Mitchell Stephens, in his *History of News* (1988), notes that in oral cultures, news was transmitted by word of mouth, by messengers, criers and singers, and by such media as smoke signals and talking drums. The introduction of writing allowed for more formal approaches to news to develop, for example news sheets such as the ancient Roman *acta* and Chinese *tipao*. The printing revolution associated with Gutenberg's mid-15th century invention gave rise to various forms of pamphlets, letters, broadsheets, *etc.*, that functioned as news media, and eventually led to the introduction of the newspaper itself beginning in the 17th century. The innovation of the printed newspaper, as a periodical published frequently and according to a regular schedule, established the media environment within which the modern concept of news could begin to emerge. Printing gave us the first form of mass communication, allowing for the mass dissemination of information, but whether and to what degree mass media actually transmit information about the environment as opposed to manufacturing news in their own image is a matter of some debate (Boorstin, 1978; Carey, 1989, 1997; Postman, 1985; Stephens, 1988; Strate, 2014; Thoreau, 1899). It is certainly the case that the content of news media is shaped by the technologies and codes used to disseminate it, which in part is what McLuhan (1964) meant in saying that the medium is the message (see also Strate, 2017).

News as we understand it today would not be possible without the printing press, but it is also the product of further technological developments occurring during the 19th century. One of the earliest and most important was the application of steam power to the press, which was previously operated largely by hand. This innovation represented a giant leap in mass production capabilities, giving rise to the first mass circulation daily newspapers, while economies of scale allowed for the papers to be sold at much cheaper prices than previously possible (e.g., the penny press in the United States). The need to fill these papers with news led to the regular employment of reporters, and with it the separation of reporting from editorial functions; at the same time, in search of content for these media, newspapers turned for the first time to covering crime on a regular basis (Schudson, 1978). It also inaugurated the shift from simply gathering the news to manufacturing the news, through innovations such as the interview, the publicity stunt, investigative reporting, and eventually the press release, press conference, and such phenomena as background briefings, trial balloons, and leaks, not to mention the entire public relations industry (Boorstin, 1978).

While publishers and editors felt free to express their opinions and endorse political candidates and initiatives, the ideal of objective reporting gained momentum over the course of the 19th century, with opinion relegated to the op-ed pages, in part in an effort to appeal to a broad and heterogeneous readership and maximize the potential for advertising revenue (Schudson, 1978). Objectivity in reporting, with its stress on the propositional character of language as a discursive symbolic form, had much to do with the popular conception of news reporting as pure information, *factual information*, so to speak. In this sense, *information* might be distinguished from *ideas*, which originate from human beings and therefore are inherently subjective in nature. The notion of a *free marketplace of ideas* is based on the assumption that competition among them will lead to the discovery of truth. There is no comparable sense of a *free marketplace of information*, because objective descriptions are assumed to be true in that they are propositions or statements of fact that can be checked for accuracy, much like scientists can test each other's findings. It would follow that news should remain essentially the same no matter which reporter or newspaper it originates from, as the reports would or should contain essentially the same information. Complementing this rational conception of news, the development of various methods of printing images, and especially incorporating photographs into print media, gave information a new form, later to be amplified by motion pictures and television. The resulting flood of visual images constitutes a new, unprecedented kind of information explosion, unquantifiable, seemingly objective but in a form that appeals to the emotions rather than to reason (Postman, 1985; Strate, 2014, 2017; Thoreau, 1899). While in some ways counterbalancing the rationality of objective journalism, ultimately the result are two extremes of irrationality and hyperrationality (Strate, 2011a, 2014).

Perhaps no technology more radically changed the concept of news than the telegraph. As previously noted, it transformed material, written documents into electronic signals for instantaneous transmission, and in this sense helped to form the modern idea of information, as well as news. As McLuhan (1964) observed, telegraphic news was associated with the breakdown of linearity in newspapers, as the storyline gave way to the dateline, a loss of narrative form that helped to give the impression of news as pure information. In place of a linear progression of events, the inverted pyramid format was introduced, where the article begins with the most important information in the first paragraph, the *who, what, where, when, why, and how,* followed by information of lesser importance in each succeeding paragraph. In this way, editors would still have the main news "story" even if transmission broke down before the full report was transmitted. And they could easily tailor the articles to fit into the available space for a particular edition of the paper, as the first paragraph could stand on its own as a complete item, as could the first two paragraphs, or the first three, etc. The speed-up brought on by telegraphy consequently led to a change in the face of the newspaper, from a relatively linear display to the *mosaic* (to use McLuhan's, 1951, 1964, term) of the modern front page, with its hypertextual mix of different, unrelated articles.

The telegraph gave rise to the wire services (e.g., Associated Press, Reuters), turning news into a commodity to be bought and sold (Carey, 1989, 1997; Innis, 1951; McLuhan, 1995); in this manner, information became a *thing*, a *product*, unto itself, existing independently of any given newspaper or material object. The buying and selling of news became an industry separate and distinct from the buying and selling of newspapers. Additionally, by 1870, telegraphic printing systems, popularly known as ticker tape machines, disseminated financial information directly to business offices. Money itself could be dematerialized and turned into a form of information though the 19th century innovation of wire transfers; individuals could visit a Western Union office in one city, pay a certain amount, and that office would message another office in another city to hand over that same amount (minus whatever service fee was being charged) to a designated individual. Even the sending of telegrams as a form of point-to-point communication involved turning a material object, a message written on a piece of paper, into a series of electrical impulses, encoded as dots and dashes, transmitted as pure information to a distant location, where the message is decoded and written down or typed on a piece of paper. Telegrams were used to deliver news, just as written messages had been hand delivered since antiquity, and postal services had been set up by governments in the modern era.

By the end of the 19th century, Marconi's wireless technology had demonstrated that information could be disseminated through the airwaves, truly giving us *news from nowhere* (the title of a late 19th century utopian science fiction novel by William Morris). With the introduction of radio, and especially following the end of the First World War, news had become more fully decontextualized than ever before, and broadcasting signaled the beginning of information overload in the 20th century, marked in Postman's (1985) estimation by irrelevance, incoherence, and a sense of impotence on the part of the audience.

Add to this the further development of telecommunications technologies, the internet, the web, social media, and mobile devices (Strate, 2014).

Information as Control

Norbert Wiener (1950, 1961) believed the function of control to be so central to the concept of information that he coined the term *cybernetics* to refer to a new science of control, paralleling Shannon's information theory (Shannon & Weaver, 1949). Wiener went so far as to declare that *communication is control*, by which he meant that the transmission of information into an environment has an influence on that environment, and therefore serves to control that environment in certain ways; this returns us to the basic point that information is a means of reducing freedom. Moreover, as opposed to *news*, which corresponds to information on the content level, *control* corresponds to information on the relationship or medium level (Bateson, 1972, 1979; Strate, 2017; Watzlawick et al, 1967). Control, then, is a form of metainformation or metanews. In military parlance, the function is referred to as *command and control*, and indeed, any medium of communication can be used for the purposes of control. Harold Innis (1951) notes that the ability to communicate over space is necessary for control over territory, so technologies of transmission and transportation are essential to organized force, i.e., military and police. Writing is a key technology for organizing armies as well as massive labor projects in the ancient world, as Mumford (1967) makes clear, and Innis particularly stresses the relationship between light media such as papyrus used as a writing surface, that is, media that are easy to transport, and the expansion of power from the settlement of cities to the conquest of empires in the ancient world. In addition to light media, the development of economical writing systems such as the alphabet was useful in carrying out such cybernetic functions, and transportations systems were essential; improvements in transportation technology, such as the building of roads and sailing ships inevitably enhanced command and control operations. Ultimately, the limitations of physical transportation, of both people and written messages, were overcome with the introduction of the electronic media beginning in the 19th century.

Heavy media, writing surfaces that are durable as opposed to transportable, can also be seen as performing the function of control, in this case over time, but information storage is a one-way form of transmission, and therefore lacks the ability inherent in two-way systems to receive feedback and adjust accordingly. Wiener (1950, 1961) argues that feedback is the key to enhanced control, indeed in his view feedback is the entire basis of cybernetics; Bateson (1979 importantly distinguishes between negative feedback which provides the constraints necessary for precise control, as opposed to positive feedback which can lead to runaway growth and systems snowballing out of control. And although Mumford's (1934) discussion of the mechanical clock precedes and therefore does not use Wiener's terminology, it is clear that this innovation, invented in 13th century Europe, was a form of information technology, a forerunner of the computer, and a cybernetic technology (Bolter, 1984; Strate, 1996). The mechanical clock produced no physical product, but rather functioned only to disseminate information. Its multiple, identical units (e.g., hours, later minutes, and seconds), while evolving out of the digital technologies of writing and the alphabet (McLuhan, 1964), set the stage for mechanization, mass production, and eventually industrialism. But most important of all, as Mumford argues, the main function of the mechanical clock was to control and coordinate human activity. First developed in monasteries as a means of getting monks to pray at the appointed times of day (i.e., the canonical hours), the technology was quickly adopted by nearby towns, where its ability to synchronize action was put to commercial use. The metaphor that time is money originates as one of the effects of the adoption of this innovation.

Printing represented a further extension of mechanization, and while lacking an effective feedback mechanism (although the exchange of written messages could still be employed), its potential for mass dissemination of information made it a very powerful blunt instrument of control; that the messages were identical in form introducing an unprecedented homogenizing force into human culture that was instrumental in establishing the modern nation-state, and its colonial empires (McLuhan, 1964, 1995; McLuhan & Fiore, 1968; Steinberg, 1996) According to Innis (1951), telecommunications in the 19th and 20th centuries for the most part further extended the emphasis on control over territory, and the drive to empire, whether it involved military control, political hegemony, or economic power. Again, the introduction of telegraphy stands as a watershed moment in the history of information, extending control over space, and opening the door to the movements of the 19th century associated with nationalism, and increased centralization of authority (Carey, 1989, 1997).

An excellent example of the cybernetic function of the telegraph was its use to solve the problem of railroad accidents. With the introduction of the steam-powered trains in the early 19th century came a significant speed-up in transportation, but no way to control railway traffic. Trains running in both directions on a single set of tracks relied on occasional shunts to avoid collision, but this also required the ability to coordinate schedules. This proved to be all but impossible as each locality set its clocks differently based on its geographical latitude and other factors, and there was no way to synchronize any timepieces—before telegraphy. Not only did the telegraph provide a means of communication that could easily outrun a speeding locomotive, but it introduced the possibility of homogenizing time. Clocks that could only serve a cybernetic function locally could be set simultaneously via the instantaneous transmission that electronic transmission of information affords. This in turn allowed trains to run on synchronized schedules and thereby minimize collisions. With the newfound ability to set the time simultaneously at myriad different locations, the railroad companies in the United States established the first time zones, whose administration was soon taken over by the federal government, an innovation that then spread across the globe. Moreover, the telegraph and telephone together provided the command and control needed for organizations to develop horizontally, to grow beyond the local and open offices in different locations, creating the foundations for the modern corporation.

In the 20th century, Marconi's wireless provided a measure of control over ships at sea that had previously been unthinkable, as once sailing beyond the line of sight, there was no way to communicate from ship to shore, or ship to ship for that matter. For this reason, governments took control of the airwaves following the outbreak of the First World War, and retained control (directly or, as in the United States, by maintaining ownership and leasing portions of the electromagnetic spectrum to private interests) after the armistice was signed. Of course, the digital computer technologies that were developed during the mid-20th century and that continue to evolve have given us new forms of information processing, and have come a long way towards fully realizing Wiener's vision of a cybernetic future. Coupled with wired technology, especially the internet, and wireless technologies that stretch from satellites orbiting overhead to handheld cell phones and mobile devices, we have gained new powers to control and coordinate our own activities, at the same time that we have become increasingly more subject to control and coordination through and by our devices. We become enveloped by a new media environment characterized by new forms of networked organization, and systems of increasing complexity, both technological and social.

In his outstanding scholarly study, *The Control Revolution: Technological and Economic Origins of the Information Society*, James R. Beniger (1986) argues that the speed-up of society due to the invention of the steam engine and the ensuing industrial revolution led to a crisis of control throughout western societies, and this crisis in turn led to the development of new technologies and techniques to help restore control. In addition to inventions such as the telegraph, Beniger points to the extension and formalization of bureaucracy and the institution of rationalized procedures in government and other organizations, new methods of data processing such as Hollerith's punch card tabulator, the development of new accounting techniques, Taylor's scientific management, Ford's assembly line, and various techniques related to advertising, public relations, sales, and marketing. This *control revolution*, as he terms it, has its origins in the 19th century, and to the extent that control is a primary function of information, this shift represents an *information revolution* as well. His specific argument concerning the 19th century can be extended backwards, to the information overload brought on by writing and printing, and to increased production due to the innovations extending out of the agricultural revolution (Hobart & Schiffman, 1998; Innis, 1951).

Information and Mediation

The concept of information represents a form of function rather than substance, the function of informing and being informed, or surveillance of the environment and dissemination of that intelligence, the function of gathering and distributing news about change and differences that make a difference, the function of reducing uncertainty, reducing freedom of choice, and the function of control. And the function of information, and communication, is nested within the function of mediation, which refers to the way in which we relate to our environment (Strate, 2011a, 2017). For example, as Alfred Korzybski (1993) notes, the process of perception involves the irritation of nerve endings within our sensory organs, which then send electrochemical signals through the nervous system to the brain, where those signals are transformed into some "sense" of the external environment. The inner "map" of the outer "territory" that we produce is a mental construct, not a direct reflection of reality, although to be functional it must bear a structural similarity to the outer world. What is it then that our sensory organs abstract out of the external environment? The answer would have to be information about the world. Again, it is important to keep in mind that information is not something physical or material, not a substance or thing that we extract from the outside world in the same sense that organisms ingest nutrients, inhale oxygen, or absorb energy from sunlight. Rather it is a matter of sensory organs responding to stimuli and sending electrochemical signals through the nervous system, which are then processed by neural activity in the brain. Admittedly, this sort of specific phrasing is complex and convoluted, so as a matter of convenience and a form of shorthand, I will still utilize the common figures of speech, including referring to information as something that can be transmitted, stored, received, and so on, with the understanding that such terminology should not be reified.

Information as it relates to mediation brings us to the topic of media ecology, a field of study that is defined as *the study of media as environments* (Postman, 1970; see also Strate, 2017). It should come as no surprise that the key terms in this field include *media* and *medium*, and *ecology* and *environment*; other key terms include *effects*, and *bias*, referring to the inherent properties or tendencies of a medium, type of material, or system (as in, the bias of a closed system is towards greater entropy), as I have discussed in my book, *Media Ecology: An Approach to Understanding the Human Condition* (2017). *Information*, while not a key term, is commonly used within the field, sometimes drawing on the precise, scientific definition put forth by Claude Shannon (Shannon & Weaver, 1949), but not always.

Central to the field of media ecology is McLuhan's (1964) famous aphorism, *the medium is the message*, a saying that has a number of different meanings (see Strate, 2017). On the surface, it may seem in some ways to conflate *medium* and *message*, but its foundation is the distinction between media and the messages they carry, also framed as a distinction between *medium* and *content*. Hence, one of its basic meanings is that we tend to ignore the medium and only pay attention to the content, but the medium has the greater significance and effect. Contrary to what some critics mistakenly assume, McLuhan did not deny the existence of content, but rather considered it secondary at best in regard to the impact of the medium or technology used to convey the message, as well as a distraction that kept individuals from paying attention to the main event, being the medium itself. In the field of media ecology, similar to the field of communication studies, the term *information* is sometimes used in ways that are somewhat synonymous with content or message, as that which is contained, preserved, and/or shared by a medium (or as a subset of the content or message). It follows that, like content or a message, information can be transferred from one medium to another, but cannot exist independently of any medium, in some abstract realm of its own. Media ecology is grounded, in part, in the materialism of modern science, and it follows that information cannot exist outside of the parameters of the physical universe. Information is produced by energy (which can also take the form of matter), Shannon defined it as the opposite of entropy (Shannon & Weaver, 1949), but the key point is that information as content or message must be based on some kind of physical form. Messages cannot be present in a vacuum as it were, devoid of situational context or physical environment. Within the study of media as environments, information can only be communicated by a medium, can only be produced through the agency of a medium, can only emerge out of a medium as system, can only exist within a medium as environment (Strate, 2017).

The term *medium* includes the material, but also incorporates the methodological, the technique as well as the technology. This would include the *code* that is used to communicate information, as it is commonly understood that messages are *encoded* and *decoded* (Shannon & Weaver, 1949). The code may be a language such as English, German, French, Hebrew, Hindi, or Mandarin; it may be a writing system that is logographic, syllabic, or alphabetic; it may be smoke signals, talking drums, semaphore flags, or Morse code; it may be C++, HTML, Java, Python, or Perl, *etc*. Codes are also sometimes referred to as symbol systems, and more generally as symbolic form (Langer, 1957). Thus, for example, Christine Nystrom (2021) states that, "because of the symbolic forms in which information is encoded, different technologies have different intellectual and emotional biases" (p. 140). Symbolic form itself may be equated with form in general, or it may be seen as a special case of form as a more general phenomenon. Either way, the longstanding contrast between form and content parallels the distinction between medium and content, indicating that the two terms are equivalent, or rather, that the concept of medium incorporates the concept of form (Strate, 2017). Apart from the code, other formal elements that may be identified within a message include style, tone, arrangement, treatment, pattern, *etc*. While the word *form* is present and visible within the larger term in*form*ation, the meaning of *information* can be understood to refer to that which resides within *form*, inside *form*, the content of *form*, and as that which is *given form*, that which is placed *in formation*.

The term *information* is commonly employed as a near synonym for *content* and *message*, but it can also be used to suggest something subordinate to the other two phenomena, as something contained within or carried by the content or message. Moreover, while *form* is in one sense an aspect of *medium*, it can also be regarded as part of the message. Formal elements such as the aforementioned style, tone, arrangement, treatment, pattern, etc., whether understood as aesthetic, poetic, or rhetorical, are sometimes viewed as aspects of a medium's content, while at the same time they in turn take information as their content. As McLuhan (1964) observed, a given medium can become the content of another medium, as for example, spoken language becomes the content of written texts, the manuscript becomes the content of print media, print media become the content of electronic text. A motion picture broadcast on television becomes the content of the television medium, while a television image incorporated into a cinematic film becomes the content of that movie. Jay David Bolter and Richard Grusin (1999; see also Bolter & Gromala, 2003) refer to this process as *remediation*, and when a physical medium is remediated by another medium, it loses its material quality and becomes a code or style, as for example when handwriting is transformed into a choice of typefaces or fonts. The process of remediation is the equivalent of the nesting of systems within systems, so that the single cell as a system is part of the larger organism as a system, which is part of the larger ecosystem. Along similar lines, McLuhan

(1964) noted that when a new environment is introduced, the older environment becomes part of its content (and recall here the definition of media ecology as the study of media as environments, which indicates that *medium* and *environment* are equivalent terms; see Strate, 2017).

McLuhan (1964) has been wrongly accused of claiming that content does not exist, which is absurd given that his argument is, in part, that content is influenced and shaped by the medium that is used (see also Strate, 2017). What his observation does suggest, however, is that there are some instances when content may in fact be entirely reducible to medium. For example, the content of a given message can be said to be pure style or aesthetics, or it may be encoded in a language not known by the receiver, or the message may be non-sensical or so garbled as to be unintelligible (but in both cases still recognizable as a message). In such cases, we may rightly conclude that there is a message, but no information is present. Similarly, a message may be said to present no information, for example if the same message is repeated over and over again, or if it is so entirely expected as to contain no *new information* (an obviously problematic phrase, in that *new information* is redundant, and *old information* oxymoronic, except in the sense that information that is old to one party may be new to another, hence the expression, *that's news to me*).

Messages that contain no information can include those associated with ritual, including the everyday rituals of phatic communication (e.g., *hello, how are you? fine, how are you?*). Following Bateson (1972, 1979), and Paul Watzlawick, Janet Beavin Bavelas, and Don D. Jackson (1967), we can understand that communication takes place on two different levels, content and relationship. Information can be exchanged on the content level, but only after channels of communication are established on the relationship level. Moreover, it is on the relationship level that instructions are provided on how to interpret information exchanged on the content level. Parallel to the content and relationship level of communication, Bateson and Watzlawick *et al.* discuss the differences between communication and *metacommunication*, the latter being defined as *communication about communication*. The relationship level of communication, along with metacommunication, insofar as they stand in contradistinction from content, are the equivalent of medium (and therefore of environment, system, context, and situation).

Content and messages lacking in information can still have meaning. Like information, *meaning* is a term that has a great deal of significance within the field of media ecology. But unlike information, which is associated with novelty and situated within the message, meaning requires familiarity and is situated within individuals and groups (Ogden & Richards, 1923). Information can be seen as a type of stimulus, while meaning is understood to be a response to a stimulus, and can take the form of behavior, for most organisms, or especially for human beings it can take the form of thought, which is itself a form of behavior (Mead, 1934; Nystrom, 2021), otherwise referred to as a semantic reaction (Korzybski, 1993). Because meaning is in the eye of the beholder, so to speak, it does not require the presence of information, but rather can be said to be based on recognition and recall (1974), and to a certain extent projection (Freud, 1918; Korzybski, 1993). Meaning is not the opposite of information, but to the extent that meaning is based on familiarity, and information on novelty, the two can be said to exist in inverse relationship to one another. Meaning is generated, in part, by the grammar, rules, structure, *etc.*, of the medium, all of which are aspects of the code or form, and all of which place constraints on the information that can be transmitted or stored, thereby providing the needed redundancy to allow information to be meaningful, rather than being reduced to noise (Campbell, 1982).

Nystrom (2021) notes that, "because of the accessibility and speed of their information, different technologies have different political biases" (p. 140). Holding aside the effects, in addition to accessibility and speed of information, different media can be distinguished by the amount or volume of information that they can produce, contain, preserve, and transfer, by their capacity for information storage, information retrieval, information transmission, and information dissemination. In other words, *information* in various ways can be used to characterize a given medium (again, this serves as a shorthand, in this case for referring to concepts such as the carrying capacity of signals, or their bandwidth, or data storage). McLuhan (1964) goes so far as to declare that, "the electric light is pure information. It is a medium without a message" (p. 7). In this instance, the concept of information is neither equivalent nor subordinate to that of content or message, but independent of them, much in the same way that the concept of medium is understood to be its own message, independent of any actual content. Similarly, information is used in a manner parallel to that of medium when it is combined with the term environment, so that the phrases *information environment* and *media environment* are essentially interchangeable. For example, in *Teaching as a Conserving Activity*, Neil Postman (1979) argues:

> Every society is held together by certain modes and patterns of communications which control the kind of society it is. One may call them information systems, codes, message networks, or media of communication. Taken together they set and maintain the parameters of thought and learning within a culture. Just as the physical environment determines what the source of food and exertions of labor shall be, the

information environment gives specific direction to the kinds of ideas, social attitudes, definitions of knowledge, and intellectual capacities that will emerge. (p. 29)

Similarly, in *Take Today: The Executive as Dropout* coauthored by McLuhan and Barrington Nevitt (1972), we find the following:

Hypnotized by their rear-view mirrors, philosophers and scientists alike tried to focus the *figure* of man in the old *ground* of nineteenth-century industrial mechanism and congestion. They failed to bridge from the old *figure* to the new. It is man who has become both *figure* and ground via the electrotechnical extension of his awareness. *With the extension of his nervous system as a total information environment, man bridges art and nature.* (p. 11)

The use of *information environment* as an alternative to *media environment* has been irregular, but not uncommon, and the phrase *information ecology* has even made an appearance (Davenport & Prusak, 1997). This suggests that understanding information as the equivalent or a subset of content or message is at best incomplete. Here, Bateson's (1972, 1979) view that content and relationship constitute different levels of communication can be helpful (see also Watzlawick et al, 1967). As noted, metacommunicational messages provide instructions on how to interpret information, and following Boolean logic, instructions can be coded in the form of information, as a form of metainformation. To a computer, basic data such as a series of numbers, and instructions such as a command to add the numbers together, both take the form of binary code, the language of the machine. In human terms, establishing a relationship as being hierarchical (I'm the boss!) or egalitarian (Treat me like an equal!) provides information that helps to interpret content level messages (e.g., Can you get me a cup of coffee?). Following this model, we can distinguish between information on the content level (the message is the message), and information on the relationship or medium level (the medium is the message).

Information as a Variable

Information on the medium level is most typically associated with *transmission*. In the well known Shannon-Weaver Model of communication, an *information source* encodes a *message* which is then sent out as a signal by a *transmitter*, over a *channel* to a *receiver* that decodes the message and sends it on to its *destination* (Shannon & Weaver, 1949). It is important to note that this model is based on electronic media such as the telegraph or telephone, and not on face-to-face conversation, or public speaking. In the case of the telegraph, the information source is the telegraph key, which is used to tap out a message in Morse Code, the message being sent as electrical impulses through wires, which are the channel (in the case of wireless telegraphy, the airwaves constitute the channel), to be received at the other end where the electrical impulses are turned into a series of long and short beeps (which the telegraph operator translates from Morse Code to written alphabet). In the case of the telephone, the microphone is the information source, encoding sound as electrical impulses that the transmitter sends through telephone lines, the channel, where the receiver turns the signal back into sound played on a speaker.

The Shannon-Weaver Model reflects the close connection between information theory and the introduction of electronic communication technology, and serves as an adequate representation of the technical aspects of information transmission via electronic media. In other words, it is a model of the medium or technology alone, and does not include the human beings and the process of human communication. For this reason, when it has been overgeneralized and used to represent communication in general, the model becomes easy to criticize as simplistic and inaccurate. Problems with the model include the fact that it does not allow for the complexities of human communication, which involve the use of numerous channels simultaneously; that it represents communication as one-way, not allowing for the fact that much of human communication entails interactions and transactions, and that these too occur over multiple channels simultaneously; and that it only represents dyadic communication, leaving out triadic situations, group contexts both small and large, and public and mass communication. Broadly, applying the model to human activity can be faulted for describing it by way of a mechanistic, technological metaphor, leaving out such vital concerns as meaning, purpose, and motivation. In the field of media ecology, the transmission or transportation view of communication that underlies the Shannon-Weaver model has been criticized and rejected in favor of metaphors emphasizing ritual and communication over time rather than space (Carey, 1989; Innis, 1951), transformation and the effects of the medium itself (McLuhan, 1995), and resonance and communication as the sharing of meaning (Ong, 1982; Schwartz, 1974). Moreover, the theoretical basis of the model, Shannon and Weaver's (1949) mathematical theory of communication, and the explosion of information technology that followed its introduction, have prompted scholars such as Walter Ong (2002) and Douglas Rushkoff (2003) to draw a sharp contrast between information, as a typically unidirectional form of signal transmission, and communication, as an interactive process of sharing. Put another way, in contrast to human communication, information represents a form of inhuman communication.

Reducing the role of the medium to the narrow notion of *channel* seems to suggest that messages can exist independently of a medium, that the sender somehow creates a message and only then determines which channel to use in sending it. In other words, the model does not recognize the prior existence of the physical medium (e.g., writing, speech, even the nervous system and brain), which has much to do not only with the creation of the message, but in the decision to send a message in the first place (Strate, 2017). Moreover, while the activities of encoding and decoding are sometimes included in the model, the prior existence of the code itself goes unmentioned, as if the message could be created without a code, rather than created by choosing units from the code itself, e.g., words, numbers (Strate, 2017). Messages are created by working with materials as well as by following formal, grammatical, structural patterns (Anton, Logan, & Strate, 2016; McLuhan & McLuhan, 2011), so that the division between channel and code is artificial if not arbitrary, as well as a form of elementalism (Korzybski, 1991), and this is also true of the divisions between source, message, channel, and receiver, not to mention the fact that noise can be present at any point in transmission, not just in the channel. Moreover, the communication that is represented by the model is without context or situation, which is to say that it is without environment.

Given the inadequacies of the Shannon-Weaver Model for representing something other than the electronic signaling, it is still possible to consider the transmission of information as a medium-specific phenomenon. For example, the way in which information is transmitted via telegraph differs from the way in which messages are transferred via telephone, and from communication by way of wireless technology. Information shared via speech can be distinguished from information shared through writing. The kind of information transmitted through images is not the same as the type of information disseminated by words. Receiving information when alone and in the comfort of one's home is not the same as receiving the same information as part of a crowd in a public place.

One of the main tenets of media ecology is that different media have different kinds of biases (one of the meanings of *the medium is the message*). To analyze the biases of different media, it is useful to break down the concept of *transmission* into more specific characteristics, such as communication over space or distance, speed of transmission, dissemination or relationship between sources and receivers, conditions of attendance for the audience, accessibility of information to the audience, access to and control of the transmission process, information storage, volume or amount of information, and the form that information takes or the code that is used (Nystrom, 2021; see also Strate,

2017). Each of these characteristics can be examined in their own right, but it is essential to remember that they are all interrelated and cannot truly be isolated from one another.

. . .

Regarding communication over space or distance, apart from the fact that voices carry over relatively short distances, it begins with what Korzybski referred to as the space-binding capacity shared by all forms of animal life, specifically our ability to travel by foot. Insofar as the human species is believed to have originated in Africa, and spread from there to the four corners of the world, information was carried along with human migration. That is, at least *in theory*, given enough time, information can be transmitted over almost any distance, even if the messenger travels on foot. In practice, information remains confined to local areas and the small networks of the clan, tribe, and village, as long as communication is conducted entirely by word of mouth. The game of telephone, originally developed to investigate the oral transmission of rumors, is a poor representation of communication within oral cultures, as it does not take into account mnemonic techniques adopted to increase redundancy and otherwise reduce noise in the transmission process. But there is no doubt that the invention of writing vastly increased our capacity to deliver messages over distance with complete fidelity. Writing is associated with the growth of settlements from small villages to the cities of the ancient world, and lightweight, easily transportable writing surfaces are closely connected to the rise of the empires of antiquity (Innis, 1951). The invention of paper and its diffusion during the medieval period, and the development of the printing press with moveable type in the early modern period, each in its own way extended the reach of human communication. Both oral and written communication across space was entirely dependent on physical transportation up until the 19th century, so that improvements in our ability to travel over land (e.g., Roman road building, and the building of railroads) and water (e.g., the introduction of carracks, caravels, and clipper ships) extended the distance over which information could be disseminated with relative ease and reliability.

More recent progress in transportation is not without significance, but has been vastly overshadowed by the electronic media's ability to transmit information instantaneously. The telegraph was the first medium to split apart information transmission from physical transport, translating material objects (*i.e.,* a written message) into energy (*i.e.,* electrical signals), and in this sense presages the splitting of the atom, with similar explosive effect on human life. While the telegraph was said to have transformed the vast continental spread of the United States into a single neighborhood (Carey, 1989; Czitrom, 1983), space was more broadly conquered by Marconi's wireless. Satellite communications extended information's reach to the entire planet, giving us what McLuhan terms the *global village* (McLuhan, 1962; McLuhan & Fiore, 1968; McLuhan & Powers, 1989), with the internet and mobile devices filling in the gaps. Electricity truly marks the turning point in this regard, so much so that the *transmission* view of communication originates in the 19th century with the advent of telecommunications (Carey, 1989; Czitrom, 1983). In response to this historical development, Postman (1985) echoes Thoreau's (1889) famous criticism of telegraphic communication in suggesting that the instantaneous transmission of information is characterized more often than not by irrelevance, and given our inability to act on the information, a sense of impotence.

• • •

Much of what pertains to communication over distance also applies to the speed of transmission, as the two are very closely interrelated. McLuhan (1964) places a great deal of emphasis on the significance of electric speed, which in turn speeds up human activity in general. Instantaneous transmission of information challenges the ability of the receiver to process information in a sequential manner, so that linearity, the idea of taking things one step at a time, is severely undermined. This is manifested in the loss of logical thought, need for consistency, sense of history and progress, and narrative plotting. McLuhan (1964) notes that longstanding linear frameworks and approaches have been giving way to pattern recognition as a means of making meaning out of simultaneous multichannel messaging. Multitasking likewise appears as a response to the speeding up of communications, albeit not necessarily an adequate response. Speed-up is a significant factor in the problem of information overload, and to an overall sense of incoherence in culture and communication (Postman, 1985, 1992).

• • •

As for the dissemination of information and conditions of attendance, the Shannon-Weaver Model represents what in technical terms would be called point-to-point transmission. In human face-to-face communication, this most closely resembles dyadic situations such as conversation and dialogue, albeit minus the back-and-forth. Such interpersonal communication can also occur in the context of small groups without much altering the essential quality of one-to-one transmission. It is also possible to have communication on a one-to-many basis, such as we associate with public address and oratory (as well as other forms of oral performance). In ancient Greece, where the written word had given rise to both a larger, more complex form of social organization in Athens and its neighbors and colonies, and a more sophisticated form of public speaking through the development of rhetoric (the use of writing to review, edit, and study oratory), the conflict between the philosophers and sophists represented a contrast between the two types of relationships, one-to-one and one-to many. And while dialogue emerged as the generally accepted ideal form of communication, public address remained highly significant in politics, law, and religion (Peters, 1999).

The printing press with moveable type introduced by Gutenberg in the mid-15th century, in mechanizing the act of copying written works, provided unprecedented possibilities for the mass production of messages. This new ability to communicate from one to many eliminated the noise introduced via scribal corruption, and made the mass dissemination of information a reality. Speed of dissemination was limited, however, by the fact that the press was for the most part powered by human muscle until the introduction of steam powered printing in the early 19th century truly ushered in the age of mass communication. By the end of the century, Marconi's wireless telegraphy opened the door to broadcasting, a new kind of mass communication, and commercial radio became commonplace during the 1920s. Mass dissemination of information is not easily separated from mass opinion, advertising and public relations, and propaganda—indeed, the term *information* has been used as an euphemism for propaganda in the United States and elsewhere (e.g., the United States Information Agency during the Cold War).

While steam-powered printing and broadcasting are similar in their potential for the mass dissemination of information, they differ in that printing requires physical transportation from the point of production out to the mass readership, reinforcing the center-margin relationships that can be traced back to the first empires of the ancient world, which were made possible by the written word and lightweight writing surfaces. Broadcasting, on the other hand, does not disseminate a fully formed message in the way that printing does, but rather sends out a signal that is transformed into a message at the point of reception by the user's radio or television set. In this, the electronic media follow the bias towards decentralization associated with electricity and electric technology more generally, as Mumford (1934) first observed. For McLuhan (1964, 1995; McLuhan & Fiore, 1968; McLuhan & Nevitt, 1972), this meant the dissolution of center-margin distinctions, so that anywhere and everywhere is potentially a center, at least as long as it is in range of broadcast signals. This shift is further realized by computer networks and mobile devices. Moreover, electronic communications facilitate many-to-many communication in a manner never before possible. The potential was first glimpsed in the early days of radio, when the medium was still dominated by amateurs, and continued in the relatively narrow part of the spectrum reserved for citizen's band and ham radio operators. It was the internet, however, that revolutionized many-to-many communication, as information was distributed, to a large extent, through decentralized networks, and disseminated from one to many via online bulletin boards, email distribution lists, chat rooms, user generated content, and social media (Levinson, 1995, 1997, 1999, 2013).

The relationship between sender and receiver is connected to the conditions of attendance by which information is received and decoded. Oral communication is communal in nature, whether it is the bond formed by dialogue between two individuals, or the fact that the audience for public speaking and oral performance form a unity, linked by the fact that they are receiving messages simultaneously in addition to their co-presence in time and space. Whereas listeners come together as a unified audience, readers must isolate themselves, at least psychologically, in order to decode written messages. Listening to a book read out loud, therefore, constitutes an entirely different experience than reading a book silently, and this affects and alters the decoding process. The cinema, appearing as an adjunct of live performance in the late 19th century, weds mass communication to the communal experience of the audience as a co-present group. During the 20th century, sound amplification created two quite distinct situations: The speech or oral performance before live audiences of unprecedented size made possible by the addition of public address systems (Leni Riefenstahl's 1935 Nazi propaganda film, *Triumph of the Will*, offers a chilling portrait of this communication context), and the radio broadcast heard at home by isolated individuals or by families and other small groups. Further, even in the privacy of the home, radio and television transmission differs markedly when attended to with others or alone, and changes dramatically when received in a public setting. Similar contrasts can be made between information received while listening with headphones or through speakers, whether indoors, in a car, or on the street. McLuhan (1964) believed that the difference between images projected onto a screen and from behind a screen made a great deal of difference in how they are decoded (see also E. McLuhan, 2000), and we may similarly consider the proliferation of screens today via smart phones, tablets, and digital TV and computer displays as providing a variety of new conditions of attendance for individuals.

* * *

Conditions of attendance have some bearing on the accessibility of information to audiences and receivers. Access to information via the spoken word is relatively open among individuals who speak the same language, albeit limited in reach and breadth of dissemination. Reliance on the written word changes patterns of access, extending accessibility in some ways, but creating significant barriers with the addition of the prerequisite of learning how to read. Complex systems of notation such as logographic writing (e.g., cuneiform, hieroglyphics, Chinese ideograms) tend to limit access, leading to the creation of what Innis (1951) referred to as *monopolies of knowledge*. Other barriers include the use of learned languages for written documents (e.g., Latin, classical Greek, ancient Hebrew), scarcity of written documents and/or writing materials, and even heavy use of calligraphy, which slows reading and detracts from legibility (Havelock, 1982; Ong, 1982). Increases in accessibility associated with the introduction of simplified writing systems, especially the alphabet, and mass production of texts and publications in vernacular languages, as occurred during the printing revolution in early modern Europe (Eisenstein, 1979; Steinberg, 1996), have resulted in the disruption of hierarchies and shifts in favor of democratization. In the modern world, for example, printing set the stage for the Protestant Reformation, breaking the monopoly of knowledge held by the Roman Catholic Church in western Europe, and for the rise of nationalism which was accompanied by the decline of the aristocracy in favor of the middle class, transitions towards various forms of democratic governments, and other manifestations of populism (Eisenstein, 1979; Innis, 1951; McLuhan, 1962, 1995; McLuhan & Fiore, 1968; Steinberg, 1996).

Printing led to a proliferation of images as well as writing, and it was the 19th century that saw the onset of what Daniel Boorstin (1978) referred to as the *graphic revolution*, an unprecedented expansion of our ability to produce and distribute visual images. Through a variety of technologies for the mass production of print graphics, the invention of photography and the motion picture, and in the 20th century the invention of television, the western world became, in many ways, an image culture. Visual communication, amplified by electronic transmission, vastly increased the accessibility of information, as it bypassed the barriers of literacy and education. Unprecedented access to information has disrupted the stability of social roles based on gender, race, ethnicity, religion, age, and socioeconomic class, and undermined authority relationships (Meyrowitz, 1985). Computers and the internet have made information even more accessible than previously thought possible, eradicating almost all vestiges of privacy and secrecy. While some concern has been raised about the digital divide, the cost of access has been steadily reduced, and options for free access increasing. And while new media at first relied almost exclusively on text-based forms of communication, as digital technology has evolved, increasingly more emphasis is being given to more accessible forms such as computer graphics, digital photography, podcasts, and online video. Moreover, McLuhan's (1964, 1995) argument that the electronic media eliminate center-margin distinctions is evidenced by the potential to access information from any location via mobile devices, which now routinely incorporate screens and cameras.

Access to information is of great significance, and can be represented by the act of reading, which suggests the question, what of writing? For typical individuals, speaking and listening are inseparable aspects of spoken language. And for the most part, we learn to read and write at the same time, although it is possible to teach reading without writing, which is unusual but not unprecedented in past eras. The printing revolution introduced a read-only emphasis, in that typography relies on heavy and expensive machinery, and the various forms of mass communication introduced in the 19th and 20th centuries have tended to amplify this disparity. The introduction of new media in the final decades of the 20th century opened up new possibilities for access to the transmission process, the ability to send as well as receive information. The shift from read-only to read-write set-ups means greater audience control. Increased access to information facilitates democratization, but that trend can be mitigated through restricted control over the source of information. Power disparities are more readily eliminated when the transmission process is open and easily accessible, but on a meta level new disparities are created based on control of the platforms used to communicate and transmit information, i.e., ownership and control of social media companies.

* * *

Transmission of information is generally discussed in regard to space, and the speed at which distance can be bridged, but transmission can also occur over time (Innis, 1951), a process otherwise known as information storage. In a sense, information needs to be stored for at least the length of time required for its transmission, and the speed at which information is transmitted is a function of time as well as space. But transmission over time is not about speed or distance, but rather is particularly concerned with duration and durability. Languages store information in the code itself, by identifying what phenomena in the environment are worthy of being named and therefore need to be attended to, and by providing the grammar to properly interpret messages (Lee, 1959; Sapir, 1921; Whorf, 1956). Symbolic communication provides a unique potential for what Korzybski (1993) referred to as time-binding, the ability to communicate information over time, from one generation to the next. The spoken word, being ephemeral, is a poor medium for storage, however, and collective memory is required to preserve language and its contents. Oral cultures clearly have limited capacity for information storage, and fidelity is likewise limited in transmission over time, although this has the virtue of providing flexibility and aiding in maintaining a society's homeostasis (Havelock, 1963, 1986; Goody, 1977; Ong, 1982).

Notational systems, and especially the written word significantly increase our storage capacity, which is why they are intimately associated with the shift from tribal society to what has traditionally been termed civilization. Durability is an important factor in storage capacity, so that monuments and architecture can be highly effective forms of information storage, and writing on stone and clay tablets, and parchment manuscripts, all of which Innis (1951) termed heavy media, help to transmit information accurately over time, albeit at the cost of reduced flexibility, and an increased rigidity of culture (see also Strate, 2011a). The copying of written texts by hand allows for variability, thereby providing new forms of flexibility, as well as new sources of noise in transmitting information over time, aka scribal corruption. Printing, in producing multiple, identical copies of a text, aided in the preservation of information and the fidelity of its transmission over time by eliminating the multiformity of oral and scribal transmission (Eisenstein, 1979; McLuhan, 1962). By the 19th century, information storage led to an unprecedented historical consciousness in the western world, further enhanced by new capacities to store visual, audile, and audiovisual information. Although broadcasting is exceedingly ephemeral, technologies for electronic recording have proliferated, and digital technologies coupled with computer databanks represent the possibility of *total recall*, a prospect at once exciting and worrying for its surveillance implications (Strate, 1996). Digital archives promise unprecedented access to stored information, but concern exists that changing formats may make older archives inaccessible. Even data stored in digital form is dependent on certain types of software needed to read the files, a form of metainformation, and there already are instances where new versions of programs cannot read the files produced by older versions of the same program.

* * *

All of the above variables contribute to the volume or amount of information that exists within a culture at any given time. Innovations in communications have generally resulted in increases in the amount of information stored and transmitted, as we have moved from oral cultures to literate cultures, from scribal cultures to print cultures, and now to electronic cultures and digital cultures. As the volume of information has grown, we have seen shifts away from material objects and towards electronic mediation, e.g., e-mail and text messaging, electronic monetary transfers, e-books, etc. In this sense, we have become aware as never before that we live in an information environment, and we have come to characterize our time as an age of information. While there are times when insufficient information is a problem that needs to be remedied, over the past century we have reached the point where information overload has become a more commonly voiced concern. Postman (1992) argues for the need to restore barriers to information, noting that ever-increasing amounts of information will not solve the basic problems associated with the human condition. Others have written popular works offering advice on how to cope with the deluge and work effectively with new media (Rheingold, 2012; Rushkoff, 2010). And while we may celebrate the demise of gatekeeping as having imposed unnecessary barriers on access to information, this change comes at the cost of a loss of editorial function, of professional expertise that aids in the evaluation of information. The tragedy of 9/11 provides a case in point, as sufficient information was gathered to warn of the attack, but intelligence analysts were unable to put the pieces together, to engage in the synthesis needed to understand its meaning and implications.

. . .

From the perspective of Shannon's information theory, the only variable that matters in regard to the code used to transmit information is quantitative, the number of units, possible messages, signals or symbols within the code (Shannon & Weaver, 1949). As previously noted, this allows for the measurement of the information contained within a series of messages, based on their probability (the larger the number of units within a code, the less probable the message, the greater the amount of uncertainty reduced by the message, the more information that it carries). This in turn allows for a measurement of the degree of complexity within a given system, but provides no insight as to the meaning of whatever is being transmitted. Moreover, such measurement is only possible if the code is digital, that is, if it is made up of discrete units. It is difficult if not impossible, however, to apply any form of measurement to analogical communication, such as images. While it is possible to digitize images in order to store or disseminate them electronically, the digital file is not itself an image, and tells us nothing about the information associated with the image itself. The image, as a picture, cannot be broken down into discrete units, but must be understood as a continuous whole, based on its resemblance to what it represents. And yet, it still performs the function of information.

The fact that digital codes such as spoken language (for the most part), writing systems, and mathematical notation consist of discrete units whose meaning or value is more or less arbitrary, conventional, and clearly defined, while analogical codes such as images, most forms of nonverbal communication, and most forms of art and direct perception are relatively continuous and cannot be broken down into discrete units (in a picture, what line or bit of color constitutes one unit clearly separate from the next?), is itself a significant difference between different types of media. As Susanne Langer (1959) notes, digital or as she terms it, *discursive* forms, while being potentially propositional in character (able to form statements that can evaluated as true or false, or at least open to falsification), make up a small portion of the symbolic forms used by human beings (Langer does not use the term code herself, but the concept of code and symbol system are essentially the same). Most of our codes, or more accurately, most of our art forms, are analogical in nature, or in Langer's terms *presentational*, and are associated with the inner world of feelings and emotion, rather than factual descriptions about the outer world. This is an example of what Nystrom (2021) refers to in stating that information encoded in different symbolic forms will have different intellectual and emotional biases. Although it is not possible to measure analogical form, Meyrowitz (1985) intuits that much more information can be communicated by pictures than by words, and in a manner much less under the control of the information source (in this sense, control is related to measurement), and this has much to do with the disruptive impact of television.

The distinction between analogical representation and digital coding of information can be seen as rooted in the difference between nonverbal and verbal modes of communication, and between direct perception of reality and the use of symbols to mediate between thought and perception (this is, admittedly, an oversimplification of a complex process). Human communication is distinguished from that of all other species, more or less, by the use of symbols, as exemplified by language, and scholars such as Bateson (1972) consider symbolic communication to be the basis for all other digital coding that humans beings employ:

> Verbal language is almost (but not quite) purely digital. The word "big" is not bigger than the word "little"; and in general there is nothing in the pattern (*i.e.*, the system of interrelated magnitudes) in the world "table" which would correspond to the system of interrelated magnitudes in the object denoted. (p. 373)

Language as a code may be essentially digital, but in practice the spoken word mixes the digital code with analogical forms of communication such as

tone of voice and other paralinguistic cues, not to mention the equally analogical use of gesture, posture, facial expression, touch, and other forms of
nonverbal communication. Symbolic communication, a creation of the mind,
may allow for digital representation, but the body is hopelessly analogical by
its very nature, and where human presence and face-to-face communication is
involved, the digital cannot be isolated from its analogical context. Some of this
is carried over into written communication (e.g., handwriting and penmanship
as analogical form), printed documents (e.g., font and layout, not to mention illustrations), and electronic communications (e.g., the mixture of language and
image on television).

The difference between digital codes/discursive form and analogical codes/
presentational form is one of the most significant in the field of media ecology, but it is also acknowledged that, within these categories, different forms or
codes have different biases. Edward Sapir (1921), Benjamin Lee Whorf (1956),
and Dorothy Lee (1959) are most often associated with the position that different languages codify reality in different ways, utilizing different grammars
as well as vocabularies, and that these differences influence the way individuals
view the world. Edward T. Hall (1959) extends this idea to culture in its entirety, arguing that each distinct culture is in its own right a symbol system or
code. Edmund Carpenter (1960) extends the idea to media, arguing that every
medium has its own grammar and vocabulary, and therefore its own worldview.

* * *

Along with the distinction between word and image, and more generally the
digital and the analogical, within the field of media ecology great emphasis is
placed on the distinction between orality and literacy, that is, the difference between speech and writing as linguistic codes. Rather than the spoken word and
the written word being two parallel symbol systems, however, writing is defined
as a secondary symbol system (Ong, 1982), used to encode the primary symbol
system of speech. As previously noted, the content of writing is speech, and this
form of remediation represents the digitization of one digital code by another.
The result is that the written word is a more abstract symbolic form than the
spoken word, one that involves a process of decontextualization, as language
is removed from the context of co-present communicators, and also from the
rich accompaniment of nonverbal communication that also acts as a form of
metacommunication (as tone of voice, facial expression, gesture, posture, *etc.*,
all are cues that can help the receiver to interpret the information associated
with the verbal message).

In addition to decontextualization, the encoding of spoken language into written form involves a translation from one sensory mode to another, from hearing to vision. This is a qualitative shift, with a variety of implications, including much improved fidelity in messages transmitted over space, the ability to evaluate messages more effectively by allowing for their review and objective analysis, an enhanced ability to formulate messages given the potential for editing and rewriting, and the enormous expansion of our capacity for information storage. All of this contributes to a great increase in the volume of information in societies with writing, especially as writing systems becomes more efficient through the development of phonetic writing, and in particular the alphabet. Again, as previously noted, this sets the stage for the information explosion resulting from the printing revolution that began in mid-15th century Europe, and that has been further extended by the many innovations in communication technology of the past two centuries.

* * *

While our present era is often referred to as *the information age*, Michael E. Hobart and Zachary S. Schiffman (1998) argue that it is simply the most recent in a series of *information ages* that begins circa 3500 BCE in Mesopotamia:

> The invention of writing actually gave birth to information itself, engendering the first information revolution. Writing created new entities, mental objects that exist apart from the flow of speech, along with the earliest, systematic attempts to organize this abstract mental world. (p. 2)

Writing, as a code that encodes a code, extends the digital quality of language, but what Hobart and Schiffman (1998) stress is writing's decontextualization of the word, as it removes language from the context of a specific time and place, while providing discourse with a degree of permanence previously inconceivable. In doing so, writing also gives us the ability to take words out of their natural context of human dialogue and oral performance alike, for example, as Goody (1977) notes, in the very basic activity of making lists, one of the first uses of the written word. In a list, we can have subjects without predicates, for instance, 12 chickens, 7 cows, 20 bushels of wheat, but in conversation, such utterances would make no sense, prompting the listener to respond, "What about them? What are you trying to say?" Writing even establishes the concept of words as separate things, each word represented by its own character or group of characters, whereas in speech words can be strung together without pause as a single vocalization or utterance. As Hobart and Schiffman (1998) explain:

> Information came into being at the cusp between orality and literacy, a singular moment that cannot itself be understood unless we first consider the nature of the oral culture that literacy would transform. In this oral world, memory functioned in sharp contrast to the way we literates conceive of it, not as a container for information but as a participatory act, commemoration, serving to maintain social consensus. The emotional power and immediacy of this activity prevented its participants from distinguishing between the context and the experience of commemoration in any consistent manner. Only with this distinction did the mental object we call information come into being, and only then could memory become a container for them. The information revolution born of literacy is all the more stunning and revolutionary when seen in stark relief against an oral world where information did not exist. (p. 2)

Hobart and Schiffman (1998) stress that the accumulation of information following the introduction of writing eventually leads to a situation of information overload, and necessitates new innovations for managing that overabundance; this is a process that Paul Levinson (1997) refers to as *remedial media*, newer media invented to remedy the problems introduced by older media (for example, the invention of windows led to the remedial medium of window shades or curtains, the invention of the telephone eventually led to the telephone answering machine, and television to the VCR and DVR). The remedy for the information overload brought on by alphabetic writing was Aristotle's methods of classification, and the logic used to govern their use, and Hobart and Schiffman make the case that this Aristotelian approach, with some modifications, was sufficient for the volume of information characteristic of chirographic media environments, that is up until the printing revolution in early modern Europe. Moreover, Robert K. Logan (2004) aptly explains how the solutions to the problems posed by the information explosion resulting from the alphabet were inherent in the alphabet itself as a medium of communication (e.g., alphabetical order, as well as the technique of analysis, breaking phenomena down into component parts, just as the alphabet divides the sounds of speech into consonants and vowels). And while Hobart and Schiffman emphasize the techniques of logical analysis, it would also follow that the material innovation of the parchment codex provided a means for improved management of information, providing greater accessibility by storing more information in one volume than scrolls are able to, and allowing for random access (flipping through pages) in a way that scrolls cannot.

In regard to the information explosion occurring in the wake of the invention of the Gutenberg printing press, the remedy that Hobart and Schiffman (1998) identify is numeracy, and Descartes' dream of mathematical rationality, leading up to the development of calculus. Here too, we can identify other efforts such as the consistent use of alphabetical order, page numbers, table of contents and indexes, footnotes and bibliographies, references and citations, not to mention the production of reference works such as dictionaries, thesauri, and encyclopedias, and more ephemeral items such as almanacs, catalogs, and calendars. Elizabeth Eisenstein (1979) notes the importance of printing in the production and distribution of the visual display of information in the form of tables (e.g., multiplication, sine, cosine, tangent, logarithm, etc.), graphs and charts, etc. Even the simple outline as a form of visual organization does not become commonplace until after the introduction of printing, and is related to the educational innovations of Peter Ramus, as Walter Ong (1958) explains; in this, we also see the origins of the school textbook as a medium for the collection and organization of information. Of course, dating back to antiquity, schools themselves along with libraries were also methods developed for storing and managing information, and both received significant impetus in the typographic era.

The communications revolution of the 19th century, which began with the application of steam power to the printing press, producing the first mass circulation daily newspapers, led in turn to the development of Boolean logic, the 19th century foundations of computer technology (e.g., Charles Babbage's unfulfilled plans for a difference engine, and the actual Hollerith punch card machines used to tabulate data), and the actualization of computer technology during the 20th century (e.g., Alan Turing, and the first electric, digital computers such as ENIAC). Currently, computer databases, hypertextual interfaces such as the World-Wide Web, and search engines such as Google, all are means for coping with information overload, albeit not always completely or successfully. The key point that Hobart and Schiffman (1998) introduce, that new information technologies lead to other new technologies and techniques for organizing information, returns us to the two levels of content/communication and relationship/metacommunication. In other words, as the introduction of new media results in increases in information on the content level, this in turn requires innovations on the medium level to assist in providing second order information, information about information, to perform the function of control.

Implications for "The Information Age"

That we are now living in the *age of information* is undoubtedly a statement that many would take as a given, would accept without question as the best way in which to characterize contemporary life. And it no doubt would be easy enough to justify this appellation by pointing to the plethora of digital devices, computer technologies, and forms of wired and wireless connectivity that dominate our activities, and our thoughts. But in contrast to the *age of typography*, which begins with Gutenberg's invention of the printing press with movable type in the mid 15th century, or the *industrial age*, which begins with James Watt's invention of the steam engine in the late 18th century, identifying the origin of the *information age* proves to be highly problematic. After all, *information* is not an invention, nor is it a phenomenon that is anchored to any particular type of technology. Indeed, information can be present in all forms of communication, in animal communication from the songs of whales to the dances of bees, in the transmission of electrochemical impulses within animal nervous systems, and in the self-replicating strands of DNA and RNA that form the basis of all known biology. The concept of information can even be applied to purely physical phenomena such as the energy output of stars. From the point of view of digital physics, the age of information could be said to begin with the Big Bang, the moment when the ultimate computer that we call the universe was turned on. Such speculation aside, it is possible, as we have seen, to argue that the information age begins with language, or with writing, or with printing, or with the revolution in communication and control that began in the 19th century. Moreover, as has been noted, it is possible to argue that there has been not just one, but several different information ages.

Having earlier noted that matter and information, atoms and bits, are not parallel phenomena that can be compared to one another, it follows that the same holds true for machines (e.g., the printing press, the steam engine) and information. So, when we speak of our time as constituting *the information age*, it is not the presence of *information* that we refer to, nor even its abundance. Instead, it might be argued that what is being referred to is the collective phenomenon of *information technology*, which more and more is part of an integrated network of *information systems*. But references to the *information society* and an *information economy* based on *information capitalism* and brought on by an *information revolution* predate the rise of the internet as a popular phenomenon during the 1990s, and have their origins in discussions of a *postindustrial* society and economy during the 1950s and 1960s. During the 1960s, computer scientists adopted the phrase *information science* to refer to a field of study closely related to their own, while simultaneously, social critics first voiced concern over the problem of *information overload*, a phrase popularized at the end of the decade through the publication of Alvin Toffler's *Future Shock* (1970).

But we can push the point of origin back, as some would no doubt argue that Shannon's introduction of *information theory* (Shannon & Weaver, 1949) signals the beginning of the information age, and there is certainly rationale for viewing this new era as a postwar development, although the first modern computers were introduced during the late 1930s and early 1940s. Indeed, information can be seen as a phenomenon closely connected to 20th century modernism, and the anxiety associated with it was famously expressed by T.S. Eliot in 1934, in the opening stanza of "Choruses" from his play entitled, *The Rock*, specifically in the lines, "Where is the wisdom we have lost in knowledge? Where is the knowledge we have lost in information?" The target of Eliot's faith-based critique is not computation, however, but communication, specifically mass communication. Although the mass production of messages can be traced back to Gutenberg, and the phenomenon of mass communication is frequently said to originate with the introduction of steam powered printing presses in the early 19th century, actual awareness of mass communication coalesces during the early 20th century. The propaganda (aka mass persuasion) campaigns of the First World War played a role in this development, as well as the beginnings of modern advertising and public relations that followed the end of the Great War. But of particular importance was the advent of broadcasting, which served as an alternative to printing. With broadcasting came the realization that there are *media of mass communication*, a phrase eventually abbreviated as *mass media*. What is significant is the plural form, *media*. Earlier use of the term *medium* tended to be in reference to the materials of expression, paint or clay as an artist's medium, language and literature as a writer's medium. By the time Eliot wrote *The Rock*, the idea that newspapers, magazines, paperback books, radio, and movies (which were formerly considered a form of exhibition, akin to stage performance) constitute a single category of *mass media* had become firmly embedded, with television soon to be added to the group. Three decades after *The Rock*, McLuhan (1964), an admirer of Eliot, would drive home the point that media are not a singular, unified phenomenon, that all media are not mass media, and that significant differences exist between different media, hence his pithy observation that the medium is the message, and his special emphasis on the distinction between electronic media such as radio and television, and the older forms of print media.

The sudden popularity of *information* and *media* within public discourse is contemporaneous in origin, and their relative absence in intellectual discourse prior to the 20th century is conspicuous. Consider, for example, that the First Amendment to the Constitution of the United States, adopted as part of the Bill of Rights in 1791, reads, "Congress shall make no law respecting an establishment of religion, or prohibiting the free exercise thereof; or abridging the freedom of speech, or of the press; or the right of the people peaceably to assemble, and to petition the Government for a redress of grievances." There is no mention of *freedom of information*, a phrase that does not enter popular discussion until after the Second World War, when the United Nations General Assembly declared it a fundamental human right in 1946, and included in its Universal Declaration of Human Rights, adopted in 1948, Article 19 of which states, "Everyone has the right to freedom of opinion and expression; this right includes freedom to hold opinions without interference and to seek, receive and impart information and ideas through any media and regardless of frontiers." In the US, the Freedom of Information Act of 1966 established that citizens have a right to access information about their government, and the phrase *freedom of information* was adopted by other nations as well during the postwar period.

Rather than information or media, the First Amendment guarantees freedom of speech and press, which corresponds to the two primary modes of verbal communication highlighted in the title of Walter Ong's best known work of media ecology scholarship, *Orality and Literacy* (1982). The right of assembly can be seen as an extension of freedom of speech, as the whole point of assembling a group of people together in one place would be to serve as an audience for public address, or otherwise engage in oral discussion, debate, and deliberation. And the right of petition can be seen as an extension of the freedom to engage in written communication, as petitions are typically written or printed documents delivered, in this case, to government officials, or alternately to deliver requests and demands orally. As for the freedom of religion clause, religion as it is understood in western culture, revolves around a sacred text, and therefore requires freedom of the press; it also entails oral expression and ritual performance, thereby relating to freedom of speech and assembly.

What sets the 20th century apart, then, is the growing use of the term *information*, as opposed to terms such as *news* and *intelligence*, as well as the growing use of the terms *media* and *medium*, as opposed to *press* and *speech*. The same period that has been dubbed *the information age* has also been referred to, on occasion, as *the media age*. Of course, *media age* is just as problematic as *information age*, in that in all previous ages, human beings relied on some various types of media as well, including speech and language; even the human body can be considered a medium within the field of media ecology (Strate, 2017). It is here that a media ecology approach helps to clarify matters by specifying that ours is an age of electronic media, and within that age, we have entered a later stage of development characterized by digital media.

Peter Drucker (1968) describes the postindustrial period as one in which knowledge workers would operate within a knowledge economy in the context of a knowledge society, but his terminology did not catch on. While increased complexity does require knowledge for effective management, continued progress in the technologies of control require less knowledge on the part of workers—witness, for example, the automatic scanning of products by cashiers today as opposed to the basic arithmetic skills required in the past. And note too the implication that information has displaced knowledge in Eliot's query, *where is the knowledge we have lost in information?* In regard to economics, the one rival to *information* as the appropriate designation for the postindustrial economy is the phrase *service economy*. But service is, arguably, a by-product of information technologies and systems, of the control and coordination of human activity, whether it is in retail sales where traditional interpersonal, oral skills of salesmanship are no longer utilized, or in the fast food industry where cooks and chefs are reduced to the status of servomechanism, or in the high end financial sector where information technology and the technological imperative of efficiency (Ellul, 1964) outstrips all human judgment, resulting in in the worst financial crises since the Great Depression in 2008, not to mention the supply chain breakdowns accompanying the COVID-19 pandemic starting in 2020. Information, in its contemporary sense, is a numbers game, a reference to digital technology based on binary code, and Claude Shannon's mathematical theory of communication (Shannon & Weaver, 1949); measurement also serves as the basis for evaluating efficiency, and therefore is foundational for the technological imperative. Information in its contemporary sense is also very closely connected to electric technology and the electronic media, a point I have endeavored to stress throughout this chapter. And as we are now associating information technology with artificial intelligence, a meta level of control (or perhaps a meta meta level?), I would suggest that the abbreviation AI could also stand for *autonomous information*.

Eliot's poetic linking of *information* to *knowledge* and *wisdom* set off a flurry of speculation on the relationships between these three concepts (as well as others, e.g., data), often based on arguments that sufficient quantities of information bring us knowledge, and sufficient amounts of knowledge bring us wisdom. As if knowledge and wisdom can be assigned numerical value in the same way that information can in the context of information theory! I do feel obliged to note that as in emphasizing the concept of information in the discussions leading up to this point, I have not been especially concerned with distinguishing it from the concepts of knowledge and wisdom. But by way of conclusion, I would suggest that the relationships between the three can be properly contextualized within the field of media ecology. Wisdom is a characteristic of the human person, whether it is regarded as an innate sensitivity and intelligence, or a product of hard won experience. Wisdom is an understanding of relationships, of relationships among people, of people's relationships with their environment, and of one's relationship to oneself. And I would argue that wisdom is intimately associated with nonliterate, oral culture and the media environment with which it is associated. Speech cannot be separated from the speaker, and memory cannot be separated from the persons who remember and commemorate. As Ong (1982) explains, in an oral culture, you can only know what you can recall, and if you cannot bring it readily to mind, in what sense do you really know it? Words of wisdom, in a traditional sense, later to be collected and referred to as wisdom literature, are proverbs, mnemonically formed sayings and aphorisms.

Writing, on the other hand, in separating the knower from the known (Havelock, 1963), transforms a process, a verb, *knowing*, into a thing, a noun, *knowledge*. Knowledge becomes something that you find in a book, that you look up when you need to know something. And whereas wisdom involves understanding relationships, which is to say that it operates on the medium or relationship level, knowledge is about content, and works on the content level. Note that wisdom does not disappear when writing appears, and neither does speech after all. But the characteristic of wisdom becomes more distant the more fully immersed we are in literate culture, becomes more mysterious and elusive. We look for it in books, but there we find only knowledge. And in tying knowledge to writing and literacy, I do not mean to imply that knowledge does not exist in oral cultures, but simply that there is no such thing as a *body* of knowledge, there is only *knowhow*, the practical ability to do things, which can be learned as an activity, and that includes the ability to remember and recite. In the absence of written documents, the only *body* of knowledge is the human body, and as Edmund Carpenter (1973) notes, this is symbolized by the fact that we talk about learning things *by heart*.

If wisdom resides in the person and in human communication, and knowledge resides in a text, a book or document, where do we find information? As we currently conceive of it, in communication*s* rather than communication, in signals transmitted through wires and airwaves, bouncing off of satellites, stored on magnetic and optical media, in computer memory and databanks. Knowledge takes time to acquire, and wisdom is the fruit of a lifetime, but information appears instantaneously, dematerialized and decontextualized, its function to reduce freedom and establish control. While popular discourse treats information as a basic human need and an unmitigated good, media ecology scholars warn that its benefits do not come without costs, and have expressed concerned about the devaluation and loss of human judgment, and liberty. The danger is in an unbalanced media environment where knowledge becomes the property of the privileged few rather than of the population as a whole, and wisdom all but disappears in the noise and clutter of information overload. At the same time, our new information technologies do have the potential for helping us achieve a more complex and ecologically sound social system, one where information serves human needs and purposes, not the least of these being human communication, and is used to create a sustainable and humane environment. The potential is there, if information can be harnessed through knowledge, and if it can be applied with wisdom.

Chapter 8

Communication and Isolation

We typically think of communication as being about linking and connecting, building bridges, coming together, finding common ground, etc. In other words, communication is generally positioned in opposition to isolation. But the two are not antonyms, and in fact they intersect in a variety of ways. This goes beyond the simple contrarian impulse to explore what may have otherwise been overlooked. To the extent that they might be considered near opposites, there is always the yin within the yang, or the yang within the yin, in this case the isolation within communication and the communication within the isolation. Or in the context of systems theory, we can understand that increasing the amount of communication can, at a certain point, result in a return back into isolation; this also relates to Marshall McLuhan's laws of media, and specifically to the fourth law that any medium pushed to its extreme will reverse or flip into its opposite (McLuhan & McLuhan, 1988). Or isolation can simply be the subject of communication, so that the two coexist on different levels, isolation on the content level, communication or rather metacommunication on the relationship level (Bateson, 1972, 1979; Watzlawick, Bavelas, & Jackson, 1967). Or isolation can be a function of communication, or its intended or unintended consequence. Isolation can even be a necessary prerequisite for certain types of communication.

We have a blind spot when it comes to understanding communication that has much to do with the dominance of Socrates and Plato in western thought, and through them, the idealization of dyadic communication, of conversation and dialogue. This extends to their denigration of rhetoric, oratory, and public communication, which extends to all manner of one-to-many forms including mass communication (Plato, 1971, 1973; see also Peters, 1999). But it also results in the general tendency to overlook or disregard intrapersonal communication in favor of interpersonal communication. Coinciding with this prejudice, individuals who are introverts, who are labeled as *shy*, who for whatever reason eschew the company of others, tend to be seen as abnormal or as unfortunate, whereas individuals who are extroverts, who are gregarious and garrulous, the outgoing, loquacious and talkative types, are seen as normal and held in high esteem. This should come as no surprise, insofar as we are social animals, and our sociability is essential for our survival (Dunbar, 1996). So it is that we look upon the loner with suspicion, and all the lonely people with pity.

And yet, there remains the line from the 1932 film, *Grand Hotel*, famously uttered by Greta Garbo: *I want to be alone*. In later life, she noted the difference between wanting to be *left alone* and wanting to be *let alone*. Isolation need not be permanent, might simply be a matter of taking a break from the pressure of social interaction. Or it may be related to hypersensitivity to social stimuli. As noted in the first chapter, the *aloneness* characteristic of individuals with autism might have something to do with a failure to connect, but often has to do with being overwhelmed and unable to process the stimuli coming from others in their environment. For typical individuals, wanting to be alone may be a response to trauma or emotional distress. Or it may be a desire for individual contemplation and meditation, the sense that I have to get away from all of the talk and activity and noise so that *I can hear myself think*. In order to engage in effective intrapersonal communication, a measure of isolation from interpersonal communication is required.

Isolation also plays a role in any type of performance before an audience. Erving Goffman (1959) argues that all forms of communication are performances, and that an important element in putting on an effective performance is the maintenance of boundaries that limit the audience's access to what he terms the *back region*. This is analogous to the backstage area in a theatre, but also includes the fact that audiences only gain admittance for the limited time during which the play is performed; typically, they are not privy to rehearsals. The point here is that preparation for a performance requires a degree of isolation from the audience, whether it involves actors learning their lines or salespersons learning the tricks of their trade. Having a back region isolated from the audience during the performance is also helpful, as performers in the front region can obtain help during the performance without the audience being aware of it.

The act of creation is often an isolated activity, requiring time and space to concentrate, free of distractions. Whether it involves the kind of oral composition associated with epic poetry and the singing of tales, or the creation of music or visual art, or and especially the writer's craft, we isolate in order to communicate. This seeming paradox that applies to the sending of messages can also apply to their reception. Apart from situations like the theatre and concerts where we are part of a co-present audience, reading, for example, is an isolated activity, requiring a quiet space, and a bit of privacy. This is especially true of print culture, as Walter Ong (1982) notes:

> In manuscript culture and hence in early print culture, reading had

> tended to be a social activity, one person reading to others in a group. As Steiner (1967, p. 383) has suggested, private reading demands a home spacious enough to provide for individual isolation and quiet. (Teachers of children from poverty areas today are acutely aware that often the major reason for poor performance is that there is nowhere in a crowded house where a boy or girl can study effectively.) (p. 131)

Indeed, literacy and print, and the activities of reading and study, are intimately associated with modern notions of privacy, conceptions that did not exist until a few centuries ago. Simply put, when we listen, even to a text being read out loud, we listen together as a group, but when we read, even if we read the exact same text at the exact same time, we read as private individuals. The visual sense is isolating and alienating, as Ong (1967, 1982) explains, whereas the acoustic sense knits us together as an audience, a singular noun, in contrast to being one of many individual readers. Electronics restores some aspects of the acoustic and the communal, as for example, in the case of broadcasting, the audience attends to the exact same program at exactly the same time. But radio and television audiences are isolated in space, watching in small groups, such as families, or often alone as discrete individuals. For radio and sound recording, increasing use of headphones and earbuds render listening a private activity. Computers too, and videogames, are most often isolating, even when they are used for the purposes of communication, and the same can be said for going online, and using social media. The fact that many of us can be co-present but spend our time not communicating with each other, but rather engrossed in communion with our cell phones and mobile devices is a commonplace in contemporary culture, as are comparisons to Narcissus staring at his own reflection. Sherry Turkle (2011) summed it all up quite eloquently in her study of robotics and digital communications: *Alone Together*—we share in our psychological isolation even when we are in close proximity to one another.

It is another form of paradox that so much of our electronic media, by extending our ability to communicate, leaves us ever more isolated from one another. And while there is much cause for concern about our self-imposed isolation, especially insofar as it is so often not something that is being consciously pursued, but rather an unintended consequence of our media use, there also are times when we do want to be let alone, or simply to be alone. With this in mind, it is worth recalling the first axiom of communication put forth by Paul Watzlawick and his colleagues, "one cannot not communicate" (Watzlawick, Bavelas, & Jackson, 1967, p. 49). Everything we do has message value; even silence and inactivity communicates. It follows that we can express a desire for isolation nonverbally as well as verbally, for example by crossing our arms in front of our body, avoiding eye contact, turning our head to look away, and walking away. Similar signals are sent by looking at our wristwatch, or in or around elevators by focusing on the floor indicator rather than others nearby. We create a sense of psychological isolation in crowded conveyances, for example mass transit during rush hour, by reading or looking (again noting that sight can isolate us), looking at ads or out the window for example. Newspapers once were a mainstay of such situations, not only as a distraction but as a formidable shield against eye contact and visual inspection. (When I was in elementary school in New York City, our teacher once instructed us in the straphanger fold, a method of reading a traditional format newspaper such as the *New York Times* while standing on a crowded subway or bus.) Nowadays, it is cell phones and mobile devices instead that send the message that we want to be let alone. All of these forms of communication can be interpreted by others as messages of rejection and disconfirmation, but most often are mutual exchanges confirming the boundaries that separate us from one another.

McLuhan (1995) observed that North Americans go outside to be alone, preferring to socialize indoors and at home, whereas Europeans go out to be sociable, and consider the home to be a private space. In other words, both artificial and natural environments can be used for the purposes of isolation. Here too, we isolate from others for the purposes of intrapersonal communication, or acts of creation and composition, or in the North American mode, to commune with nature (something not confined to any one continent or culture, of course). Further, while I have been focusing on social isolation up to this point, human beings also seek out environmental isolation. We may retreat to the natural environment to go far from the madding crowd, but also far from the unpleasant aspects of city life, the noise and the noisome and unsightly surroundings. This amounts to a reversal of our overall trajectory, which has been the creation of artificial environments to isolate ourselves from nature and shield ourselves from the elements. That includes the building of dwellings and other constructions, both to achieve actual isolation and to communicate a sense of security; architecture isolates the inside from the outside, and can establish private spaces internally. Walls and fences are obvious boundary markers, and while roads are often seen as connecting different places, they create a separation from the off-road areas, and isolate the two sides of the road from each other. Settlements, villages, cities, and other forms of urban, suburban, and exurban environments all create various forms of isolation from the natural environment. On a smaller scale, we can also consider various forms of confinement, such as prison and asylums (Goffman, 1961; see also Foucault, 1977), as well as how imposed isolation is altered by the addition of electronic media, which reduce the sense of being cut off from the outside world (McLuhan, 1964; Meyrowitz, 1985). In its most extreme form, environmental isolation includes the sensory deprivation tank, its function being to isolate the individual mind from all external sensation, allowing for the ultimate form of intrapersonal communication.

McLuhan (1964) refers to media and technology as extensions of our bodies and biology. The idea of technology as an extension of ourselves was not original to McLuhan, having been invoked by Ralph Waldo Emerson (1883) in the 19th century, but McLuhan also argued that every extension is also an amputation. In this way, he invokes the paradoxical sense that as we extend our abilities to communicate, we do so by becoming increasingly more isolated from one another, and from our surroundings. An extension of ourselves by definition must come between ourselves and our environment, and therefore must also separate us from our environment, shielding us from direct contact with it. In doing so, our extensions become our new environment (Strate, 2017), but at the cost of isolating ourselves from our old environment, interposing an artificial environment between ourselves and the natural environment. As Max Frisch observed in his cybernetics-inspired novel *Homo Faber* (1959), "technology is the art of never having to experience the world" (p. 178). Our isolation from the natural world certainly has much to do with our current crisis involving climate change, and our inability to date to deal with it in an effective manner.

It is not isolation itself that is inherently dysfunctional, however. From a systems perspective, all systems must isolate themselves to some extent from their environment, maintaining a boundary in order to establish and maintain their integrity and identity as systems. In fact, it is only by closing itself off from its environment to a significant degree that a system can organize itself in the first place, in the process termed autopoiesis (Maturana & Varela, 1980, 1992). Healthy systems are neither entirely open nor entirely closed, but maintain a balance between the two (Klapp, 1978). In other words, what we need is a balance between communication and isolation.

Communication and Solipsism

In considering the relationship between communication and isolation, we might begin with the following model (with apologies to Harold Lasswell, 1948): *Who is isolated from whom or what, how, and with what effects?* The *effects* refer to the positive and negative consequences of isolation. *How* refers to the method of isolation, including the ways in which various forms of communication perform the function of isolation. *Who is isolated from whom* refers to the different types of isolation: individuals may be isolated from other individuals, or from groups (and by groups here I mean small and large groups, audiences, organizations, societies, etc.); groups may be isolated from individuals or other groups. I also include *who is isolated from what* because individuals and groups may be isolated from something other than fellow human beings; in its most general sense, *what* can refer to individuals and groups being isolated from their environment. This type of isolation may be physical or psychological. And perhaps the most extreme form of psychological isolation from the environment, that is, from reality, is solipsism.

By *solipsism*, I am in particular referring to *reality solipsism* or *metaphysical solipsism*, the idea that nothing exists except for the self. It is impossible to determine when such doubts first were raised, but Descartes is generally credited with introducing metaphysical solipsism as a philosophical problem (Haldane & Ross, 1911; Rollins, 1967). By making *I think therefore I exist* the first principle of his philosophy, Descartes suggests that all other knowledge might be subjective, if not illusory. The positions of subjectivism and solipsism are also inherent in the empiricism of Locke (1961) and Hume (1965); if knowledge can only be based on the individual's sense perceptions, then the validity of those perceptions, and the very existence of the objects of those perceptions, can be called into question. Descartes, Locke, and Hume rejected solipsism, as have most other philosophers. Solipsism not only defies common sense, but if true, would put an end to philosophical dialogue—in other words, it would put philosophers out of business. This does not mean that solipsism has been disproved, however; on the contrary solipsism is generally described as "implausible but incapable of being refuted" (Rollins, 1967, p. 488).

For most philosophers, attempting to disprove the solipsistic position is an intellectual challenge, akin to solving a logical puzzle (see, for example, Teensma, 1974). But solipsism is not just an academic exercise or a matter of scholarly discourse, but also a psychological phenomenon. According to T.Z. Lavine (1984):

> Solipsism is dangerously close to being a philosophical expression of the form of insanity called schizophrenia. One striking feature of the schizophrenic personality is his withdrawal from the common world of reality into his own private world, in which his mind and his thoughts are all that exist for him, are the only reality. (p. 100)

A more common form of psychological solipsism is what A.D Nuttall (1974) refers to as *solipsistic fear*:

> the fear that the external world of trees, tables, bricks and mortar may

not exist at all. Solipsism as a settled system of belief is quite properly regarded as something absurd, or even comic; no one but a philosopher—no, a lunatic philosopher—could believe that. But it sometimes happens that an idea which is in the strictest sense of the word incredible can prove a fertile source of disquiet.... Thus, although there have been few doctrinaire solipsists, the number of those touched by an intermittent solipsism has, since the eighteenth century, been very great.... Among the philosophers we find an argument, with a life of its own, making persistent head against natural belief and intuition. But meanwhile among the novelists and poets... Feelings, of unreality, intuitions of solipsism become more frequent, and the deeper skepticism of Hume or Bradley finds a distorted echo in the poetry of Wordsworth or Eliot. (p. 11)

It is clear that the effects of solipsism can be positive as well as negative. Doubts about the existence of an external reality can serve as a source of artistic and intellectual inspiration, while solipsistic fear can be extremely disturbing, and total acceptance of the solipsistic position can be dysfunctional.

In considering solipsism, I have so far answered the questions, *who is isolated from what?*, the individual from reality, and *with what effects?*, being both positive and negative. The question that remains is *how?*, that is, *how does communication isolate the individual from reality?* The relationship between communication and reality has itself been an area of interest for social scientists and communication theorists. Peter L. Berger and Thomas Luckman (1967) argue that reality is a social construction, Paul Watzlawick (1976) asserts that there are, "many different versions of reality... all of which are the results of communication, and not reflections of eternal, objective truths" (p. xi). Earnest G. Bormann (1972) maintains that social reality is rhetorically constructed through *dramatizing communication*. And David L. Altheide and Robert P. Snow (1979) state that, "social reality is constituted, recognized, and celebrated with media" (p. 12). Given that our idea of reality is constructed through communication, and media of communication, it follows that our ideas about the nature of reality might be constructed in the same way. I would therefore suggest that that the solipsistic position is a byproduct of the written word and literacy. Of course, this is true in a facile sense, as there was no formal study of philosophy before writing, indeed no formal study whatsoever before writing, but my argument is something more significant: that solipsism specifically is an outgrowth of the psychological effects of literacy and the literate mindset.

To put it another way, members of a nonliterate, oral society do not entertain doubts about reality. Scholars such as Ong (1982), Eric Havelock

(1963), and Jack Goody (1977) point out that the oral mindset is concrete, situational, and operational. In other words, nonliterates are not comfortable with high-level abstractions; instead, they rely on modes of expression and conceptualization that are, as Ong puts it, "close to the human lifeworld" (p. 42). What Ong means by this is that the oral mindset is closely linked to the commonsense world of practical experience. According to A.R. Luria (1976), when nonliterates are asked to define a tree, a typical response is something like, "Why should I? Everyone knows what a tree is, they don't need me telling them" (p. 86). To such individuals, the nature of reality is patently obvious, and accessible to all. In an oral culture, no one would use formal logic to establish the existence or the non-existence of reality, nor would anyone abstractly differentiate between sensory experience and the external world; to a nonliterate, it is taken for granted that all percepts relate to some form of objective reality, and this includes even dreams and hallucinations. Moreover, in an oral culture, individual identity is submerged within that of the group; when Luria asked nonliterates to explain the type of person they are, a typical response was, "we behave well—if we were bad people, no one would respect us" (p. 15). In this kind of culture, identity refers to *we* and *us*, not *I* and *me*; the individual has no identity outside of the group, and western style individualism is inconceivable. Thus, the nature of reality is established through the group's oral communication, reinforced by group consensus, and sanctified by the group's traditions.

Orality binds groups together, while literacy breaks them apart. Reading and writing are, at least potentially, private, isolating activities. Of course, literacy can also be used to supplement orality, as texts can be composed through dictation, and read out loud to others. But literacy makes it possible for individuals to isolate themselves intellectually and psychologically in ways not conceivable in oral societies. Oral communication requires the physical presence of both sender and receiver; written communication allows senders and receivers to be separated in space and in time. Moreover, consider the difference between speaking to oneself and writing to oneself. Due to the immediacy of speech, we hear our own words as we speak them, but when we write to ourselves, we read our own words at a later point in time. Reading our own words after the passage of time creates a sense of disassociation, a splitting apart and fragmenting of the self, creating the impression that the writer, our earlier self, is a different person from the reader, our present self. Writing to ourselves can also create a kind of schizophrenic split, as we are addressing a future self. This occurs, for example, in the case of diary-writing:

> The personal diary is very late literary invention, in effect unknown
> until the seventeenth century. The kind of verbalized solipsistic reveries

it implies are a product of consciousness shaped by print culture. And for which self am I writing? Myself today? As I think I will be ten years from now? As I hope I will be? For myself as I imagine myself or hope others may imagine me? Questions such as this can and do fill diary writers with anxieties and often enough lead to the discontinuation of diaries. The diarist can no longer live with his or her fiction. (Ong, 1982, p. 102)

It is no coincidence that diaries and solipsism are introduced during the same period; the 17th century marks the end of printing's incunabula, and the beginning of a truly typographically literate culture in the west. Understand that I am not suggesting that diary-writing is the cause of solipsism, but rather that the two are both effects of the printing revolution, both related to literacy's capacity to psychologically isolate the individual. Writing isolates the reader from the writer, and the writer from the reader (even when the two are one and the same), and it also isolates individuals from their communities and their traditions. In doing so, literacy makes objectivity possible, and objectivity, I would argue, is the first step on the road to solipsism, as paradoxical as that may seem.

In oral societies, knowledge is preserved in the form of a dramatic oral performance, one in which all of the members participate. The participants recreate the traditional narratives that they have committed to memory, empathizing with the heroes of those stories, and symbolically reenacting their actions (Havelock, 1963; Ong, 1982). Through performance, through mimesis, individuals merge with their traditions, and through commemoration, traditions are merged with individuals. When tradition is transferred to a written form, however, it is physically separated from the individual, which in turn allows for psychological separation. Literacy makes possible, in Havelock's (1963) memorable phrasing, "the separation of the knower from the known" (p. 197). That is, when knowledge is stored in a written document, it is moved from within the self to outside of the self. And knowledge being literally transformed into an object through writing opens the door to the position of objectivism, the idea that the external world can be known and perceived as if we were outside of it, as if we were isolated from it. The position of the reader *is* the position of objectivism. And the position of objectivism is a necessary prerequisite for the formal study of abstract concepts, that is, for philosophy. Havelock (1963) goes so far as to suggest that Plato's theory of the forms is not much more than a device for dramatizing the division between objective reality and the subject who thinks about it. The main point, however, is that objectivity is derived from literacy's isolating potential.

The worldview associated with oral cultures is implicitly subjective, in the sense that they see themselves inside of their environment, central to their world, and view everything in their environment as subjects characterized by spirit and consciousness; this is consistent with the concept of acoustic space, as when we listen, the sounds of the world surround us and envelop us (Carpenter & McLuhan, 1960; Ong, 1982). Nonliterates are therefore not objective, but neither are they explicitly subjective, which is to say that they are not self-consciously aware of each person's unique subjectivity, and skeptical of any claim to objective knowledge. Rather, they inhabit the commonsense world shared by most human beings as they go about their everyday lives, casually assuming that what they perceive the world to be is, in fact, what it *is*. They believe that what they know and perceive of reality *is* reality, and not an individual interpretation of it that would differ from one person to another.

Nonliterates do not themselves embrace either subjectivity or objectivity; both are, in a formal sense, literate inventions, and in order to invent subjectivism, objectivism had to be invented first. This is not just because subjectivity is objectivity's counterpart, but because subjectivity is a product of objectivity and self-reflexiveness. I should note here that self-reflexiveness is a characteristic of our capacity for language and symbolic communication (Korzybski, 1993), as we can talk about talking, and talk about ourselves talking (and ourselves talking about talking, etc.). But self-reflexiveness is particularly facilitated by the abstract thinking characteristic of the literate mindset. Writing divides the self whenever we are writing to ourselves, or simply whenever we are reading back what we have already written down. Writing allows thought, which is to say it allows a portion of the mind, to be separated from the individual and frozen in a form that can be viewed and reviewed. In other words, writing facilitates the self-reflexive examination of thought, that is, thought about thought. And by taking the position of objectivism when thinking about thinking, the mind is able to examine itself as if it were outside of itself. Self-reflexive objectivity allows us to ask questions about our ability to understand and observe the external world, and thereby come to realize our limitations, thus paving the way for subjectivity. The process is aided by comparing our own thought as it changes over time, and by reading the thought of others, internalizing their thinking while making it possible to compare different worldviews by comparing different texts.

Again, it is indeed paradoxical that objectivity applied to itself in self-reflexive fashion can lead to the conclusion that the position of objectivism itself has no objective support, and therefore cannot be justified, leading to the invention of subjectivism. And once we accept the idea that we cannot know the external world directly, then we open the door to the possibility that there is no external world at all, outside of ourselves. In this manner, literacy gives rise to objectivity and amplifies self-reflexiveness, and consequently permits the positions of subjectivity and solipsism to emerge. To be perfectly clear, I am not arguing that literacy necessarily leads to objectivity, subjectivity, and solipsism, only that literacy is required to arrive at the position of objectivism, that literacy and objectivity is required to arrive at the position of subjectivism, and that all three are necessary prerequisites for solipsism. Each one creates an intellectual, psychological, and cultural system or environment within which the next can emerge.

So far, I have argued that writing isolates and fragments the self, and makes it possible to question the self's relationship to external reality. There is a further connection between writing and solipsism that has yet to be mentioned: that writing makes it possible to generate fictional realities. In oral cultures, narrative takes the form of myth, a traditional story with a traditional plot. According to Mircea Eliade (1963), within such cultures, myth "is regarded as... a 'true history,' because it always deals with realities" (p. 6). It is only after writing is invented, and written narrative is developed, that distinctions are made between fiction and nonfiction (Scholes & Kellogg, 1966). Unlike myth, fictional narrative is recognized by writer and reader alike as imaginary, as something that resembles but does not correspond to external reality. In effect, fictional narrative presents the reader with a world that seems real, but only exists in the reader's mind. By introducing the idea that an imaginary world can seem real, fictional narrative carries within it the seeds of the notion that the real world might, in fact, be imaginary. And as in the case of personal diaries, it is no coincidence that the rise of the novel, the most realistic of fictional narratives, along with the introduction of a clear distinction between the literary categories of fiction and nonfiction, occur during the same period that solipsism is introduced, the 17th and 18th centuries (Scholes & Kellogg, 1966).

In sum, in regard to the question of *who is isolated from whom or what, how, and with what effects?*, in the form of psychological isolation known as solipsism, it is the individual who is isolated from reality, the effects range from inspiration to fear and insanity, and the agency is the written word, literacy, and typography. Although writing and printing revolutionized our ability to communicate across space and time, it also made unprecedented forms of isolation possible. This suggests a further generalization that whenever a new medium of communication is introduced, it will be accompanied, at least potentially, by new forms of isolation.

Media, Journalism, and the Culture of Solipsism

The process I have so far detailed, that writing allows for the separation of the knower from the known, making possible the position of objectivism; that literacy also opens the door to enhanced forms of self-reflexiveness; that the self-reflexive examination of the mind and of objectivity turned back onto itself allows for the position of subjectivism; and that the combination of objectivism, self-reflexiveness, and subjectivism together suggest the possibility of solipsism, is a philosophical and psychological process. In other words, we are dealing here either with intellectual puzzles and games or the building of systems of thought, or with the problem of existential fear and dread and the possibility of neuroses or even psychoses. As serious as this may be, they are problems for the individual, intellectual and emotional problems that plague a small minority of a given population. But this process also helps to shed light on a parallel social and cultural phenomenon, one that has been characteristic of the west, and especially the United States, for some time now: We are in danger of becoming a solipsistic society, in many ways we already have become one, and this development is related to current forms of communication.

First, I should note that my reference to *the culture of solipsism* is a nod to the 1979 book by Christopher Lasch, *The Culture of Narcissism*. The connection here is more that one of parallel construction, as both solipsism and narcissism are worldviews centered around the self. Narcissism, as discussed by Lasch, is more than simple selfishness and preoccupation with the self; drawing on the tradition of Freudian psychoanalysis he argues that "narcissism blur[s] the boundaries between the self and the world of objects" (p. 79), and therefore "the narcissist... sees the world as a mirror of himself and has no interest in external events except as they throw back a reflection of his own image" (p. 96). Both the narcissist and the solipsist deny the distinction between the self and its environment, seeing the external world as an extension of the self and nothing more. Both narcissism and solipsism, as psychopathologies, are associated with feelings of fear, anxiety, and alienation. Lasch follows in the footsteps of Freud by psychoanalyzing the public as well as the individual mind; his diagnosis is that late 20th century America is a narcissistic society, "a society that gives increasing prominence and encouragement to narcissistic traits (p. 23). My intent here is not refute Lasch, as his critique applies quite well to American culture in the 21st century, and not the least to American politics. I merely wish to supplement his arguments by noting how our society has slipped into a solipsistic position as well.

This development coincides with what some have dubbed the postmodern age, an age that Jean-François Lyotard (1984) argues is characterized by "incredulity toward metanarratives" (p. xxiv). Metanarratives can be defined as "those universal guiding principles and mythologies which once seemed to control, delimit and interpret all the diverse forms of discursive activity in the world" (Connor, 1989, p. 9). The postmodern condition is one in which a babel of narratives, principles, and ideologies coexist, none of which are given priority over the rest, all of which are suspect. The authority once invested in metanarratives such as religion and science is now decentralized, localized, ultimately diffused; the hierarchy under which all forms of social activity were organized and ordered has been replaced by a heterarchy that borders on anarchy. In the postmodern age, the only ruling idea is that there are no ruling ideas. Of course, these cultural changes have been commented on long before the rise of postmodern theory, for example in the work of media ecology scholars such as Neil Postman (1995, 1999) and Christine Nystrom (2021).

Certainly, the advent of cultural relativism, which Allan Bloom bemoans in *The Closing of the American Mind* (1987), constitutes a preface to postmodernity. Relativists recognize that every culture has its own metanarrative, from which is derived all of the standards and criteria for judging human behavior, and consequently they may dismiss any attempt at evaluation as ethnocentrism. Extreme relativism asserts the equality of all metanarratives, and in doing so, ultimately denies their status as true metanarratives. For a concrete example, we need look no further than the way in which people talk about opinions. It is of course a traditional American belief that individuals are entitled to their own opinions, and free to express them without reservation. In the past, opinions were the key to opening discussions, a welcome exchange of viewpoints, engaging in the ideal form of rational communication established by Plato, dialogue. Now, however, opinions are used to close off conversation, as a final rejoinder after which no further discussion is possible, for example by saying, *well, that's your opinion!*, or for that matter, *well, that's my opinion!* Where once expressing opinions was seen as a means of arriving at truth via the free marketplace of ideas, now statements of opinion amount to a denial of the existence of truth, or at least the denial of the possibility of arriving at any agreement as to what might be true or false, in turn calling into question whether truth is at all accessible to human beings.

Extreme relativism, then, can be understood as a form of cultural solipsism. The relativist denies the possibility that any metanarrative can be evaluated objectively, that any worldview could be an accurate reflection of objective reality. And it is a short step from relativism to radical constructivism (Berger & Luckmann, 1967; Watzlawick, 1976, 1984), a position that denies the very existence of the external world, arguing that reality is a social construction. That constructivism is essentially another name for solipsism is not a new argument, and the constructivist response is that solipsism refers to the creation of reality by the individual, whereas constructivism refers to the creation of reality by the community (Foerster, 1984). But the *ipse* in solipsism refers to *self*, not individual, and it is possible to talk about group identity and the personality of an organization or a nation; it is also possible to psychoanalyze a society, as Lasch does, and therefore it is possible to speak of a *collective self*. It is in this sense that I refer to *cultural solipsism*, the belief that nothing exists outside of the collective self, the culture, and that external reality is not much more than a figment of the communal imagination. I should note that cultural solipsism does not preclude individual solipsism; in fact, it creates a climate quite conducive to it. Just as we may look at the group as if it were a single individual, we may also look at individuals as if they were groups, a microculture of one (paralleling the way that, in linguistics, the idea of the dialect can be brought down to the level of the individual idiolect). In this sense, individual solipsism may be seen as an extreme form of cultural solipsism. I do want to make it clear at this point that I am not saying that most individuals have embraced solipsism personally; most people still hold to commonsense beliefs about objective reality. But for western cultures as a whole, it is on that macro scale that we see the symptoms of cultural solipsism, resulting in a significant degree of solipsistic fear and anxiety which manifests in a variety of socially dysfunctional ways.

Turning now to the ways in which cultural solipsism relates to contemporary communications, by way of an example consider the case of journalism. As solipsism is a form of isolation from the environment, it would make sense to consider the form of communication dedicated to the surveillance of the environment: the news. That journalists have long labored working from the position of objectivism is common knowledge. Historians of journalism such as Michael Schudson (1978) trace the origin of objectivity in reporting back to the 1870s, and note its close relationship to another innovation in communications: the telegraph. Telegraphy served to undermine the concept of news as a partisan expression of opinion on political issues and events, allowing for its substitution by, as Susan Maushart (1986) puts it,

> the interesting notion that "news" exists as an objective category of phenomena. According to this view, news is a sort of commodity, and the reporter merely an agent who effects its transfer from "enacted" reality (say, an event) to an "encoded" reality (a news story). The particular character of the agent is seen as irrelevant to the task at hand—or very nearly so. Writing styles admittedly differ, but styles of perceiving, it is presumed, do not. (p. 273)

Whereas writing in general allows for the separation of the knower from the known, telegraphy intensified the separation of the reporter from the re-ported, and thereby intensified the objectification and commodification of news. Telegraphic news emphasizes timeliness over thoughtfulness (Postman, 1985), reliability over righteousness, and consequently, factuality over ideology. The separation of the reporter from the reported gave journalists the distance necessary for self-reflexive examination of the journalistic enterprise, and one result was the canonization of objective and impersonal reporting (also the es-tablishment, in the United States, of college courses and schools of journalism). Around the same time as the introduction of commercial telegraphy, a very different kind of innovation in journalism was introduced: the interview. As self-reflexiveness made possible the critical examination of news, it also allowed for its artificial manufacture; the interview was only the first of a multitude of media-made events, what Daniel Boorstin in *The Image* (1978) refers to as *pseudo-events*. And while interviewers could maintain the stance of objectivity and the style of impersonality (Maushart, 1986), such media events suggest the possibility that all news is artificially manufactured (McLuhan, 1964, 1995), and therefore subjective. Self-conscious subjectivity in journalism, as opposed to the unselfconsciousness of the pre-telegraphic partisan press, manifested it-self in a variety of ways during the 20th century, for example in interpretive reporting in the 1930s, and in the New Journalism associated with Tom Wolfe originating during the 1960s, culminating in the gonzo journalism of Hunter S. Thompson in the 1970s. Effectively reversing the longstanding impersonal style of print journalism, Wolfe, Thompson, and other injected their personal-ities and literary voice directly into their reporting, going as far as to establish a first-person form in which the reporter is the protagonist of the story being reported. This was not a return to the partisan press, which emphasized argu-ments based on political positions, and which often could be delivered anony-mously, as was the case for the Federalist papers authored by Alexander Hamil-ton, James Madison, and John Jay under the pseudonym, Publius. Rather, this new form of journalism was all about the reporters, their subjective experienc-es, and their subjectivity.

At the same time that the of New Journalism was being introduced, jour-nalistic objectivity was declared a myth (Schudson, 1978), and it is no accident that both coincide with the widespread adoption of television and its rise to dominance in American culture. Broadcasting more generally mounted a se-rious challenge to objective reporting, with radio restoring the reporter's dis-tinctive voice, and with it a sense of subjectivity. Television took it even fur-ther by bringing the newscaster's appearance and manner into people's homes, eliminating the distance and impersonal quality of print media. Television is by far an intimately personal medium (McLuhan, 1964), and its anchors and reporters could not help but restore the individual personality to journalism. Not only are newscasters evaluated based on their personal credibility (Postman, 1985; Strate, 2014), but they cannot avoid being part of the story they are reporting; their presence on screen guarantees it. It is not surprising therefore that television anchors and reporters actually become the subjects of news stories themselves, for example when they are in conflict with management over salary and other issues, when they are fired, promoted, move to another network, when they have babies, when they die, and most certainly when they find themselves in conflict with politicians and public officials. And it is not surprising that television, in promoting the news, plays up the star qualities of its newscasters. In this sense, television transforms journalists into objects and commodities, and thereby encourages self-reflexive examination of their role as journalists. Consequently, it allows them to focus on the process of reporting and manufacturing the news. Increasingly self-conscious as to the subjectivity of their reports, it is quite natural for newscasters to begin to emphasize the construction of news in their reports. Thus, the process of producing the news becomes part of the story on television; this is particularly apparent when it comes to investigative reporting, where the process is usually presented as a kind of detective story or courtroom drama (Arlen, 1978), and often is of greater interest than the actual results of the investigation.

Self-reflexiveness is perhaps most evident in political reporting, however. While journalists were the first to discover that they could self-consciously manipulate and manufacture the news, others soon realized that they could create their own news, and have it publicized, and so was born the public relations industry. Nowhere else did this have a greater impact than in the political sector (Moran, 1984), particularly as television became the dominant medium of communication. Television's self-conscious response has been to reveal the politician's attempts at media manipulation, calling into question all of the candidate or official's actions and motivations. Election coverage is dominated by discussion of image-building, the choice of setting and timing for political events, the use of spin doctors, etc. The result is a sense that the campaign, the issues, and all political actions exist only insofar as they are reported. The same doubts appear in other spheres as well—for example, is an act of terrorism carried out for the sake of being reported on television?

What began with broadcasting has only been intensified with the expansion of offerings via cable and satellite television, especially via cable news networks, and by way of the internet, the web, and further developments such as blogs, podcasts, video uploads, and social media (see Strate, 2014). User generated content has broken the monopoly of knowledge once held by professional journalists, resulting in a flood of information minus any editorial filters or gatekeeping. Distinctions between reporting and expressions of opinion are blurred and dissolved, and communicators devote more time and space to dele-gitimizing other sources than they to do providing information and rational analysis. By 2016, accusations of *fake news* become commonplace, competing claims for *alternate facts* surface, as do declarations that we are in an age of *post-truth*. Can there be any denying that ours is a culture of solipsism?

Note that this process follows the evolution of the electronic media. The telegraph was associated with the rise of objectivity and self-reflexiveness in journalism, while television is related to journalism's increasing self-conscious-ness of its subjectivity, of its role in the events it is supposed to be reporting. Unable to reestablish a sense of objective reality, journalists instead made man-ifest the subjectivity of the surveillance function. Surveillance, then, is turned inward, to the collective self of the news media, and this metastasizes as the technology to publish and distribute audiovisual content is made broadly avail-able via the internet, web, and social media. The combination of subjectivity and self-reflexiveness constitutes a kind of *media solipsism*, in which the exis-tence of events apart from the (mainly electronic) media is met with skepti-cism. While there may be good reasons for these doubts in some instances, they also make political action increasingly more difficult. If nothing is real outside of the electronic media, then nothing is real except for the electronic media. Why attempt to change the environment when it does not exist, when the only thing can be changed is the channel, or when change is only a click away? Media solipsism then is related to the general disinterest in public activity in contem-porary culture, to our narcissism, and to our political paralysis, even in the face of existential threats to democracy, and to human life due to climate change. In other words, it is related to our increasing sense of isolation from our social and physical environment. To the extent that culture is communication (Hall, 1959), cultural solipsism is media solipsism. And while some postmodernists revel in our cultural solipsism, we have yet to determine whether a solipsistic society can survive.

Hyperreality and Media Solipsism

In diagnosing our culture as solipsistic, I do not want to give the impression that I am presenting another conservative critique in the tradition of Allan Bloom (1987) and Arthur Schlesinger, Jr. (1992). I myself am something of a relativist, and have often relied upon the constructivist perspective in my schol-arship, finding it both sensible and useful. The problem is when constructivism is taken to an extreme, to the point of absurdity, as Postman (1999) argues, and when relativism is so absolute as to disallow any form of judgment or evaluation. For our survival, we have to be able to apply reality-testing to situations, and we have to engage in some form of moral or ethical evaluation. To the extent that I am a relativist, I am hesitant to pass judgment on postmodernity in its entirety. But I am not certain if our doubts about reality reflect a healthy skepticism, the kind that makes us want to go and check things out and determine what exactly is going on, or if they are a byproduct of our culture's narcissism (Lasch, 1979), and our collective form of solipsistic fear and anxiety. Given that our slide towards cultural solipsism has been associated with our population's general disinterest in public activity and in political paralysis, I have serious doubts regarding the survival value of a solipsistic society. Again, this is not a conservative critique, nor a reactionary call for a return to a simpler, more comprehensible culture (although we might wind up in that situation due to breakdowns brought on by environmental catastrophe). Rather, this is a plea for understanding how we are isolating ourselves from our environment, and for understanding the role that our communication technologies play in that process.

My argument thus far has been that media of communication influence us psychologically, socially, and culturally. Writing and literacy intensify self-reflexiveness and made it possible to conceive of the position of objectivism, which in turn led to the position of subjectivism, and finally to solipsism, as both intellectual and psychological developments. Printing and telegraphy did the same for journalism, giving rise to self-reflexiveness and the idea of objectivity, which eventually led to a subjective turn, and finally to the solipsism that characterizes contemporary electronic media, and contemporary society and culture. The two processes share the same pattern, the difference being one of scale. I now want to return to another connection between communication technologies and forms of solipsism: the ways in which media allow us to create realistic fictions. Here too there is a parallel between writing and individual solipsism on the one hand, and contemporary media and cultural solipsism on the other.

The distinction we make between fictional and nonfictional narratives is a byproduct of the invention of writing and the emergence of literate cultures (Kittay & Godzich, 1987; Lima, 1988; Scholes & Kellogg, 1966). Oral cultures do not make such distinctions (Ong, 1982), and instead measure truth by adherence to local tradition (Lord, 1960; Nagy, 1981) and fidelity to sacred myth (Eliade, 1963). The tyranny of oral tradition is necessary for cultural survival, as the only way to preserve knowledge is through collective human memory. Writing reduces the need for memory, separates the knower from the known, and therefore individuals from their tradition, and allows the communicator to transcend the local audience for an oral performance. The introduction of writing, then, constitutes a declaration of independence from oral tradition, freeing narrative to evolve into the oppositional forms of nonfiction and fiction. As Scholes and Kellogg (1966) put it, nonfictional narrative "replaces allegiance to *mythos* with allegiance to reality," while fiction "replaces allegiance to *mythos* with allegiance to the ideal" (p. 13). Freed from the constraints of tradition, ancient and medieval writers created imaginary ideal worlds in the form of the romance and the didactic fable.

The shift from imaginary idealism to imaginary realism in fiction following the Renaissance has been described as a response to modern science (Lima, 1988). Elizabeth Eisenstein's (1979) study of the printing revolution in early modern Europe makes clear that the scientific emphasis on accurately describing and explaining the natural world was very much a product of typographic communication. In this sense, Gutenberg's invention fostered the development of both modern science and the modern literary form known as the novel. According to Northrup Frye (1957):

> the essential difference between the novel and romance lies in the conception of characterization. The romancer does not attempt to create 'real people' so much as stylized figures which expand into psychological stereotypes.... The novelist deals with personality, with characters wearing their *personae* or social masks. He needs the framework of a stable society, and many of our best novelists have been conventional to the verge of fussiness. (pp. 304-305)

In this we can recognized another connection between printing and the novel, based on typography's association with the rise of individualism (Eisenstein, 1979; McLuhan, 1962, 1964, 1969).

All forms of fictional narrative present imaginary worlds that, depending on internal coherence and the reader's own powers of imagination, seem to be not actual but possible (Maitre, 1983). The development of the novel is of particular significance because it presents the possible world in a particularly realistic fashion, populated by realistic, well-rounded mimetic (or ironic) characters with individualistic personalities (Frye, 1957; Ong, 1982). Scholes & Kellogg (1966) go so far as to argue that the novel represents a synthesis of idealistic fiction and empirical nonfiction. Consequently, the novel presents a possible world that resembles but does not correspond to external reality, a world that seems real, but only exists in the reader's mind (and the writer's). Not surprisingly, *realism*, the semblance of the real, becomes one of the main criteria used to evaluate the literary merit of a given work. In this way we are introduced to the idea that an imaginary world might, in fact, seem real, to the point that it might even be hard to determine truth from fiction, that it might even be the cause of delusions and madness, which is the theme of what is often considered the first true novel, *Don Quixote* by Miguel de Cervantes. And if an imaginary world might be taken for real, this carries with it the seeds of the notion that the real world might be imaginary. It is no accident, then, that Nuttall (1974) finds frequent evidence of solipsistic fear among novelists and modern poets such as Wordsworth and Eliot. Nor is it a coincidence that the rise of the novel occurs during the same period that the positions of subjectivism and solipsism are introduced in philosophy, during the 17th and 18th centuries.

According to critics such as Jean Baudrillard (1983) and Umberto Eco (1986), modernity's emphasis on realism has given way to a postmodern hyper-reality. The hyperreal is more real than real (Baudrillard, 1983; Eco, 1986; Kellner, 1989), so that it is an extension of realism that results in a reversal of realism (in accordance with the laws of media put forth by McLuhan & McLuhan, 1988). Realism is based on representation, and we judge a given representation realistic based on its resemblance to the thing it represents. Hyperreality, according to Baudrillard, is based on simulation, and a simulation "bears no relation to any reality whatever: it is its own pure simulacrum" (p. 11). And as Eco (1986) puts it: "The 'completely real' becomes identified with the 'completely fake'. Absolute unreality is offered as real presence" (p. 7). In other words, the simulation does not resemble or represent anything in reality, but is presented and perceived as being real. Baudrillard's concept of hyperreality is in many ways an extension of the work of Walter Benjamin (1968). Benjamin was one of the first to point out that mechanical reproduction alters the relationship between the original and the copy, and that film all but abolishes that distinction. For example, while it is possible to film an actor's performance in its entirety as it occurs, in which case the motion picture would be a representation of the actual performance, more often than not, the performances we see on the screen never quite occurred as we see them, but rather are creations of the filmmaker, through the editing of recorded fragments of the performance (in some of the fragments actors may not even be aware that they are performing or being filmed). The result is not a reproduction of a performance that actually occurred; it is a "reproduction" that is *not* a reproduction of anything in reality, not a representation, but a simulation of a performance. And this simulation in many ways seems more realistic, and more real than a live theatrical performance.

Working along the same lines, Gary Gumpert (1987) notes that sound editing technology has allowed musicians to record performances that never actually occurred, that could not actually occur, and that they are incapable of reproducing in live concerts. Such sound recordings are simulations of musical performance, and here too the simulation comes across as more real than the unmediated performance. A related parallel can be found in Daniel Boorstin's (1978) identification of pseudo-events, events set up entirely for the purpose of being reported or reproduced by the news media, e.g., interviews, press conferences, publicity stunts, press releases, leaks, etc. Boorstin notes that pseudo-events crowd out real events in news media because they are easier to include, being created specifically to fill pages and programs, more interesting because they are created specifically for that purpose, and more plentiful. Ultimately, then, most of what we read or see as "news" consists of pseudo-events, and even when there is a real event, something that would have happened even if there was no one to cover it, it is immediately surround by pseudo-events (e.g., interviews, press conferences, leaks), and thereby overshadowed. Pseudo-events, being hyperreal, leave us confused about what is real, and accepting of a post-truth world of alternative facts.

Realism is asymptotic to reality, approaching it, but never quite getting there; hyperrealism surpasses reality. Realism is subordinate to reality, but hyperreality takes the dominant position. Alluding to Korzybski's (1993) famous dictum that the *map is not the territory* (p. 58) and his concern with instilling in individuals a consciousness of abstracting, Baudrillard (1983) insists:

> Abstraction today is no longer that of the map, the double, the mirror or the concept. Simulation is no longer that of territory, a referential being or a substance. It is the generation by models of real without origin or reality: a hyperreal. The territory no longer precedes the map, nor survives it. Henceforth, it is the map that precedes the territory. (p. 2)

In the postmodern age, then, reality must make the futile attempt to catch up to hyperreality. This can be seen in the relationship between Hollywood and Broadway. Whereas in the past the movie industry routinely adapted stage plays for the screen, for decades now some of the most popular shows in American theatre involve the recreation and adaptation of movies, starting with *The Wizard of Oz, Captains Courageous, My Favorite Year, The Goodbye Girl*, and *The Kiss of the Spider Woman* (Richards, 1992); Disney has enjoyed great success with theatrical versions of its animated films such as *Beauty and the Beast, The Lion King*, and *Aladdin*, and some other examples include *Monty Python's Spamalot, Mama Mia!, The Producers, Little Shop of Horrors, Moulin Rouge, Beetlejuice*, and many more. This follows a pattern similar to the relationship between sound recordings and live performance. Gary Gumpert (1987) points out that in the past recordings were considered inferior reproductions of live performances, but for many decades now audiences have been attending concerts with the expectation of hearing reproductions of sound recordings. The pressure to match the perfection of edited recordings has led many performers to use prerecorded music, and even lipsynching in their "live" concerts. Computer generated music adds a further level of ambiguity, as the music is preprogramed but not actually recorded, so that in one sense it is played "live" but as a simulation of performance.

Moreover, the pressure to recreate the hyperreality of the televised performance and the music video has resulted in the commonplace presence of giant television screens projecting both close-ups of the performers and prerecorded clips to the audience (Connor, 1989). This same technology is used at sporting events and political conventions in an attempt to make the live event as real as its televised simulation. Inevitably, images of the audience itself will be projected, so that the audience takes part in its own simulation. And simulations of the television audience, from the Loud family in the 1973 PBS documentary *An American Family*, to the studio audience in talk shows such as *The Oprah Winfrey Show*, *The Ellen DeGeneres Show*, and the like, are no longer unusual. This has been taken even further over the last few decades in the form of reality programs, such as *Survivor*, *Big Brother*, and *The Amazing Race*, not to mention the program that launched a presidency, *The Apprentice*. But even this is surpassed by user generated content on the web and social media, where the vast gulf between sender and receiver characteristic of mass media essentially vanishes. Along similar lines, Baudrillard (1983) in his characteristically hyperbolic style argues that simulation dissolves the distinction source and spectator:

> We are witnessing the end of perspective and panoptic space... and hence the *very abolition of the spectacular*. Television... is no longer a spectacular medium... The medium is no longer identifiable as such, and the merging of the medium and the message is the first great formula of this new age. There is no longer any medium in the literal sense: it is now intangible, diffuse and diffracted in the real, and it can no longer even be said that the latter is distorted by it. (p. 54)

McLuhan (1964) provides a clearer understanding in arguing that television is a cool medium, one that demands participation from its audience, so much so that it draws viewers into itself in implosive fashion. In that sense, the boundary between audience and medium is less distinct, the merger between audience and medium more complete, than in older forms such as print media. As McLuhan (1995, 2003) explains, the user becomes the content of the medium, and in broadcasting the communicator becomes the message that is electronically transmitted by the medium. As for Baudrillard (1983), he goes on to point to "the dissolution of TV into life [and] the dissolution of life into TV," referring to media as "a sort of genetic code which controls the mutation of the real into the hyperreal" (p. 55).

Neil Postman (1985) presents a similar argument in a much more comprehensible fashion by suggesting that television is the command center of our society, that it forms the basis of our epistemology and our culture. What this means is that the biases of television as a medium can be found not just on the screen, but throughout our society; we have reshaped ourselves and the world around us in the image of the electronic media, and therefore in the image of the simulation. Eco (1986) discusses how hyperreality has permeated our museums and even our zoos (which are now designed along the lines of the nature film), and Baudrillard (1986) argues that it has penetrated to the very core of our culture, and to the highest levels of society: Thus, the real fear of those in power is not the fear of losing power, but the fear that power might no longer exist, except as a simulation. It also leads to what Baudrillard identifies as "the characteristic hysteria of our time: the production and reproduction of the real" (p.44), when all that is and can be produced are more and more simulations. Ultimately, he believes that "it is now impossible to isolate the real, or to prove the real" (p. 41).

Clearly, what Baudrillard (1983) describes as the postmodern condition is a solipsistic society. And the connection between cultural solipsism and audiovisual simulation that he alludes to parallels the relationship between individual solipsism and fictional narrative. As the audiovisual media create simulations that are not real and yet are experienced as being more real than real, they introduce the idea that our non-mediated or immediate reality is somehow less than real, or that it is just another type of simulation. And because the audiovisual media externalize imaginary reality, solipsism is fostered on a cultural as well as individual level. Critics of Baudrillard (e.g., Connor, 1989; Kellner, 1989) find his description of postmodernity too extreme, and accuse him of exaggeration, but I interpret him as speaking in the prophetic mode. The true function of prophecy is not to predict the future, but to deliver a warning about our present direction. At the time that he was writing about simulation and hyperreality, Baudrillard was not demonstrating that we are living in a solipsistic culture, but rather pointing to then present solipsistic tendencies, outlining the trends that could lead us to complete cultural solipsism.

We have certainly seen the merging of the real and the simulation over the past several decades in a variety of ways. This includes the breakdown of the distinction between fiction and nonfiction in merging genres, such as the docudrama and re-enactment, infotainment and edutainment, advertorial and in product placement. Film narratives that question reality abound, including *The Matrix* where Baudrillard's book on simulation makes an appearance. And it is especially in the realm of computing and digital media that we find unprecedented opportunities for the manipulation and creation of reality. In 1982, much concern was raised about the fact that electronic imaging was used to move the pyramids so that they could better fit the cover of *National Geographic*, and not long after similar technology was used to create seamless Coke commercials in which pop stars danced and sang alongside dead movie actors (Ritchin, 1990). What came to be known as photoshopping images has been criticized for creating unrealistic images of feminine beauty, but otherwise is taken as a matter of course; filters and editing tools are now part of the basic equipment for the cameras incorporated into our smart phones and mobile devices, as well as social media platforms such as Instagram. Digital technology has been used to create artificial scenery, for example in the *Avatar* and *Lord of the Rings* movies, and to de-age living actors and resurrect dead ones, for example in the *Star Wars* sequels. One of the most serious causes for concern in the second decade of the 21st century is the deep fake video, which is becoming harder and harder to tell apart from genuine recordings. That people are willing to interact with artificial intelligence programs as if they were real is a phenomenon first identified in the 1960s (Weizenbaum, 1976); neither is there anything new about ascribing human consciousness to technological devices (Turkle, 1984). The proliferation of bots, chatbots, intelligent agents, and the like only add to the confusion. And then of course, there is virtual reality, a buzzword in the early 90s that has come back into vogue in the last few years, especially in regard to Facebook's proposed metaverse. Along with augmented reality (AR) and mixed reality (MR), VR technology is still primitive enough to make obvious the fact that the simulation is an illusion, and the same is true of holographic technology, but we have every reason to believe that continued technological innovation will eventually bring us fully into the realm of hyperreal environments.

The danger is not that we may mistake our illusions for reality—human beings have been making that type of error throughout our history. The danger is that we may mistake our reality for illusions. In order to meet the needs of a changing environment, and the challenges and demands that we are currently facing, as well as those we cannot even imagine right now that we will inevitably face in the future, we must be able to accurately assess our environment, and evaluate our actions and activities. And how can we do so if the communication technologies that we depend upon to connect us to our environment cause us to be psychologically and sociologically isolated from that environment?

Chapter 9

Human Communication and Human Technology

Thinking About (How We Think About) the Future

The topic I wish to take up here is the future. The future of the field of communication, and the future of academia in general. At the same time, I well recall how the sense of the future that we all shared prior to 9/11 was shattered along with the twin towers of the World Trade Center, and how we found ourselves at war across the globe and on our highest alert for terrorist attacks at home. And how the sense of the future we all shared prior to the COVID-19 global pandemic of 2020 was completely upended by the deadly disease. And yet, the future is at once entirely different, and much the same as it was before. If this is the *eve of destruction*, well then most of us, at least those of us of a certain age, have been there before. The sixties were a time of such extremes. We lived with the threat of atomic war. I recall from my childhood in Queens, New York, that the air raid siren would ring every weekday at noon, and I remember seeing the little signs displayed on the outside of many office and apartment buildings indicating that there was a fallout shelter inside. I also remember the drills we ran in school, one where we left the classroom and lined up in the hall, away from the windows, and another where we simply hid underneath our desks. One night when I was about nine, one of the networks ran the motion picture *Fail-Safe*, which ended with an A-bomb dropping on New York—and why was it always New York in these stories, I wondered, why my hometown? I had nightmares for years after that.

But accompanying extreme anxiety was extreme optimism. Some of my fondest childhood memories are of the vision of the future that was embodied in the 1963-1964 New York World's Fair. Looking out of the window of our fifth story apartment in Kew Gardens I could see, off in the distance, the Fair's major structures such as the Unisphere. At night, we would watch the fireworks, sometimes walking up to the roof of our building for a better view. And whenever we could, we would head over to the fair grounds to experience such futuristic devices as monorails, moving sidewalks, and video-telephones. One of my favorite exhibits was General Electric's Carousel of Progress, designed by Walt Disney, whose theme song promised that, "there's a great big beautiful tomorrow, shining at the end of every day." There was a tremendous sense of hope and enthusiasm about the future, born out of faith in science, technology, and human progress.

I know I am only scratching the surface of the agonies and the ecstasies of the sixties, but what I am trying to emphasize are the extremes. If these two kinds of feelings about the future seem contradictory, let me quote to you from a 1964 essay by Buckminster Fuller (1969):

> This moment of realization that it soon must be Utopia or Oblivion coincides exactly with the discovery by man that for the first time in history Utopia is, at least, physically possible of human attainment. (p. 292)

What utopia and oblivion both reflect is a common concern with the future. It was also in 1964 that the cybernetics and communication theorist Norbert Wiener wrote that:

> The world of the future will be an ever more demanding struggle against the limitations of our intelligence, not a comfortable hammock in which we can lie down to be waited upon by our robot slaves. (p. 69)

And that same year, that most celebrated of media ecology scholars, Marshall McLuhan (1964) wrote that "after three thousand years of explosion, by means of fragmentary and mechanical technologies, the Western world is imploding" (p. 3). We were reeling from the force of the future, so much so that the great management theorist, Peter Drucker (1968), said that ours is an "age of discontinuity" (p. 3). We were suffering from *future shock* according to Alvin Toffler (1970), which he described as "the shattering stress and disorientation that we induce in individuals by subjecting them to too much change in too short a time" (p. 2). The answer was to train futurists to study the future, just as historians study the past.

But somehow the future grew less shocking as time wore on, the discontinuities less abrupt. Our futures came to be seen as merely markets during the 20th century's fourth quarter, and futurism was reduced to predicting trends by lifestyle analysts like Faith Popcorn. Walt Disney's celebration of the future, Tomorrowland, came to be marketed nostalgically by the Disney Corporation as "the tomorrow that never was," while his proposal for a city of the future, the Experimental Prototype Community of Tomorrow was turned into a Disneyworld theme park, Epcot Center, a permanent World's Fair. The idealistic future of the *Star Trek* television series that Gene Roddenberry introduced in 1964, gave way to the *Star Wars*, George Lucas's temporally challenged fairy tale of a film, in which the future happened "a long time ago, in a galaxy far, far away." With the fall of the Soviet empire, Francis Fukuyama (1992) said that we had seen *the end of history*, and that meant the end of the future as well, or at least the end of discontinuities. From here on in, history would be brought into the present by endless instant replays, while what was left of the future would be programmed on computer, run in the present as simulations and scenarios before being implemented. After all, that is how we fixed the millennium bug in our computer programs. No wonder *The Matrix* offered us a future in which it always seemed to be the late 1990s.

But with the celebrations of the new millennium still fresh in memory, 9/11 brought us back to the future, and the shock returned with a vengeance. The destruction of the Twin Towers recalled the threat of Oblivion, as does the specter, a little over two decades later, of World War Three and nuclear exchange that followed Russia's invasion of Ukraine. And so, we find that we are challenged to counter that threat with a vision of Utopia. But, where do we find the futurists of today, and tomorrow? Let me suggest that the field of communication would be a great place to start. Communication studies has no choice but to be forward-looking. We must pay attention to and account for the waves of technological innovation that are always altering the ways in which people communicate. That is why our communication scholars work harder than many others from other fields. The things that other scholars study—history, literature, society, for example—do not change all that much from year to year, while the object of *our* study is on an eighteen-month cycle of obsolescence. Toffler (1970) explained that the focus of futurism is not technological innovation or scientific progress, but rather on human adaptation. And the fundamental method we rely upon for adaptation to our environment is our capacity for communication. As communication scholars, we already are futurists, and we must answer the call of history, and more so, the call of the future.

Human Communication

We have to begin by knowing our field. Speech is one method of communication, and it is arguably the most basic and most important form of communication. But it is our job to study all of the modes and media of communication. I have heard speech specialists dismiss the study of media, and I have heard media specialists dismiss the study of speech, and quite frankly I think that both attitudes are foolish. We are not the only ones who study speech—it is studied by speech pathologists, and by linguists—but when *we* study speech, we study it as a form of communication. We are not the only ones who study media—media can be studied as art forms, as literature, as social institutions, or as engineering projects, but when *we* study media, we study them as media *of communication*. And we are not the only ones to study culture—culture is studied by anthropologists, archeologists, historians, and scholars of the fine arts—but when *we* study culture, we follow Edward T. Hall's (1959) suggestion that we treat "culture in its entirety as a form of communication" (p. 28).

Underlying our studies is the understanding that communication is a singular phenomenon, by which I mean both unique and unified. In other words, there are characteristics common to all forms of communication. For example, there is Kenneth Burke's (1950) observation that communication fosters identification and increases common ground among participants, and Gregory Bateson's (1972, 1979; Ruesch & Bateson, 1968) perception that communication involves messages about relationships as well as the sending and receiving of information (see also, Watzlawick et al, 1968). I should note that, as we bring this holistic approach to the study communication, we also specialize in the study of *human* communication, to invoke a phrase coined by Frank Dance (see Dance, 1976; Dance & Larson, 1982). Our study of the unity of human communication speaks to our understanding of the unity of humanity, an understanding that needs to be emphasized especially in times of war. We are not the only ones who study communication. Computer scientists and engineers study machine communication. Biologists study animal communication, the transfer of messages on a cellular level, and the transmission of information via genetic coding. Chemists and physicists study forms of communication that are natural but not organic. *We* study human communication, but in seeking the unity of all communication, it also falls to us to relate these other types of communication to our field. Our study of the unity of all communication speaks to our consciousness of the unity of the universe, a spiritual matter to be sure, but our field does not exclude matters of the spirit.

Without a conception of communication as a whole, we have no field. But with only a conception of communication as a whole, we do not have much of a field. That is why we also study those *differences that make a difference*, to use Gregory Bateson's (1972) phrase. We therefore distinguish between interpersonal communication and mass communication, group communication and organizational communication, dialogue and public speaking, for example. These are some of our most fundamental concepts. And along the same lines, in the media ecology tradition we distinguish between literate and nonliterate or oral modes of expression and thought; between ideographic and alphabetic modes of written communication; between the scribal copying of documents and the mass production of printed materials; between material interchange made through persons and objects on the one hand, and energy-based connections involving the transmission and reception of electrons, radio waves, microwaves, or photons on the other. Media ecology's first principle is summed up in McLuhan's (1964) famous statement, "the medium is the message" (p. 7). By this, he meant that we must attend to the different methods and materials used to communicate, because these are differences that make a difference.

Human Technology

During the early sixties, McLuhan (1964) correctly identified communication technology as the single most potent factor in shaping the future. We now take it for granted that we do business in an information economy, are governed through image politics, and fight our wars not just with gunpowder, but with gigabytes. And that is why we need to understand technology as we study communication, or else we will not be the futurists that we need to be. I believe that the dichotomy that is often set up between communication and technology is a false one, that is, that technology is hard and communication is soft, that technology is artificial and communication is natural. And so, I now propose that we start talking about human technology, just as we talk about human communication. The idea of human technology is neither redundant nor oxymoronic, for there are indeed nonhuman technologies. On one end of the spectrum, in the age of computers we can now talk about computer programs written by other computer programs, machines that are designed and manufactured by other machines, high tech untouched by human hands. On the other end of the spectrum, there are animal technologies as well, as Lewis Mumford make eminently clear in his 1967 study, *Technics and Human Development*:

> In any adequate definition of technics, it should be plain that many insects, birds, and mammals had made far more radical innovations in the fabrication of containers, with their intricate nests and bowers, their geometric bee hives, their urbanoid anthills and termitaries, their beaver lodges, than man's ancestors had achieved in the making of tools until the emergence of *Homo sapiens*. In short, if technical proficiency alone were sufficient to identify and foster intelligence, man was for long a laggard, compared with many other species. The consequences of this perception should be plain: namely, that there was nothing uniquely human in tool-making until it was modified by linguistic symbols, esthetic designs, and socially transmitted knowledge. At that point, the human brain, not just the hand, was what made a profound difference; and that brain could not possibly have been just a hand-

made product, since it was already well developed in four-footed creatures like rats, which have no free-fingered hands. (p. 5)

Mumford's (1967) point is extraordinarily significant for two reasons. First, he counters a view that prevailed through much of the 19th and 20th centuries, that we human beings are best characterized as tool-using animals. Much is made of the utility of our opposable thumb, but from Mumford's point of view, it is of secondary importance. As our ancestors came down from the trees to the grasslands, their hands were freed to perform tasks other than clinging to branches and climbing up tree trunks. Their hands could now carry objects, which meant that it was no longer necessary to carry things in our mouths. In this way, our mouths were freed to perform the function of communication, and clearly natural selection favored those hominids who were most proficient at vocalization (see also Nystrom, 2022). In short, Mumford favors the view that it is speech and symbolic communication that makes us human, not tools and technology.

The second reason why Mumford's observation concerning animal technology is so significant is that it forces us to see technology as natural, rather than artificial. All living things try to adapt to their environments in order to survive, and they also try to modify their environments in order to enhance their possibilities for survival. Animals use technologies as a form of adaptation, and to make their environments less threatening, and this extends to the human animal. One of the commonly voiced objections to viewing speech and language as forms of media and technology is that speech and language are natural, part of our biology, while media and technology are artificial, a product of our culture. Again, I would suggest to you that this is a false dichotomy. It is true that we are born with the genetic predisposition for language use, which is then activated by interaction with significant others. But we are also born with the genetic predisposition towards tool use, an instinct we share with other species, a trait that natural selection also seems to have favored in us. As a species, we are born with opposable thumbs just as we are born with opposable tongues.

It is actually interesting to note the close connection between the two. The hand and the mouth are our two most aggressive body parts, the two main ways that we instinctively attack or otherwise actively manipulate objects in our environment. They are also both centers of tactile perception, as the most sensitive areas on the body are the fingertips, tongue, lips, and the nearby tip of the nose. Both touch and taste, which is monopolized by the tongue, require direct contact with the object being sensed, in contrast to the other main senses of sight, hearing, and smell. And in communication, the mouth is source of speech, song, and other forms of meaningful vocalizations, so that clearly in this respect it is of primary importance. But the hand is a significant backup system for when speech fails, for example in the case of the hearing impaired, for whom sign language is a functional alternative. All very young children are in fact quite receptive to learning hand signals, which they sometimes find easier to master than the spoken word. Of course, we also supplement speech with gesture, and we also use our hands to draw pictures, and to carve, chisel, or mold images. Perhaps most significantly of all, we take pen in hand and write, or we sit down at the keyboard and let our fingers do the talking.

Human technology encompasses the human body, and the human brain. That is why Lewis Mumford argued that the first machines were made of flesh and blood, and appear early in antiquity. As he writes in his 1961 study, *The City in History*, in the ancient world:

> gigantic forces of nature were brought under conscious human direction: tens of thousands of men moved into action as one machine under centralized command, building irrigation ditches, canals, urban mounds, ziggurats, temples, palaces, pyramids, on a scale hitherto inconceivable. As an immediate outcome of the new power mythology, the machine itself had been invented: long invisible to archaeologists because the substance of which it was composed—human bodies—had been dismantled and decomposed. (p.34)

The first machines were what Mumford (1967) termed "invisible machines" (p. 188) because they were based on the coordination of human labor, for engineering, architectural, or military purposes. Such complex coordination only became possible after the introduction of writing as a medium of organizational communication. Eventually, the fallible human parts of early machine technology would be replaced with more reliable inorganic components. But the important point is that today, as in the past, human techniques, procedures, and organizations are technologies comparable to tools, machines, and computers. And as José Ortega y Gasset (1944) put it: "An institution is a machine in that its whole structure and functioning must be devised in view of the service it is expected to perform" (pp. 27-28). Social institutions are more than patterns of behavior—they are methods of achieving certain ends. For example, the institution of marriage (traditionally) has been a technology for managing biological reproduction, among other things, and the institution of education is a technology for managing social and cultural reproduction, among other things. Both are technologies that deal with the manufacture of replacement parts for our invisible machines.

Human technologies cannot function without human communication, for control and coordination in the case of organizations and institutions, or to provide operating instructions, software, and interfaces, in the case of mechanical and electronic devices (Ellul, 1964, 1965). Human communication does not function without human technology, without some sort of system or method for sending messages and making meanings.

Both communication and technology converge around the concept of media, for communication involves the mediation between ourselves and others, and technology involves the mediation between ourselves and our surroundings. In both instances, our media extend us into the world at the same time that they shield us from the world. Our media allow us to manipulate our environment at the same time that they come between ourselves and our environment. In this sense, our media become our environment, and McLuhan himself wrote that "to say that any technology or extension of man creates a new environment is a much better way of saying that the medium is the message" (McLuhan & Parker, 1969, p. 31). McLuhan, among others, used the term media ecology to refer to the study of media as environments (as defined by Postman, 1968, 1970; see also Strate, 2017).

Since the sixties, the notion of media as environments has worked its way into public discourse and popular culture. During the nineties, it became commonplace to associate computers and telecommunications with the concept of *cyberspace*, and with electronic *frontiers*, information *superhighways*, and virtual *communities* (for further discussion, see Strate, 1996, 1999; Strate, Jacobson, & Gibson, 2003); more recently, the shortened form of *cyber* has been used to refer to the internet, while Mark Zuckerberg has popularized the term *metaverse* to refer to virtual environments. These metaphors can be superficial and naive, that is often the case when scholarship is diffused to a mass audience, but they point the way to a more sophisticated understanding of the nature of technology and communication. As environments, media exert a great deal of influence on the content of our communication, on our modes of cognition and emotion, on our very consciousness, and on our culture and social organization. That is why changes in our media environments are differences that make so much of a difference.

Higher Education

We ourselves are not immune to these changes. As scholars, we share a commitment to the written word and print culture. But we live in an electronic media environment, and this means that we are not quite the bookish individuals that our predecessors were. We live between two worlds, the old world of ink and paper, and the new world of audiovisual simulation and stimulation;

we live between the old world of face-to-face dialogue and lecture, and the new world of virtuality and telepresence. We are not immune to these changes, and neither is our field. The modern study of communication coalesces during the 20th century, at the same time as we experience a revolution in communication technologies. Many communication programs and departments were founded following the Second World War, paralleling the development of the first electronic computers, as Claude Shannon's information theory (Shannon & Weaver, 1949) and Norbert Wiener's (1950, 1961) cybernetics held out hope for a science of communication. During the second half of the century, older terms such as *speech* and *the press* come to be overshadowed by newer ones such as *communication*, *information*, and *media*. And as the internet and the web have come to dominate our consciousness, programs, departments, and schools of communication across the United States have been engaged in restructuring or reorganization of some sort or another.

Our field is not immune to the effects of a changing media environment, and neither is higher education in its entirety. One sign of change is the interest in distance education, online learning, distributed education, and the like, gradually increasing with the development of the online communication, and vastly accelerated with the COVID-19 pandemic. I should point out that we had distance education long before the internet, except that we called it large lecture classes, and we generally do not consider it to be a pedagogical improvement over classes where you can get to know all of your students' names and faces.

But let us not fool ourselves. Individual faculty members may decide whether to be dinosaurs or digital gods, but the system-wide decision-making power is rarely in our hands. College administrators generally decide when and how to implement online programs, based on their efficiency and profitability, but ultimately their hands are being forced by factors beyond their control. The invisible hand of the educational marketplace is at work here, and some of the competition is coming from companies that specialize in online education, many of which are profit-making concerns, and even nonprofit institutions have been setting up for-profit units to deliver distance education for many years now. Profitability, and commercialism, are both significant issues, but I want to stress the fact that the invisible hand is a byproduct of the opposable thumb, that markets are made by visible hands and their human technologies.

Right now, faculty teaching online courses are mostly concerned with how best to make such courses work, and administrators may also be concerned with how to make them profitable. The unspoken assumption is that we are adding an alternate method of delivering education to our existing university system, and that this will not affect the existing educational system. We expect the existing educational system to remain unchanged, and we expect the new delivery method to mold itself to existing arrangements such as semesters and traditional concepts of coursework. But innovations are rarely so cooperative, and even a small addition to a large system can result in large changes. We need to anticipate such ecological changes if we want to avoid another round of future shock.

We can start by thinking about the institution of higher education as an invisible machine, a human technology whose parts are controlled and coordinated by human communication. One of the primary functions of the university is to serve as a knowledge machine, a technology for producing knowledge, but especially for storing and retrieving knowledge, both in the form of written documents, and in the form of human experts conversant in those documents. The first schools of any kind appeared in ancient Mesopotamia, following the introduction of the first known writing system, cuneiform (Logan, 2004). The first forms of coherent study appeared in ancient Greece, following the introduction of the Greek alphabet. The first university appeared in medieval Paris, following the diffusion of paper from China to Europe in the 12th century. The first colleges appeared in the 15th century, and were closely associated with the printing revolution initiated by Johann Gutenberg. And many of the procedures of our modern institutions of higher education, such as grading, written examinations, and credit-hours took form in the 19th century, along with the rise of industrialism and the mass production of print media. Since then, colleges have become increasingly more book oriented, library collections have become a key indicator of educational quality, and university presses have become major or at least mid-sized publishing houses. And in the 21st century, universities have also become digital repositories, online platforms, and increasingly more web and social media oriented.

In addition to being a knowledge machine, the university is also a diploma machine. The power to certify, to confer credentials based on the completion of a curriculum, is what powers the academic machine. The machine's final product is produced through the technology of writing, traditionally the sheepskin or parchment diploma, and it sometimes seems to be the only product. How often have we heard of students saying that all they really want out of their college education is to get their diplomas?

It is also quite clear that the university has been a coming of age machine, by which I mean that it is a mechanism for transforming youth into adults. Traditionally, the college experience has been a rite of passage for members of the elite, who had the luxury of extending their youth past their teens. In postwar America that rite has been more widely shared among the middle classes, thereby becoming part of our dominant culture. Rising costs and stagnant or declining salaries have made higher education increasingly more difficult for many to afford, but the sense among the middle class that this is a necessary ritual remains. Completing this rite of passage is symbolized by the diploma, and requires a series of trials that depend upon mastery of the written word. But the ritual itself is rooted in face-to-face communication, and centered in the college campus.

The university machine performs other functions as well, but knowledge, credentials, and adulthood are certainly its main products. And these products will most likely continue to be in demand in this century, perhaps more so than ever. Back in the sixties, Peter Drucker (1968) argued that we are becoming a knowledge society, based on a knowledge economy. The value of the traditional university as a means of storing and retrieving knowledge can only decline in our current media environment, as electronic technologies make online articles, electronic books, and virtual libraries easily accessible, while human experts are only an e-mail message or tweet away. Cyberspace can substitute for the classroom as a learning environment, and even laboratories can be simulated electronically. The new knowledge machines are distributed across electronic networks, rather than centralized and concentrated in the college campus. So far, universities remain important nodes of these networks, but they can no longer be the isolated ivory towers of the past, nor can they maintain the monopoly on knowledge production that they once held. Arguably, their isolation and monopoly ended in 1969, the year that Stanford University, the University of California, Los Angeles, the University of California, Santa Barbara, and the University of Utah formed the first four nodes of the ARPANET, the beginning of what would become the internet.

In a knowledge society, credentials will become increasingly important. In fact, contrary to contemporary wisdom, by the end of the century doctoral degrees may in fact be plentiful and highly valued in business, industry, and politics. Considering the fact that we now have a First Lady with an Ed.D., Dr. Jill Biden, there is even a possibility that an individual with a Ph.D. could be elected president before the century is over. Perhaps even a professor of communication. But as knowledge becomes more widely distributed across networks, this calls into question the power of certification. State governments have been willing to legitimize distance education providers and virtual universities, not to mention commercial and for-profit educational programs. Alternative modes of education will most likely make it cheaper and easier to earn degrees than ever before. But the idea of pursuing education for its own sake, and not bothering with the specific requirements for a degree, has become increasingly more feasible, and attractive. Given the likes of Bill Gates and Mark Zuckerberg, the 1972 book by McLuhan and Barrington Nevitt, *Take Today: The Executive as*

Dropout, is clearly prophetic.

And the most valued credentials of all will be those that certify adulthood. Joshua Meyrowitz (1985) and Neil Postman (1982) both have argued that the electronic media have blurred the boundaries between child and adult. And the less clear the biological boundaries are, the more we need symbolic markers such as rites of passage. In all probability, the traditional campus experience will remain an initiation ritual for the elite segments of society, but online education will be hard put to provide the same sense of social transition for others. Instead, the older rite of passage based on military service may make a comeback, or perhaps a broader notion of a period of public service.

As a knowledge machine, diploma machine, and coming of age machine, the contemporary university is obsolescent, and this becomes increasingly apparent if you consider all of the negative publicity, criticism, and delegitimation that higher education has been subjected to in recent years. Back in the sixties, we heard the slogan, "tune in, turn on, drop out." McLuhan argued that "the dropout represents the rejection of nineteenth century technology as manifested in our educational establishments" (McLuhan & Fiore, 1967, p. 101), and he and others suggested that this was due to the instantaneous transmission of television. The call went out for greater student involvement in learning, more emphasis on discovery, and more connection to the outside world (see, for example, Postman & Weingartner, 1969). Along the same lines, for some time now we have seen various proposals for more student empowerment and the establishment of learning communities, for more experiential and service learning, and engagement with the world beyond the ivory tower.

More significant are the many ways in which the university is being directly delegitimized. Questions are raised about its finances, about the high cost of tuition, about the big business of college sports, about the dependence on grant money from government and industry, about partnerships with corporations, about top heavy administrations that value money over mission. Questions are raised about our faculty's teaching ability, about their focus on research and publication over pedagogy, about the use of teaching assistants, adjuncts, and the like, about grade inflation, and about the tenure system. Questions are raised about academic turf wars, the rise of political correctness and cultural politics, and the radicalization of the college campus. And questions have been raised about the value of a college education, given the success of entrepreneurs like Gates and Zuckerberg. But what matters is not so much Gates and Zuckerberg as potential role models, as the computer revolution that they had so much to do with, which now presents us with a viable alternative to both print media and to physical situations such as the campus and classroom.

Whether the university machine is breaking down, running out of steam, or just facing competition from a newer model, it is clear that we are in a period of transition. The idyllic experience of going to college, which was opened up to so many in late 20th century America, may be vanishing along with our innocence about the world. The privileged position of professional faculty may be vanishing as well, as we are transformed into genuine knowledge workers in a gig economy. At the same time, online environments make available more alternatives and affords us greater flexibility in the pursuit of knowledge and credentials, and this can be a very exciting time indeed, if we are prepared for it.

Of course, another function of the institution of higher education is to manufacture the future. The task is much easier in times of stability and continuity, much harder now that things seem to be unpredictable and in flux. That is why we need futurists, why we need communication scholars to be futurists. We need communication scholars working on the future of higher education, and working on finding the ways to avoid oblivion and approach utopia. We need to think about the future of human communication and the future of human technology. We need to come of age as a field by thinking about the future of humanity, and find a way for us to come of age as a species (Korzybski, 1950). This is the mission that we are called upon to undertake in the 21st century. Let's get to work.

Chapter 10
My Lambda Pi Eta Address

The following is a keynote address delivered on October 23, 2016, at the annual induction ceremony of Fordham University's chapter of the Lambda Pi Eta Communication Honor Society. Lambda Pi Eta is the official honor society for the National Communication Association, with over 500 chapters at four-year colleges and universities throughout the United States. This speech was delivered to an audience consisting of the undergraduate inductees, their parents, friends, and family, and select members of the faculty and administration.

First and foremost, I want to congratulate all of the inductees and current members of Lambda Pi Eta, and their families. We are here to honor you, but speaking as a faculty member, I want to say that we too are honored, honored to have students of your caliber, honored to have joined together with you for these few years in an adventure that can and should last a lifetime: the adventure of learning.

I believe it is customary in these situations for the speaker to begin with a humorous anecdote, and so I will begin by telling you about an incident that occurred when I was an undergraduate, a communication major myself. The university that I attended had many large lecture classes, unlike Fordham, and this included the Introduction to Communication Theory class that I took as a first-year student. The professor who taught the course was a senior faculty member, an old guy (unlike me), and he had a "no nonsense" approach to education. As the course was required for all majors, the professor was free to make it as difficult and demanding as he liked. And he relished the reputation he gained for his strict and severe grading. His finals were especially tough essay exams, and at the beginning of the test, the professor would warn his students that they must stop writing when he announces that the test is over. Otherwise, they would be given a failing grade for the final, and fail the course.

When I was taking the final, I noticed that the students who completed the exam early would drop their examination booklets on the desk in the front of the room. Being an insecure young student, I myself kept writing until the professor announced that time had run out. And like everyone else, I put down my pen, afraid to risk the professor's wrath, and we added our bluebooks to the enormous pile on his desk. As I was turning to leave, I looked back and noticed that there still was one student who was furiously writing away. I watched as he finished up and, in open defiance of the professor, walked to the front of the class with his booklet. The professor looked at him sternly, and told him that he would not accept his exam, and that the student would receive a failing grade. The student looked the professor squarely in the eye and said: "Do you know who I am?" The professor responded: "No I do not, and frankly I couldn't care less!" The student then said "Good!" and stuck his final into the middle of the pile of booklets, and ran away.

Now, I must confess to you that this is not a true story. I took it from a book of urban legends written by the American folklorist Jan Harold Brunvand (1986). Actually, Brunvand refers to this particular story as one of the legends of academe, but the important point is that it is truly a legend, a story passed on and preserved by word of mouth. It has been told on many different college campuses, but always told as a true story that happened right here, at our school, at some time in the recent past. Nowadays, when so much of our attention is captured by our electronic technologies and digital communications, it is both important and humbling to recall that speech is still the foundation of human culture, and that oral traditions have yet to be extinguished altogether.

At the same time, it is clear that the urban legends of today are but a faint echo of the orality that existed before writing took hold. We have no living tradition of orally composed epics such as the *Iliad* and *Odyssey*, *Gilgamesh*, or *Beowulf*. We have no nonliterate singers of tales whose bardic performances maintain cultural continuity from generation to generation. We do not depend on collective memory alone for the preservation of knowledge. And poetry, proverbs, and other such oral media no longer serve as our dominant mode of public communication.

The legend of the professor and student originates as an oral form of communication, but its content is very much derived from literate culture. The setting of the school represents the institutionalization of literacy, and the university symbolizes literacy in its highest form. The professor is an embodiment of the literate mindset, demanding that his students proceed *by the book*, and that his instructions be followed *to the letter*. In other words, his rigidity mirrors the fixity of the written word, in contrast to the flexibility and multiformity of oral traditions. Also, the professor is an elitist, treating his students as if they were beneath contempt. The word "elite" I am told comes from the same root as "literacy," both referring to the distinction between the lettered and the unlettered. And, of course, the legend revolves around an examination, where the main activity is writing, and it is the student's refusal to stop writing that gets him into trouble.

The student's ultimate triumph is derived from the fact that the examination booklets are mass produced products, each one identical to the other, insuring his anonymity. They are, in fact, print media, a point we tend to overlook because most of what is printed does not consist of words, or pictures, but of straight lines to guide our handwriting.

The professor in our legend does not understand media. He is fully immersed in literate culture, and dismisses alternatives, or cannot imagine them in the first place. The student, on the other hand, is the central figure in an oral narrative, and very much resembles the trickster character of oral myth and legend, such as the Native American Coyote god, the ancient Greek Titan Prometheus, or the Norse pantheon's Loki. The student has much in common with these heroes of oral culture, but at the same time, he is literate enough to pursue higher education. And given the fact that this is a contemporary legend, I think it safe to assume that the student is in fact postliterate, a product of the electronic media environment. Much like the computer hacker, he steps outside of the system, uncovers its code, and alters it to his own benefit. The literate culture that the school manifests is an invisible environment to the professor. But literate culture's structure, and its flaws, stand exposed to the students of the electronic era.

My point is not to denigrate literate culture, however. Our goal today is to step outside of our own contemporary media environment, dominated as it is by our electronic, digital technologies. We need to engage in clear-headed evaluation of the costs as well as the benefits of all of our innovations and modes of communication. To ask, not only what we *can* do with them, but what we *should* do with them. To ask what uses are appropriate and what are not, as well as how to use them most effectively. To gain a measure of control over our media environment. Which begins with understanding media, and to do so we need to use every tool in our toolbox, and most especially language, words, both spoken and written. Speech and dialogue, together with reading and writing, form the basis of knowledge and education. It all begins with communication.

Marshall McLuhan (1964), who once was on the faculty of Fordham University, famously said that *the medium is the message* (p. 7). *The medium is the message* expresses in a succinct and compressed form the most basic idea in the field of media ecology, my own area of specialization. And I would suggest to you that it forms the basis for some of the most important insights in the study of communication, media, and just about everything else. But like all great notions, it is not original, but actually quite ancient. The idea it expresses, or aspects of that idea, can be found in the Bible, for example in the 115th Psalm of David, in the following passage:

Their idols are silver and gold,
The work of men's hands.
They have mouths, but they speak not;
Eyes they have, but they hear not;
Noses have they, but they smell not;
They have hands, but they handle not;
Feet have they, but they walk not;
Neither speak they through their throat.
They that make them shall be like unto them;
Yea, every one that trusteth in them. (vv. 4-8)

Apart from the critique of idolatry and graven images as a symbolic form, these lines also represent a warning about the effects of technology, *the work of men's hands*. And the key phrase is, *they that make them shall be like unto them*, which suggests that our technology, our media, feed back into us, reshaping us in their image. A similar idea is expressed in the Gospel of Matthew, in the well known declaration, "all that live by the sword shall die by the sword" (26:52). There have been a number of occasions in the past, and just recently, when I have seen critics comment in relation to political candidates, live by TV, die by TV.

Working our way across the Mediterranean to ancient Greece, Aesop of fable-telling fame is the source of the saying, *ask a silly question, get a silly answer*. That moral can be generalized to say that the kinds of questions we ask have much to do with the answers that we receive, so if you ask a serious question, you get a serious answer. By the same token, ask a political question and you are likely to get a political answer, ask an economic question and you will most probably get an economic answer, ask a psychological question and you can expect to get a psychological answer. In fact, the foundation of every field and discipline and profession is made up of a particular set of questions. The philosopher Susanne Langer (1957) put it this way:

> A question is really an ambiguous proposition; the answer is its determination. There can be only a certain number of alternatives that will complete its sense. In this way the intellectual treatment of any datum, any experience, any subject, is determined by the nature of our questions, and only carried out in the answers. (p. 4)

Along similar lines, as I was growing up, my mother was fond of the saying, *how you make your bed, so you shall sleep*, which has its origins as a 15th century French proverb, the English version, *you made your bed, go sleep in it!*, being more judgmental and less media ecological. In the 19th century, Henry David Thoreau (1899) remarked, "we do not ride on the railroad; it rides upon us" (p. 67). And Mark Twain quipped that when you have a hammer in your hand, everything looks like a nail (quoted in Eastham, 1990, p. 17). In the 20th century, Winston Churchill said, "We shape our buildings; thereafter they shape us" (quoted in Greenberg, 2012, p. 85). Another former Fordham faculty member, communications scholar John Culkin (1967) generalized Churchill's quote as: "We shape our tools and thereafter they shape us" (p. 52). With a somewhat different tone, the philosopher Hannah Arendt (1978) insisted that "there are no dangerous thoughts; thinking itself is dangerous" (p. 176). In other words, she is saying that it is the medium of thinking more than any specific thoughts that matters, whether we characterize the activity as dangerous, particularly to those who wish to exercise power over others, or as liberating. And so, you might say that it is the business of your faculty to make you as dangerous as possible.

Related to this idea, one of McLuhan's direct sources of inspiration for *the medium is the message* came from the anthropologist, Ashley Montagu (1958), who wrote, "in teaching it is the method and not the content that is the message" and that education "does not depend upon the transmission of knowledge, but upon the manner in which the knowledge is transmitted by the teacher" (p. 62), and that, "the good teacher is often the instrument of something greater than himself" (p. 63). Montagu suggests that a teacher is a medium through which you can participate in a dialogue that has been taking place for centuries, indeed for millennia.

And then there is Aldous Huxley (1958), best known as the author of the novel, *Brave New World*; Huxley advises us that, "the ends cannot justify the means, for the simple and obvious reason that the means employed determine the nature of the ends produced" (p. 10). So, one way to sum it all up, then, is that *the medium is the message* is about the way that we do things, the idea being that the way that we do things has much to do with what we end up doing, and what we end up with when we do the things we do, as well as who we end up becoming by doing the things that we do.

The medium is the message expresses in concise and compressed form the concepts that form the basis of media ecology, which is defined as the study of media as environments. And this saying stands as one of the most important tenets in the field of communication. But I want to take this opportunity to share with you some of the other quotes and sayings from scholars in communication and related disciplines that I think express ideas of value and consequence for this, and any occasion.

Let me begin with a quote from a book entitled *The Pragmatics of Human*

Communication by Paul Watzlawick, Janet Bavelas, and Don Jackson (1967). This is what they put forth as the first axiom of communication: *One cannot not communicate* (p. 49). Despite the double negative, the meaning is fairly clear, that all behavior functions as a form of communication and it is impossible not to behave, that whatever we do or do not do has message value, that even silence and inaction have meaning. *One cannot not communicate* serves as the basis for the behavioral study of communication, directing our attention to the function of communication, as opposed to the intent of the communicator, acknowledging the possibility of unintended communication, and suggesting that most of our communication consists of messages we did not intend to send, and are not even aware of sending.

What I would emphasize, however, is that the act of communication is meaningful in and of itself, apart from whatever content we might exchange. In this, *one cannot not communicate* expresses the same basic idea as *the medium is the message*. Through our communication, we recognize each other as human beings, and we establish and maintain our relationships with each other. That is why we exchange greetings when we meet, participate in small talk, and gossip with one another. Such forms of phatic communication are ways in which we simply confirm each other's existence, and establish and maintain our relationships with each other. And this is much more basic, foundational, and significant, than any content, any information, that we might exchange.

One cannot not communicate is especially relevant in this political season, as it serves as a reminder that there is no such thing as not voting. Whether we enter a voting booth or not, we are in effect casting a vote. And it is worth recalling the quote from Malcom X (1989): "It's the ballot or the bullet" (p. 44). Put another way, it has been said that you can vote with ballots or vote with bullets. I think we all know which form of communication is preferable.

On the subject of politics and civic engagement, the French social critic and theologian, Jacques Ellul (1981), embraced the saying, *think globally, act locally* (p. 21). Thinking globally means understanding the big picture, which I would suggest means thinking not only about humanity as a whole, but the earth as our environment. A global perspective would also, I believe, require thinking in terms of time as well as space, understanding the past, learning from history, and preparing for the future. Acting locally means recognizing what is taking place right in front of us, paying attention to the concrete reality that immediately surrounds us, taking responsibility for our communities, understanding that the best kind of change comes from the bottom up, working side by side with others. In this regard, the words of another former Fordham faculty member come to mind, the anthropologist Margaret Mead, who said, "Never doubt that a small group of thoughtful, committed, citizens can change the world.

Indeed, it is the only thing that ever has" (quoted in Lutkehaus, 2008, p. 4).

Another of my favorite sayings comes from Alfred Korzybski (1993), the founder of the discipline of general semantics. Korzybski (1993) was often known to say, the *map is not the territory* (p. 58). By this, he meant that our representations of the world, even our perceptions of the world, are not the same thing as the actual reality out there. Our words and symbols are not the things they represent. And this may seem obvious enough, but have you ever driven the wrong way because your GPS guidance systems gave you faulty directions? I know I have. It is important to understand that some maps are better than others, but all maps are incomplete, all representations are at best selections and simplifications of what they represent. That is why we need to engage in fact-checking and reality-testing. Most important of all is understanding that things are constantly changing, that our world is a system and network of dynamic relationships. Our maps and words and symbols and representations suggest that our world is made up of *things*, of *objects*, when all that really exists, as Albert Einstein explained over a century ago, are relationships, and events in spacetime. I want to emphasize this point because what it tells us is that we should be mindful of the world around us, savor every moment, treasure every relationship, because permanence is an illusion, because every event presents us with experiences and opportunities that will soon pass away.

This brings to mind one of my favorite quotes from the Jesuit scholar Walter Ong (1982). By way of explaining the difference between speech and writing, Ong said, *Sound only exists when it is going out of existence* (p. 32). In saying the word existence, by the time I say—*tence, exist*—is gone, never to be retrieved. If you hit pause on a video, the image freezes, but the audio is silenced. Sound only exists in time, it signals change. While this is especially relevant for understanding oral cultures, I would suggest that sound represents a truer map of the world than vision. We need to think more in terms of the auditory and acoustic, speech and song, rhythm and melody, harmonies that resonate, voices that echo. Helen Keller, being both blind and deaf, was once asked if she could restore one of her senses, which would she choose. Her answer was the sense of hearing. Why, you might ask. Because sound is how we connect to other people, talk is the basis of relationships. Another of Ong's sayings brings this home: *sight isolates, sound incorporates* (p. 72).

Ong (1982) also says, "You know what you can recall" (p. 33). No doubt you've left an exam at some point in your lives saying to yourself, I knew the answer, I just couldn't remember it. But if you can't remember it, in what sense do you know it? In this age in which answers are just a Google search away on our smart phones, it is worthwhile to recall that there is no knowledge without a knower, there is no knowledge without an act of knowing. And there is no better place to store knowledge than in the human mind, and no better way to share knowledge than by communicating with one another. Memory is not what is on a hard drive, or in the cloud. Memory is a remembering, it is not a thing, it is what we do, individually and collectively. And nothing can quite take its place.

Another one of my media ecological aphorisms comes from my mentor, Neil Postman, from a book he wrote entitled *The Disappearance of Childhood* (1982). He began that book by saying, "Children are the living messages we send to a time we will not see" (p. xi). Postman asks us, as adults, to think about the importance of childhood as an institution, and as a means of cultural continuity, of preservation of knowledge, and as a medium of communication with the future. I suspect you probably do not want to be referred to as children, but for those of us who are parents, it is worth considering the kinds of messages we are sending to the future through our children. And for those of us who are teachers, we can also think of our students as living messages we send to a time we will not see. And as living messages, all of us are not simply passive carriers conveying packets of information from the past, but active participants in a living tradition, tasked with the responsibility of carrying forward to the next generation the light of learning, of civilization, of a humane way of life. And we would all do well to ask ourselves how well we are doing our part in this sacred mission, as children and as adults.

My last quote is not quite an aphorism, but rather a very evocative phrase. It comes from the scholar Gregory Bateson (1972), whose work spanned the fields of communication, anthropology, psychiatry, biology, ecology, systems, and cybernetics. His phrase is, *a difference which makes a difference* (p. 453). That is what we are concerned with in the field of communication, differences that make a difference. That is the key to understanding information, that it is a difference that makes a difference. Information isn't a thing, it's a function, an action and event, to inform and to be informed. If a message is a difference that makes a difference, if it reduces uncertainty or resolves ambiguity, then it counts as information. If not, it was just data.

Everything that we do or do not do makes a difference. And everything that happens or doesn't happen makes a difference. Events in spacetime are differences. Relationships are based on differences. And in communication we are concerned with differences. The differences between senders and receivers, writers and readers, speakers and audiences. The differences between different types of messages, different types of sources, different types of audiences. And in my view, most importantly of all, the differences that different means, modes, and methods of communication make, in the way that senders construct messages, and receivers make meaning out of them.

As members of Lambda Pi Eta, each one of you have distinguished your-selves through your academic achievements, and your membership in this ex-clusive honor society, and for that I offer, once again, my congratulations. You have demonstrated your differences in learning and education. The question that remains for you, going forward, is, will your differences make a difference, for yourselves, your families, your communities, and your world? And you may well ask, how can we be differences that make a difference? The answer, or at least one of them, can be found in the very name of our honor society, Lambda Pi Eta.

As you know, the three letters stand for the three main forms of persua-sion identified by Aristotle (1954) in his treatise on rhetoric: *logos*, *pathos*, and *ethos*. Logos, which stands for reason, points to the importance of reason and rationality as we engage in dialogue with one another. Pathos, which stands for emotion, points to the significance of passionate commitment as we work to-wards our goals of making our world a better place. And ethos, which stands for credibility, points to the indispensable value of character and ethical conduct in all that we do and say. If you will aspire to these high ideals, if you stay true to the goal of being a difference that makes a difference, then you will truly be worthy of honor. And most importantly of all, unlike the student and professor of urban legend, *you* will have made *us*, your faculty, look good. Thank you.

About the Author

Lance Strate is Professor of Communication and Media Studies at Fordham University, where he has previously served as department chair, graduate director, director of the undergraduate program, and designed and directed an interdisciplinary major in Professional Studies in New Media. He held the 2015 Harron Family Chair in Communication at Villanova University, and received an honorary appointment as Chair Professor in the School of Journalism and Communication at Henan University in Kaifeng, China, in 2016. He earned his PhD in the Media Ecology Program at New York University, his MA from the Communication Arts and Sciences Department at Queens College of the City University of New York, and a BS degree from Cornell University.

Dr. Strate is a Trustee and President of the Institute of General Semantics, and Secretary and Past President of the New York Society for General Semantics. He is the Co-Chair of the Global Listening Centre's Academic Board, as well as a Past President of the New York State Communication Association. He is also one of the founders of the Media Ecology Association, served as the MEA President for over a decade, and is presently a member of the MEA's Board of Directors. He is also a Trustee and Past President of Congregation Adas Emuno of Leonia, New Jersey.

Lance Strate is the author of nine books, including *Media Ecology: An Approach to Understanding the Human Condition* (2017), *Amazing Ourselves to Death: Neil Postman's Brave New World Revisited* (2014), *On the Binding Biases of Time and Other Essays on General Semantics and Media Ecology* (2011), *Echoes and Reflections: On Media Ecology as a Field of Study* (2006), and the poetry collections *Diatribal Writes of Passage in a World of Wintertextuality* (2020) and *Thunder at Darwin Station* (2015). He is also the co-editor of 7 anthologies, including *Taking Up McLuhan's Cause: Perspectives on Media and Formal Causality* (2017), *The Medium is the Muse: Channeling Marshall McLuhan* (2015), *Korzybski and...* (2012), *The Legacy of McLuhan* (2005), and two editions of *Communication and Cyberspace: Social Interaction in an Electronic Environment* (1996, 2003). Additionally, he has served as editor of the *Speech Communication Annual*, the *General Semantics Bulletin*, and *Explorations in Media Ecology*, a journal he founded and edited for 9 years (2002-2007, 2017-2019). Among his many major addresses, Dr. Strate delivered the 10th Annual Cardinal Newman Lecture at Manhattan College, the 10th Annual

Bernard B. Gilligan Memorial Lecture at Fordham University, the 66th Annual Alfred Korzybski Memorial Lecture for the Institute of General Semantics, and the Fifth Annual Harron Family Endowed Chair Public Lecture at Villanova University.

Lance Strate is the recipient of the Global Listening Centre's 2020 Outstanding Research Award, the Eastern Communication Association's 2019 Distinguished Research Fellow Award, the Media Ecology Association's 2018 Marshall McLuhan Award for Outstanding Book and its 2013 Walter Ong Award for Scholarship, the New York State Communication Association's 2019 Neil Postman Mentor Award and its 1998 John F. Wilson Fellow Award for exceptional scholarship, leadership, and dedication to the field of communication, and the Proclamation by Mayor Wellington E. Webb, in honor of his keynote address to the Rocky Mountain Communication Association, "that February 15, 2002 be known as Dr. Lance Strate Day in the City and County of Denver."

About the Artist

The artwork included on the cover of this book was created especially for *Concerning Communication* by Thomas O'Meara, who is 25 years old, and a participant at Quest Autism Program. Thomas has many strengths, but his greatest is art. Thomas has always been passionate when he draws and is a perfectionist.

Along with his artistic abilities he has a desire for various languages and has taught himself Japanese, Chinese and Korean.

In June, 2017, Thomas was introduced to Arts Unbound in Orange, New Jersey. Thomas was paired with his teacher, Malik Whitaker, who has brought out the best of him. Truly, every finished piece is more amazing than the last.

Thomas lives in Wyckoff, New Jersey with his mother, Patti O'Meara, and her partner, Tom.

References

Altheide, D.L. & Snow, R.P. (1979). *Media logic*. Beverly Hills, CA: Sage.

Anton, C., Logan, R.K., & Strate, L. (2016). *Taking up McLuhan's cause: Perspectives on formal causality and media ecology*. Bristol: Intellect.

Arendt, H. (1978). *The life of the mind*. San Diego, CA: Harvest.

Aristotle. (1954). *The rhetoric and the poetics of Aristotle* (W.R. Roberts & I. Bywater, Trans.). New York: The Modern Library.

Aristotle. (1998). *The metaphysics* (H. Lawson-Tancred, Trans.). London: Penguin.

Arlen, M.J. (1978). *The camera age: Essays on television*. Hammondsworth, England: Penguin.

Baron-Cohen, S. (1995). *Mindblindness: An essay on autism and theory of mind*. Cambridge, MA: MIT Press.

Baron-Cohen, S. (2003). *The essential difference: The truth about the male and female brain*. New York: Basic Books.

Baron-Cohen, S., & Bolton, P. (1993). *Autism: The facts*. Oxford: Oxford University Press.

Barthes, R. (1977). *Image, music, text* (S. Heath, Trans.). New York: Hill and Wang.

Bateson, G. (1972). *Steps to an ecology of mind: Collected essays in anthropology, psychiatry, evolution, and epistemology*. New York: Bantam Books.

Bateson, G. (1979). *Mind and nature: A necessary unity*. New York: Bantam Books.

Baudrillard, J. (1983). *Simulations* (P. Foss, P. Patton, &P. Beitchman, Trans.). New York: Semiotext(e).

Becker, E. (1971). *The birth and death of meaning: An interdisciplinary perspective on the problem of man* (2nd. ed.). New York: The Free Press.

Bellah, R.N., Madsen, R., Sullivan, W.M., Swidler, A., & Tipton, S.M. (1985). *Habits of the heart: Individualism and commitment in American life*. New York: Perennial Library.

Beniger, J.R. (1986). *The control revolution*. Cambridge, MA: Harvard University Press.

Benjamin, W. (1968). *Illuminations* (H. Zohn, Trans.). New York: Harcourt, Brace, & World.

Bennett, W.J. (Ed.). (1996). *The book of virtues for young people: A treasury of great moral stories*. Parsippany, NJ: Silver Burdett Press.

Berger, E. (2022). *Context blindness: Digital technology and the next stage of human evolution*. New York: Peter Lang.

Berger, P.L. & Luckmann, T. (1967). *The social construction of reality*. Garden City, NY: Anchor.

Berne, E. (1964). *Games people play*. New York: Grove.

Berne, E. (1972). *What do you say after you say hello?* New York: Grove.

Bertalanffy, L.v. (1969). *General system theory: Foundations, development, applications*. New York, G. Braziller.

Bettelheim, B. (1967). *The empty fortress: Infantile autism and the birth of the self*. New York: Free Press.

Bloom, A. (1987). *The closing of the American mind*. New York: Simon & Schuster.

Bolter, J. D. (1984). *Turing's man*. Chapel Hill, NC: University of North Carolina Press.

Bolter, J.D. & Gromala, D. (2003). *Windows and mirrors: Interaction design, digital art, and the myth of transparency*. Cambridge, MA: MIT Press.

Bolter, J.D., & Grusin, R. (1999). *Remediation: Understanding new media*. Cambridge, MA: MIT Press.

Boorstin, D.J. (1978). *The image: A guide to pseudo-events in America*. New York: Atheneum.

Bormann, E.G. (1972). Fantasy and rhetorical vision: The rhetorical criticism of social reality. *Quarterly Journal of Speech* 58(4), 396-407.

Boroditsky, L. (2011, February). How language shapes thought. *Scientific American*, 63-65.

Boulding, K.E. (1956). *The image: Knowledge in life and society*. Ann Arbor: University of Michigan Press.

Braudy, L. (1986). *The frenzy of renown: Fame and its history*. New York: Oxford University Press.

Broucek, F.J. (1991). *Shame and the self*. New York: Guildford Press.

Brown, N.O. (1985). *Life against death: The psychoanalytical meaning of history* (2nd ed.). Hanover, NH: Wesleyan University Press.

Brunvand, J. H. (1986). *The Mexican pet*. New York: W. W. Norton.

Buber, M. (1952). *Eclipse of God: Studies in the relation between religion and philosophy*. New York: Harper Torchbooks.

Buber, M. (1970). *I and Thou* (W. Kaufmann, Trans.). New York: Charles Scribner's Sons.

Buber, M. (2014). *Between man and man* (R.G. Smith, Trans.). Mansfield Centre, CT: Martino.

Burke, K. (1945). *A grammar of motives*. Berkeley, CA: University of California Press.

Burke, K. (1950). *A rhetoric of motives*. Berkeley, CA: University of California Press.

Burke, K. (1965). *Permanence and change: An anatomy of purpose* (2nd rev. ed.). Indianapolis: Bobbs-Merrill.

Burke, K. (1966). *Language as symbolic action*. Berkeley, CA: University of California Press.

Campbell, J. (1973). *The hero with a thousand faces*. Princeton: Princeton University Press.

Campbell, J. (1982). *Grammatical man: Information, entropy, language, and life*. New York: Simon & Schuster.

Capra, F. (1996). *The web of life: A new scientific understanding of living systems*. New York: Anchor Books.

Capra, F. (2007). *The science of Leonardo: Inside the mind of the great genius of the Renaissance*. New York: Anchor Books.

Carey, J. W. (1989). *Communication as culture*. Boston: Unwin Hyman.

Carey, J. W. (1997). *James Carey: A critical reader* (E. S. Munson & C. A. Warren, Eds.). Minneapolis: University of Minnesota Press.

Carpenter, E. (1960) The new languages. In E. Carpenter & M. McLuhan, (eds.), *Explorations in communication* (pp. 162–179). Boston, MA: Beacon Press.

Carpenter, E. (1973). *Oh, what a blow that phantom gave me!* New York: Holt, Rinehart & Winston.

Carpenter, E., & Heyman, K. (1970). *They became what they beheld*. New York: Outerbridge & Dienstfrey.

Carpenter, E. & McLuhan, M. (1956). The new languages. *Chicago Review 10*(1), 46-52.

Carpenter, E. & McLuhan, M. (1960). Acoustic space. In E. Carpenter & M. McLuhan, (eds.), *Explorations in communication* (pp. 65–70). Boston, MA: Beacon Press.

Cassirer, E. (1944). *An essay on man*. New Haven: Yale University Press.

Cassirer, E. (1953). *The philosophy of symbolic forms*. New Haven: Yale University Press.

Centers for Disease Control and Prevention. (2022, April 7). *Key findings: CDC releases first estimates of the number of adults living with autism spectrum disorder in the United States*. Autism Spectrum Disorder. https://www.cdc.gov/ncbddd/autism/features/adults-living-with-autism-spectrum-disorder.html

Centers for Disease Control and Prevention. (2020, March 27). *Prevalence of autism* spectrum disorder among children aged 8 years—*Autism and developmental disabilities monitoring network, 11 sites, United States, 2016.* Morbidity and Mortality Weekly Report. https://www.cdc.gov/mmwr/volumes/69/ss/ss6904a1.htm

Chomsky, N. *Language and mind.* (1972). New York: Harcourt Brace Jovanovich.

Cohen S. (1998). *Targeting autism: What we know, don't know, and can do to help young children with autism and related disorders.* Berkeley: University of California Press.

Connor, S. (1989). *Postmodern culture.* Oxford: Basil Blackwell.

Culkin, J. (1967). Each culture develops its own sense ratio to meet the demands of its environment. In G. Stearn (Ed.). *McLuhan: Hot and cool* (pp. 49-57). New York: New American Library.

Czitrom, D.J. (1983). *Media and the American mind: From Morse to McLuhan*; Chapel Hill, NC: University of North Carolina Press.

Dance, F.E.X. (Ed.). (1982). *Human communication theory: Comparative essays.* New York: Harper & Row.

Dance, F.E.X. & Larson, C.E. (1976). *The functions of human communication: A theoretical approach.* New York: Holt, Rinehart & Winston.

Davenport, T.H. & Prusak, L. (1997). *Information ecology: Mastering the information and knowledge environment.* New York: Oxford University Press.

Dawkins, R. (1989). *The selfish gene.* New York: Oxford University Press.

Deacon, T.W. (2012). *Incomplete nature: How mind emerged from matter.* New York: W. W. Norton.

Derrida, J. (1976). *Of grammatology* (G.C. Spivak, Trans.). Baltimore: Johns Hopkins University Press.

Dewdney, C. (1998). *Last flesh: Life in the transhuman era.* Toronto: HarperCollins.

Donald, M. (1991). *Origins of the modern mind: Three stages in the evolution of culture and cognition.* Cambridge: Harvard University Press.

Douglas, M. (1973). *Rules and meanings: The anthropology of everyday knowledge.* Harmordsworth, England: Penguin Education.

Drucker, P.F. (1968). *The age of discontinuity.* New Brunswick, NJ: Transaction.

Dunbar, R. (1996). *Grooming, gossip, and the evolution of language.* Cambridge, MA: Harvard University Press.

Duncan, H.D. (1962). *Communication and social order.* New York: Bedminster Press.

Duncan, H.D. (1968). *Symbols in society.* New York: Oxford University Press.

Durig, A. (1996). *Autism and the crisis of meaning.* Albany: State University of New York Press.

Eastham, S. (1990). *The media matrix: Deepening the context of communication studies*. Lanham, MD: University Press of America.

Eco, U. (1986). *Travels in hyperreality* (W. Weaver, Trans.). New York: Harcourt Brace Jovanovich.

Ehrenfeld, D. (1978). *The arrogance of humanism*. Oxford: Oxford University Press.

Eisenstein, E.L. (1979). *The printing press as an agent of change: Communications and cultural transformations in early modern Europe* (2 vols.). New York: Cambridge University Press.

Eisenstein, E.L. (2011). *Divine art, infernal machine: The reception of printing in the west from first impressions to the sense of an ending*. Philadelphia: University of Pennsylvania Press.

Eisenstein, S. (1942). *The film sense* (J. Leyda Trans.). New York: Harcourt Brace.

Eisenstein, S. (1949). *Film form* (J. Leyda Trans.). New York: Harcourt Brace.

Eliade, M. (1963). *Myth and reality* (W.R. Trask, Trans.). New York: Harper & Row.

Eliot, T.S. (1934). *The rock*. London: Faber & Faber.

Ellul, J. (1964). *The technological society* (J. Wilkinson, Trans.). New York: Knopf.

Ellul, J. (1965). *Propaganda: The formation of men's attitudes* (K. Kellen & J. Lerner, Trans.). New York: Knopf.

Ellul, J. (1981). *Perspectives on our age: Jacques Ellul speaks on his life and work* (W.H. Vandenburg, Ed., J. Neugroschel, Trans.). New York: Seabury Press.

Emerson, R.W. (1883). *The conduct of life, and society and solitude*. London: Macmillan.

Erikson, E.H. (1950). *Childhood and society*. New York: W.W. Norton.

Erikson, E.H. (1980). *Identity and the life cycle*. New York: W.W. Norton.

Foerster, H.V. (1984). On constructing a reality. In P. Watzlawick (Ed.), *The invented reality: How do we know what we know? Contributions to constructivism* (pp. 41-61). New York: W.W. Norton.

Forsdale, L. (1981). *Perspectives on communication*. Reading, MA: Addison-Wesley.

Foucault, M. (1977). *Discipline and punish: The birth of the prison*. New York: Random House.

Freud, S. (1918). *Totem and taboo* (A.A. Brill, Trans.). New York: Moffat, Yard.

Freud, S. (1961). *Civilization and its discontents* (J. Strachey, Trans.). New York: W. W. Norton.

Freud, S. (1966). *Introductory lectures on psychoanalysis* (J. Strachey, Trans.). New York: W. W. Norton.

Frisch, M. (1959). *Homo faber: A report* (M. Bulloock, Trans.). San Diego: Harcourt

Brace Jovanovich.

Frith, U. (1989). *Autism: Explaining the enigma.* Oxford: Blackwell.

Fromm, E. (1965). *Escape from freedom.* New York: Avon Books.

Fukuyama, F. (1992). *The end of history and the last man.* Free Press.

Fuller, R.B. & Applewhite, E.J. (1975). *Synergetics: Explorations in the geometry of thinking.* New York: Macmillan.

Gardner, H. (1983). *Frames of mind: The theory of multiple intelligences.* New York: BasicBooks.

Gardner, H. (1993). *Multiple intelligences: The theory in practice.* New York: BasicBooks.

Gardner, H. (1997). *Extraordinary minds: Portraits of exceptional individuals and an examination of our own extraordinariness.* New York: BasicBooks.

Geertz, C. (1973). *The interpretation of cultures: Selected essays.* New York: Basic Books.

Gelb, I.J. (1963). *A study of writing* (Rev. ed.). Chicago: University of Chicago Press.

Gergen, K.J. (1991). *The saturated self.* New York: BasicBooks.

Gibson, W. (1984). *Neuromancer.* New York: Ace Books.

Giddens, A. (1991). *Modernity and self-identity: Self and society in the late modern age.* Stanford, CA: Stanford University Press.

Gilman, P. (1992). *Something from nothing.* New York: Scholastic.

Gitlin, T. (1995). *The twilight of common dreams: Why America is wracked by culture wars.* New York: Metropolitan Books.

Gleick, J. (1987). *Chaos: Making a new science.* New York: Viking Penguin.

Goffman, E. (1959). *The presentation of self in everyday life.* Garden City: Anchor Books.

Goffman, E. (1961). *Asylums: Essays on the social situation of mental patients and other inmates.* Garden City: Anchor Books.

Goffman, E. (1963). *Behavior in public places: Notes on the social organization of gatherings.* New York: Free Press.

Goffman, E. (1967). *Interaction ritual: Essays on face-to-face behavior.* Garden City: Anchor Books.

Goody, J. (1977). *The domestication of the savage mind.* Cambridge: Cambridge University Press.

Goody, J. (1986). *The logic of writing and the organization of society.* Cambridge: Cambridge University Press.

Gordon, W.T. (1997). *Marshall McLuhan: Escape into understanding.* New York:

Basic Books.

Gorman, M. (1962). *General semantics and contemporary Thomism*. Lincoln: University of Nebraska Press.

Gozzi, R. Jr. (1999). *The power of metaphor in the age of electronic media*. Cresskill, NJ: Hampton Press.

Grandin, T. (1995). *Thinking in pictures and other reports from my life with autism*. New York: Random House.

Grandin, T., & Scariano, M.M. (1986). *Emergence: Labeled autistic*. Novato, CA: Arena Press.

Gray, C.H. (Ed.). (1995). *The cyborg handbook*. New York: Routledge.

Greenberg, K. (2012). *Walking home: The life and lessons of a city builder*. Toronto: Vintage Canada.

Greenspan, S. I., Wieder, S., & Simons, R. (1998). *The child with special needs: Encouraging intellectual and emotional growth*. Reading, MA: Addison-Westey.

Griffin, J., & Tyrrell, I. (2008). Parallel processing. *Human Givens 15*(4), 11–17

Gumpert, G. (1987). *Talking tombstones and other tales of the media age*. New York: Oxford University Press.

Haddon, M. (2003). *The curious incident of the dog in the night-time*. New York: Doubleday.

Haldane, E.S. & Ross, G.R.T. (Eds.). *The philosophical works of Descartes, Vol. 1*. Cambridge: Cambridge University Press.

Hall, E.T. (1959). *The silent language*. Garden City: Doubleday.

Hall, E.T. (1966). *The hidden dimension*. Garden City: Doubleday.

Hall, E.T. (1976). *Beyond culture*. Garden City: Anchor Press.

Hall, E.T. (1983). *The dance of life: The other dimension of time*. Garden City: Anchor Press.

Haraway, D.J. (1991). *Simians, cyborgs, and women: The reinvention of nature*. New York: Routledge.

Haslam, G.W. & Haslam, J.E. (2011). *In thought and action: The enigmatic life of S. I. Hayakawa*. Lincoln, NE: University of Nebraska Press.

Havelock, E.A. (1963). *Preface to Plato*. Cambridge, MA: The Belknap Press of Harvard University Press.

Havelock, E.A. (1978). *The Greek concept of justice: From its shadow in Homer to its substance in Plato*. Cambridge, MA: Harvard University Press.

Havelock, E.A. (1982). *The literate revolution in Greece and its cultural consequences*. Princeton, NJ: Princeton University Press.

Havelock, E.A. (1986). *The muse learns to write: Reflections on orality and literacy from antiquity to the present*. New Haven, CT: Yale University Press.

Hayakawa, S.I. & Hayakawa, A.R. (1990). *Language in thought and action* (5th ed.). San Diego: Harcourt Brace.

Hayles, N.K. (1999). *How we became posthuman: Virtual bodies in cybernetics, literature, and informatics*. Chicago: University of Chicago Press.

Herman, E.S., & Chomsky, N. (1988). *Manufacturing consent: The political economy of the mass media*. New York: Pantheon.

Hobart, M. E., & Schiffman, Z. S. (1998). *Information ages: Literacy, numeracy, and the computer revolution*. Baltimore: John Hopkins University Press.

Hobbs, R. (2004). Media literacy, general semantics, and K-12 education. *ETC: A Review of General Semantics 61*(1), 24-28.

Hoffman, G., & Johnston, P. D. (1997). *Mapping the media: A media literacy guidebook*. Whitefish Bay, WI: M & T Communications.

Howlin, P., Baron-Cohen, S., & Hadwin, J. (1999). *Teaching children with autism to mind-read: A practical guide*. Chichester: John Wiley & Sons.

Hume, D. (1965). *A treatise on human nature*. Oxford: Clarendon Press.

Huxley, A. (2012). *Ends and means: An inquiry into the nature of ideas*. New Brunswick, NJ: Transaction. Original work published 1937

Innis, H.A. (1951). *The bias of communication*. Toronto: University of Toronto Press.

Innis, H.A. (1972). *Empire and communication* (rev. ed.). Toronto: University of Toronto Press.

Jameson, F. (1972). *The prison-house of language: A critical account of structuralism and Russian formalism*. Princeton: Princeton University Press.

Jameson, F. (1991). *Postmodernism, or, the cultural logic of late capitalism*. Durham, NC: Duke University Press.

Jaynes, J. (1976). *The origin of consciousness in the breakdown of the bicameral mind*. Boston: Houghton Mifflin.

Johnson, W. (1946). *People in quandaries: The semantics of personal adjustment*. New York: Harper & Row.

Jung, C.G. (1969). *The archetypes and the collective unconscious* (R.F.C. Hull, Trans.). Princeton: Princeton University Press

Jung, C.G. (1978). *Aion: Researches into the phenomenology of the self* (R. F. C. Hull, Trans.). Princeton: Princeton University Press

Kauffman, S. (1995). *At home in the universe: The search for the laws of self-organization and complexity*. New York: Oxford University Press.

Kellner, D. (1989). *Jean Baudrillard: From Marxism to postmodernism and beyond*.

Stanford, CA: Stanford University Press.

Kirk, G.S. (1962). *The songs of Homer*. Cambridge: Cambridge University Press.

Kittay, J. & Godzich, W. (1987). *The emergence of prose*. Minneapolis, MN: University of Minnesota Press.

Klapp, O.E. (1978). *Opening and closing: Strategies of information adaptation in society*. New York: Cambridge University Press.

Korzybski, A. (1950). *Manhood of humanity* (2nd ed.). Lakeville, CT: The International Non-Aristotelian Library/Institute of General Semantics. Original work published 1921

Korzybski, A. (1993). *Science and sanity: An introduction to non-Aristotelian systems and general semantics* (5th ed.). Englewood, NJ: The International Non-Aristotelian Library/Institute of General Semantics. Original work published 1933

Kranowitz, C.S. (1998). *The out of sync child: Recognizing and coping with sensory integration dysfunction*. New York: Perigee.

Kuhn, T.S. (1996). *The structure of scientific revolutions* (3rd ed.). Chicago and London: University of Chicago Press.

Kuhns, W. (1996). The war within the word: McLuhan's history of the trivium. *McLuhan Studies 1*(1), np.

Laing, R.D. (1965). *The divided self: An existential study in sanity and madness*. Harmondsworth: Penguin.

Laing, R.D. (1969). *Self and others* (2nd ed.). Harmondsworth: Penguin.

Lakoff, G. & Johnson, M. (1980). *Metaphors we live by*. Chicago: University of Chicago Press.

Lakoff, G. & Johnson, M. (1989). *More than cool reason: A field guide to poetic metaphor*. Chicago: University of Chicago Press.

Lakoff, G. & Johnson, M. (1999). *Philosophy in the flesh: The embodied mind and its challenge to Western thought*. New York: Basic Books.

Lane, H. (1977). *The wild boy of Aveyron*. Cambridge, MA: Harvard University Press.

Langer, S. K. (1953). *Feeling and form: A theory of art*. New York: Scribner.

Langer, S.K. (1957). *Philosophy in a new key: A study in the symbolism of reason, rite and art* (3rd ed.). Cambridge, MA: Harvard University Press.

Lasch, C. (1979). *The culture of narcissism: American life in an age of diminishing expectations*. New York: Warner Books.

Lasswell, H.D. (1948). The structure and function of communication in society. In *The communication of ideas* (L. Bryson, ed.). New York: Harper.

Lavine, T.Z. (1984). *From Socrates to Sartre: The philosophic quest*. New York: Bantam.

Laszlo, E. (1972). *The systems view of the world: The natural philosophy of the new developments in the sciences*. New York: G. Braziller.

Ledgin, N. (2000). *Diagnosing Jefferson: Evidence of a condition that guided his beliefs, behavior, and personal associations*. Arlington, TX: Future Horizons.

Lee, D. (1959). *Freedom and culture*. Englewood Cliffs, NJ: Prentice-Hall.

Lévi-Strauss, C. (1966). *The savage mind*. Chicago: University of Chicago Press.

Levinson, P. (1995). *Learning cyberspace*. San Francisco: Anamnesis Press.

Levinson, P. (1997). *The soft edge*. London & New York: Routledge.

Levinson, P. (1999). *Digital McLuhan*. London & New York: Routledge.

Levinson, P. (2013). *New new media* (2nd ed.). New York: Penguin.

Lima, L.C. (1988). *Control of the imaginary: Reason and imagination in modern times* (R.W. Sousa, Trans.). Minneapolis, MN: University of Minnesota Press.

Linton, S. (1998). *Claiming disability: Knowledge and identity*. New York: New York University Press.

Locke, J. (1961). *An essay concerning human understanding, Vols. 1 & 2*. New York: Dutton.

Logan, R.K. (2004). *The alphabet effect: A media ecology understanding of the making of western civilization*. Cresskill, NJ: Hampton Press.

Logan, R. K. (2007). *The extended mind: The emergence of language, the human mind, and culture*. Toronto: University of Toronto Press.

Logan, R. K. (2010). *Understanding new media: Extending Marshall McLuhan*. New York: Peter Lang.

Lord, A.B. (1960). *The singer of tales*. Cambridge, MA: Harvard University Press.

Lovaas, O.I. (1981). *Teaching developmentally disabled children: The ME book*. Austin, TX: Pro-Ed.

Luhmann, N. (1982). *The differentiation of society* (S. Holmes & C. Larmore, Trans.). New York: Columbia University Press.

Luhmann, N. (1989). *Ecological communication* (J. Bednarz, Jr., Trans.). Chicago: University of Chicago Press.

Luhmann, N. (1990). *Essays on self-reference*. New York: Columbia University Press.

Luhmann, N. (1995). *Social systems* (J. Bednarz, Jr. with D. Baecker, Trans.). Stanford: Stanford University Press.

Luhmann, N. (2000). *The reality of the mass media* (K. Cross, Trans.). Stanford: Stanford University Press.

Lum, C.M.K. (1996). *In search of a voice: Karaoke and the construction of identity in Chinese America*. Mahwah, NJ: Lawrence Erlbaum.

Luria, A.R. (1976). *Cognitive development: Its cultural and social foundations* (M. Lopez-Morillas & L. Solotaroff, Trans.). Cambridge, MA: Harvard University Press.

Luria, A.R. (1981). *Language and cognition* (J.Y. Wertsch, Trans.). Washington, DC: V.H. Winston.

Lutkehaus, N.C. (2008). *Margaret Mead: The making of an American icon*. Princeton, NJ: Princeton University Press.

Lyotard, J.-F. (1984). *The postmodern condition: A report on knowledge* (G. Bennington & B. Massumi, Trans.). Minneapolis, MN: University of Minnesota Press. (Original work published 1979)

Madaule, P. (1994). *When listening comes alive: A guide to effective learning and communication* (2nd ed.). Norval, ON: Moulin.

Maitre, D. (1983). *Literature and possible worlds*. London: Middlesex Polytechnic Press.

Malcom X. (1989). *Malcom X speaks: Selected speeches and statements*. New York: Pathfinder Press.

Marchand, P. (1989). *Marshall McLuhan: The medium and the messenger*. New York: Ticknor & Fields.

Maturana, H.R. & Varela, F.J. (1980). *Autopoiesis and cognition: The realization of the living*. Boston: D. Reidel.

Maturana, H.R. & Varela, F.J. (1992). *The tree of knowledge: The biological roots of human understanding* (revised ed., R. Paolucci, Trans.). Boston: Shambhala.

Maurice, C. (1993a). *Let me hear your voice: A family's triumph over autism*. New York: Fawcett Columbine.

Maurice, C. (Ed.). (1993b). *Behavioral intervention for young children with autism: A manual for parents and professionals*. Austin, TX: Pro-Ed.

Maushart, S. (1986). Self-reflexiveness and the institution of journalism. *ETC: A Review of General Semantics 43*(3), 272-278.

McGilchrist, I. (2009). *The master and his emissary: The divided brain and the making of the western world*. New Haven: Yale University Press.

McLuhan, E. (1998). *Electric language: Understanding the message*. New York: Buzz Books.

McLuhan, E. (2000). The Fordham experiment. *Proceedings of the Media Ecology Association 1*, 23-27.

McLuhan, M. (1951). *The mechanical bride: Folklore of industrial man*. New York: Vanguard.

McLuhan, M. (1962). *The Gutenberg galaxy: The making of typographic man.* Toronto: University of Toronto Press.

McLuhan, M. (1964). *Understanding media: The extensions of man.* New York: McGraw Hill.

McLuhan, M. (1989). Violence of the media. In G. Sanderson & F. Macdonald (eds.), *Marshall McLuhan: The man and his message* (pp. 92-98). Golden, CO: Fulcrum.

McLuhan, M. (1995). *Essential McLuhan* (E. McLuhan & F. Zingrone, eds.). New York: BasicBooks.

McLuhan, M. (2003). *Understanding me: Lectures and interviews* (S. McLuhan & D. Staines, Eds.). Cambridge, MA: MIT Press.

McLuhan, M. (2006). *The classical trivium: The place of Thomas Nashe in the learning of his time* (W.T. Gordon, Ed.). Madera, CA: Gingko Press.

McLuhan, M. & Fiore, Q. (1967). *The medium is the massage: An inventory of effects.* New York: Bantam.

McLuhan, M. & Fiore, Q. (1968). *War and peace in the global village.* New York: Bantam.

McLuhan, M., & McLuhan, E. (1988). *Laws of media: The new science.* Toronto: University of Toronto Press.

McLuhan, M. & McLuhan, E. (2011). *Media and formal cause.* Houston: NeoPoiesis Press.

McLuhan, M. & Nevitt, B. (1972). *Take today: The executive as dropout.* New York: Harcourt Brace Jovanovich.

McLuhan, M. & Parker, H. (1969). *Counterblast.* New York: Harcourt Brace & World.

McLuhan, M. & Powers, B.R. (1989). *The global village: Transformations in world life and media in the twenty-first century.* New York: Oxford University Press.

Mead, G.H. (1934). *Mind, self and society from the standpoint of a social behaviorist* (C.W. Morris, Ed.). Chicago: University of Chicago Press.

Merrill, J.C. (1997). *Journalism ethics: Philosophical foundations for news media.* New York: Bedford St. Martin's Press.

Meyrowitz, J. (1985). *No sense of place.* New York: Oxford University Press.

Milgram, S. (1974). *Obedience to authority: An experimental view.* New York: Harper & Row.

Montagu, A. (1958). *The cultured man.* Cleveland, OH: World.

Moran, T.P. (1984). Politics 1984: That's entertainment. *ETC: A Review of General Semantics, 41*(2), 117–129.

Mumford, L. (1934). *Technics and civilization*. New York: Harcourt Brace.

Mumford, L. (1967). *The myth of the machine: I. Technics and human development*. New York: Harcourt Brace & World.

Mumford, L. (1970). *The myth of the machine: II. The pentagon of power*. New York: Harcourt Brace Jovanovich.

Nachmanovitch, S. (2019). *The art of is: Improvising as a way of life*. Novato, CA: New World Library.

Nagy, G. (1981). *The best of the Achaeans*. Baltimore: Johns Hopkins University Press.

Negroponte, N. (1995). *Being digital*. New York: Knopf.

Nuttall, A.D. (1974). *A common sky: Philosophy and literary imagination*. Berkeley: University of California Press.

Nystrom, C.L. (1973). *Toward a science of media ecology: The formulation of integrated conceptual paradigms for the study of human communication systems*. Unpublished doctoral dissertation, New York University.

Nystrom, C.L. (2021). *The genes of culture: Towards a theory of symbols, meaning, and media, Vol. 1*. New York: Peter Lang.

Nystrom, C.L (2022). *The genes of culture: Towards a theory of symbols, meaning, and media, Vol. 2*. New York: Peter Lang.

Ogden, C.K. & Richards, I.A. (1923). *The meaning of meaning: A study of the influence of language upon thought and of the science of symbolism*. New York: Harcourt, Brace.

Olson, D.R. (1994). *The world on paper: The conceptual and cognitive implications of writing and reading*. Cambridge: Cambridge University Press.

Olson, D.R. (2016). *The mind on paper: Reading, consciousness and rationality*. Cambridge: Cambridge University Press.

O'Neill, J.L. (1999). *Through the eyes of aliens: A book about autistic people*. London: Jessica Kingsley.

Ong, W.J. (1958). *Ramus, method, and the decay of dialogue*. Cambridge, MA: Harvard University Press.

Ong, W.J. (1967). *The presence of the word: Some prolegomena for cultural and religious history*. New Haven, CT: Yale University Press.

Ong, W. J. (1977). *Interfaces of the word*. Ithaca, NY: Cornell University Press.

Ong, W. J. (1981). *Fighting for life: Contest, sexuality, and consciousness*. Ithaca, NY: Cornell University Press.

Ong, W.J. (1982). *Orality and literacy: The technologizing of the word*. London: Methuen.

Ong, W.J. (1986). *Hopkins, the self, and God.* Toronto: University of Toronto Press.

Ong, W.J. (2002). *An Ong reader* (T.J. Farrell and P.A. Soukup, Eds.). Cresskill, NJ: Hampton Press.

Ortega y Gasset, J. (1944). *Mission of the university* (H. L. Nostrand, Trans.). New York: W.W. Norton.

Ovid. (1955). *Metamorphoses* (R. Humphries, Trans.). Bloomington: Indiana University Press.

Parry, M. (1971). *The making of Homeric verse: The collected papers of Milman Parry* (A. Parry, Ed.). Oxford: Clarendon Press.

Peirce, C. S. (1991). *Peirce on signs: Writings on semiotic.* Chapel Hill: University of North Carolina Press.

Peters, J.D. (1999). *Speaking into the air: A history of the idea of communication.* Chicago, IL: University of Chicago Press.

Pfeiffer, J. E. (1982). *The creative explosion: An inquiry into the origins of art and religion.* New York: Harper & Row.

Piaget, J. (1954). *The construction of reality in the child* (M. Cook, Trans.). New York: Basic Books.

Plato. (1971). *Gorgias* (W. Hamilton, Trans.). London: Penguin.

Plato. (1973). *Phaedrus and Letters VII and VIII* (W. Hamilton, Trans.). Harmondsworth: Penguin.

Popper, K. (2002). *The logic of scientific discovery.* London New York: Routledge.

Poster, M. (1990). *The mode of information.* Chicago: University of Chicago Press.

Postman, N. (1961). *Television and the teaching of English.* New York: Appleton-Century-Crofts.

Postman, N. (1968, November 29). Growing up relevant. Address delivered at the 58th annual convention of the National Council of Teachers of English, Milwaukee, WI.

Postman, N. (1970). The reformed English curriculum. In A.C. Eurich (Ed.), *High school 1980: The shape of the future in American secondary education* (pp.160-168). New York: Pitman.

Postman, N. (1974). Media ecology: General semantics in the third millennium. *General Semantics Bulletin 41-43,* 74-78.

Postman, N. (1976). *Crazy talk, stupid talk.* New York: Delacorte.

Postman, N. (1979). *Teaching as a conserving activity.* New York: Delacorte.

Postman, N. (1982). *The disappearance of childhood.* New York: Delacorte.

Postman, N. (1985). *Amusing ourselves to death: Public discourse in the age of show business.* New York: Viking.

Postman, N. (1988). *Conscientious objections: Stirring up trouble about language, technology, and education.* New York: Alfred A. Knopf.

Postman, N. (1992). *Technopoly: The surrender of culture to technology.* New York: Alfred A. Knopf.

Postman, N. (1995). *The end of education: Redefining the value of school.* New York: Alfred A. Knopf.

Postman, N. (1999). *Building a bridge to the eighteenth century: How the past can improve our future.* New York: Alfred A. Knopf.

Postman, N. (2000). The humanism of media ecology. *Proceedings of the Media Ecology Association 1*, 10-16.

Postman, N. (2006). Media ecology education. *Explorations in Media Ecology 5*(1), 5-14.

Postman, N. & Weingartner, C. (1966). *Linguistics: A revolution in teaching.* New York: Delta.

Postman, N. & Weingartner, C. (1969). *Teaching as a subversive activity.* New York: Delta.

Postman, N. & Weingartner, C. (1971). *The soft revolution: A student handbook for turning schools around.* New York: Delacorte.

Postman, N., Weingartner, C., & Moran, T.P. (Eds.). (1969). *Language in America.* New York: Pegasus.

Putnam, R.D. (2000). *Bowling alone: The collapse and revival of American community.* New York: Simon & Schuster.

Rheingold, H. (1988). *They have a word for it: A lighthearted lexicon of untranslatable words and phrases.* Louisville, KY: Sarabande Books.

Rheingold, H. (2012). *NetSmart: How to thrive online.* Cambridge, MA: MIT Press.

Richards, D. (1992, October 11). You saw it on film, now see it on stage. *New York Times*, sect. 2, p. 5.

Richards, I.A. (1929). *Practical criticism: A study of literary judgment.* New York: Harcourt, Brace.

Richards, I.A. (1936). *The philosophy of rhetoric.* New York: Oxford University Press.

Riesman, D., Denney, R., & Glazer, N. (1950). *The lonely crowd: A study of the changing American character.* New Haven: Yale University Press.

Rimland, B. (1964). *Infantile autism: The syndrome and its implications for a neural theory of behavior.* New York: Appleton-Century-Crofts.

Ritchin, F. (1990). *In our own image: The coming revolution in photography.* New York: Aperture.

Rollins, C.D. (1967). Solipsism. In P. Edwards (Ed.), *The encyclopedia of philosophy*, vols. 7 & 8 (pp. 487-491). New York: Macmillan and the Free Press.

Romanyshyn, R.D. (1989). *Technology as symptom and dream*. London: Routledge.

Ruesch, J., & Bateson, G. (1968). *Communication: The social matrix of psychiatry*. New York: W.W. Norton.

Rushing, J.H., & Frentz, T.S. (1995). *Projecting the shadow: The cyborg hero in American film*. University of Chicago Press.

Rushkoff, D. (2003). The information arms race. In L. Strate, R. Jacobson, & S.G. Gibson, (eds.), *Communication and cyberspace: Social interaction in an electronic environment* (2nd ed., pp. 349–359). Cresskill, NJ: Hampton Press.

Rushkoff, D. (2010). *Program or be programmed: Ten commands for a digital age*. New York: OR Books.

Russell, B. (1968). *The impact of science on society*. New York: Simon & Schuster.

Sacks, J. (2003). *The dignity of difference: How to avoid the clash of civilizations* (Rev. ed.). London: Bloomsbury.

Sacks, O. (1987). *The man who mistook his wife for a hat and other clinical tales*. New York: Perennial Library.

Sacks, O. (1995). *An anthropologist on Mars*. New York: Random House.

Sapir, E. (1921). *Language: An introduction to the study of speech*. New York: Harcourt Brace Jovanovich.

Sanders, B. (1994). *A is for ox: The collapse of literacy and the rise of violence in an electronic age*. New York: Vintage.

Sartre, J-P. (2010). *Critical essays* (C. Turner, Trans.). London: Seagull.

Saussure F.d. (1983). *Course in general linguistics* (C. Bally & A. Sechehaye with A. Riedlinger, Eds., R. Harris. Trans.). LaSalle, IL: Open Court.

Schiller, H.I. (1973). *The mind managers*. Boston: Beacon Press.

Schlessinger, A.M., Jr. (1992). *The disuniting of America*. New York: W.W. Norton.

Schmandt-Besserat, D. (1978), *An archaic recording system and the origin of writing*. Malibu, CA: Undena.

Schmandt-Besserat, D. (1992). *Before writing: From counting to cuneiform* (2 vols.). Austin: University of Texas Press.

Schmandt-Besserat, D. (1996). *How writing came about*. Austin: University of Texas Press.

Schneider, E. (1999). *Discovering my autism: Apologia pro vita sua (with apologies to Cardinal Newman)*. London: Jessica Kingsley.

Scholes, R.E. & Kellogg, R. (1966). *The nature of narrative*. New York: Oxford University Press.

Schudson, M. (1978). *Discovering the news: A social history of American newspapers*; Basic Books: New York, NY.

Schwartz, T. (1974). *The responsive chord*. Garden City, New York: Anchor Books.

Selfe, L. (1977). *A case of extraordinary drawing ability in an autistic child*. London: Academic Press.

Shannon, C.E. & Weaver, W. (1949). *The mathematical theory of communication*. Urbana, IL: University of Illinois Press.

Shippey, T. (2000). *J.R.R. Tolkien: Author of the century*. Boston: Houghton Mifflin.

Shlain, L. (1998). *The alphabet versus the goddess: The conflict between word and image*. New York: Viking.

Shlain, L. (2003). *Sex, time and power: How women's sexuality shaped human evolution*. New York: Viking.

Siegel, B. (1996). *The world of the autistic child: Understanding and treating autistic spectrum disorders*. New York: Oxford University Press.

Smith, T., Groen, A.D., & Wynn, J.W. (2000). Randomized trial of intensive early intervention for children with pervasive developmental disorder. *American Journal on Mental Retardation 105*(4), pp. 269-285.

Steinberg, S.H. (1996). *Five hundred years of printing* (rev. ed., J. Trevitt). New Castle, DE: Oak Knoll Press.

Steiner, G. (1967). *Language and silence: Essays on language, literature, and the inhuman*. New York: Athenaeum.

Stephens, M.A. (1988). *History of news: From the drum to the satellite*; New York: Viking.

Strate, L. (1996). Cybertime. In L. Strate, R. Jacobson, & S.G. Gibson, (eds.), *Communication and cyberspace: Social interaction in an electronic environment* (pp. 351–377). Cresskill, NJ: Hampton Press.

Strate, L. (1999). The varieties of cyberspace: Problems in definition and delimitation. *Western Journal of Communication 63*(3), 382-412.

Strate, L. (2000). Narcissism and echolalia: Sense and the struggle for the self. *Speech Communication Annual 14*, pp. 14-62.

Strate, L. (2003). Something from nothing: Seeking a sense of self. *ETC.: A Review of General Semantics 60*(1), pp. 4-21.

Strate, L. (2006). *Echoes and reflections: On media ecology as a field of study*. Cresskill, NJ: Hampton Press.

Strate, L. (2011a). *On the binding biases of time and other essays on general semantics and media ecology*. Fort Worth, TX: Institute of General Semantics.

Strate, L. (2011b). The enigma of autism. *Samyukta: A Journal of Women's Studies*

6(2), pp. 17-48.

Strate, L. (2012). Sounding out Ong: Orality across the media environments. In T.J. Farrell & P. Soukup, (Eds.), *Of Ong and media ecology: Essays in communication, composition, and literary studies* (pp. 91-116). Cresskill, NJ: Hampton Press.

Strate, L. (2014). *Amazing ourselves to death: Neil Postman's brave new world revisited*. New York: Peter Lang.

Strate, L. (2016). The effects that give cause and the pattern that directs. In C. Anton, R.K. Logan, & L. Strate (Eds.), *Taking up McLuhan's cause: Perspectives on formal causality and media ecology* (pp. 93-121). Bristol: Intellect.

Strate, L. (2017). *Media ecology: An approach to understanding the human condition*. NY: Peter Lang.

Strate, L. (2018). The medium is the membrane. *ETC: A Review of General Semantics* 75(3-4), pp. 307-316.

Strate, L., Freeman, L., Gutierrez, P., & Lavalle, J. (2010). *The future of children's television programming: A study of how emerging digital technologies can facilitate active and engaged participation and contribute to media literacy education*. Washington, D.C.: Time Warner Cable Research Program on Digital Communications.

Strate, L., Jacobson, R. & Gibson, S.B. (2003). Surveying the electronic landscape: An introduction to *Communication and Cyberspace*. In L. Strate, R. Jacobson, & S.B. Gibson (Eds.), *Communication and cyberspace: Social interaction in an electronic environment* (2nd ed., pp. 1-26). Cresskill, NJ: Hampton Press.

Tannen, D. (1990). *You just don't understand! Women and men in conversation*. New York: Harper.

Teensma, E. (1974). *Solipsism and induction*. Assen, Netherlands: Van Gorcum.

Thoreau, H.D. (1899). *Walden or life in the woods*. Philadelphia, PA: Henry Altemus.

Toffler, A. (1970). *Future shock*. New York: Random House.

Tomatis, A. (1996). *The ear and language*. Norval, ON: Moulin.

Trujillo Liñán, L. (2022). *Formal cause in Marshall McLuhan's thinking*. Forest Hills, NY: Institute of General Semantics.

Tuan, Y.-F. (1982). *Segmented worlds and self: Group life and individual consciousness*. Minneapolis: University of Minnesota Press.

Turkle, S. (1984). *The second self: Computers and the human spirit*. New York: Simon and Schuster.

Turkle, S. (1995). *Life on the screen: Identity in the age of the Internet*. New York: Simon & Schuster.

Turkle, S. (2011). *Alone together: Why we expect more from technology and less from each other*. New York: Basic Books.

Turkle, S. (2015). *Reclaiming conversation*. New York: Penguin.

U.S. Federal Trade Commission. (2002). *ID theft: When bad things happen to your good name.* Retrieved May 1, 2022 from https://www.gardencitymi.org/DocumentCenter/View/159/ID-Theft-Pamphlet-PDF

Volk, T. (1995). *Metapatterns: Across space, time and mind*. New York: Columbia University Press.

Volkmar, F.R. (1989). Medical problems, treatments, and professionals. In M. D. Powers (Ed.), *Children with autism: A parents' guide* (pp. 55-77). Bethesda, MD: Woodbine House.

Vygotsky, L.S. (1986). *Thought and language* (revised ed., A. Kozulin, Trans. & Ed.). Cambridge, MA: MIT Press.

Wachtel, E. (1995). To an eye in a fixed position: Glass, art, and vision. In J. C. Pitt (Ed.), *New directions in the philosophy of technology* (pp.41-61). Amsterdam: Kluwer.

Waldrop, M.M. (1992). *Complexity: The emerging science at the edge of order and chaos*. New York: Simon & Schuster.

Watzlawick, P. (1976). *How real is real?* New York: Vintage.

Watzlawick, P. (Ed.). (1984). *The invented reality: How do we know what we know? Contributions to constructivism*. New York: W.W. Norton.

Watzlawick, P., Bavelas, J.B., & Jackson, D.D. (1967). *Pragmatics of human communication: A study of interactional patterns, pathologies, and paradoxes*. New York: Norton.

Watzlawick, P., Weakland, J.H., & Fisch, R. (1974). *Change: Principles of problem formation and problem resolution*. New York: Norton.

Weizenbaum, J. (1976). *Computer power and human reason*. San Francisco: W.H. Freeman.

Whitehead, A.N. & Russell, B. (1925-1927). *Principia mathematica* (2nd ed., 3 vols.). Cambridge: The University Press.

Whorf, B.L. (1956). *Language, thought, and reality*. Cambridge, MA: MIT Press.

Whyte, W.H., Jr. (1956). *The organization man*. New York: Touchstone.

Wiener, N. (1950). *The human use of human beings: Cybernetics and society*. Boston: Houghton Mifflin.

Wiener, N. (1961). *Cybernetics: Or control and communication in the machine and animal*. Boston: Houghton Mifflin.

Wiener, N. (1964). *God and golem, Inc.: A comment on certain points where cybernetics impinges on religion*. Cambridge, MA: MIT Press.

Wilden, A. (1980). *System and structure: Essays in communication and exchange*.

London: Routledge.

Wilden, A. (1987). *The rules are no game*. London: Routledge.

Williams, D. (1992). *Nobody, nowhere: The extraordinary autobiography of an autistic*. New York: Times Books.

Williams, D. (1994). *Somebody, somewhere: Breaking free from the world of autism*. New York: Times Books.

Williams, D. (1996). *Autism: An inside-out approach*. London: Jessica Kingsley.

Williams, D. (1998). *Autism and sensing: The unlost instinct*. London: Jessica Kingsley.

Williams, D. (1999). *Like colour to the blind: Soul searching and soul finding*. London: Jessica Kingsley.

Wilson, F. (2000, August 29). Why is there so much autism in kids today?! *2worlds Listserv* Retrieved September 23, 2000 from http://groups.yahoo.com/group/2worlds/message/79

Wittgenstein, L. (1961). *Tractatus logico-philosophicus* (D.F. Pears & B.F. McGuinness, Trans.). London: Routledge.

Wittgenstein, L. (1963). *Philosophical investigations* (G.E.M. Anscombe, Trans.). Oxford: Basil Blackwell.

Wolf, M. (2007). *Proust and the squid: The story and science of the reading brain*. New York: Harper.

Wolf, M. (2018). *Reader come home: The reading brain in a digital world*. New York: Harper

Wolfe, T. (2016). *The kingdom of speech*. New York: Little, Brown.

Wood, D.N. (1996). *Post-intellectualism and the decline of democracy: The failure of reason and responsibility in the twentieth century*. Westport, CT: Praeger.

Wright, C.R. (1959). *Mass communication: A sociological perspective*; New York: Random House.

Yates, F.A. (1966). *The art of memory*. Chicago: University of Chicago Press.

Zingrone, F. (2001). *The media symplex: At the edge of meaning in the age of chaos*. Cresskill, NJ: Hampton.

Index

O

objectivism, 68, 83, 166-169, 171-192
Odyssey, 28-29, 46, 57, 87, 196
Ogden, C.K., 37, 94, 101, 118, 134, 221
Olson, David R., xv, 46, 67, 221
O'Meara, Thomas, xv, 207
O'Neill, Jasmine Lee, 54, 69, 221
Ong, Walter J., xv, 5, 19, 25, 28-29, 35, 37, 45-46, 48, 52, 58, 67-69, 75, 79, 81, 83, 85, 87, 91, 95, 100-101, 104, 106, 116, 118, 119, 137, 143, 145, 148, 151, 154, 156, 159-160, 164-167, 175-176, 201, 206, 221-222
The Oprah Winfrey Show, 179
orality, oral culture, 3, 25-26, 29, 35, 37, 42, 45-46, 48-49, 52, 57, 67-69, 75-76, 80, 82-84, 87, 91, 98-99, 106-107, 125, 139, 141-142, 145, 148-150, 154-156, 159, 164-168, 175-176, 185, 196-197, 201
Ortega y Gasset, José, 188, 222
Orthodox Christian, 54
Orwell, George, 95
Ovid, 42, 46-47, 75, 222

P

Parenthood, 55
Parker, Harley, 189, 220
Parry, Milman, 28-29, 222
pattern, 21-23, 26, 29, 36, 53, 56, 133, 135, 138, 140, 147, 175, 178, 188. *See also* metapattern
Peirce, Charles Sanders, 37, 222
perception, x, 4, 8, 18, 34, 38, 40, 45-46, 50, 56-57, 59-60, 62, 64, 68, 78-80, 92, 94, 99-103, 117-118, 131, 147, 163, 186-187, 201. *See also* hearing, vision
Peters, John Durham, 141, 158, 222
Pfeiffer, John E., 67, 222
phatic communication, 134, 200
philology, 3, 95, 99-100
philosophy, x, xi, 19-21, 23, 25, 37, 40, 47-48, 54, 60, 87, 90-96, 104, 136,

141, 163-164, 166, 169, 177, 198-199
photography, 25, 126, 143, 161, 185
Piaget, Jean, 57, 222
Plato, x, 18-20, 24-25, 32, 39-40, 46, 60, 76, 87, 90, 92, 158, 166, 179, 222
poetry, 3, 28, 35, 42, 46-47, 77, 84, 87, 90, 101, 133, 155, 159, 164, 177, 196
politics, 30, 32, 43, 47, 52-53, 74-75, 86, 90, 107, 112, 117-119, 126, 129, 135, 141, 169, 171-175, 179, 186, 193-194, 200
Popper, Karl, 30, 222
Poster, Mark, 48, 222
Postman, Neil, ix, xiv, 8, 30, 36, 37, 41, 47, 49, 68-69, 86, 97-99, 103-105, 108, 113-117, 119, 125-127, 135, 140, 146, 170, 172, 174, 180, 189, 193, 202, 205-206, 222-223, 226
postmodern, postmodernism, 35, 47, 169-170, 174-175, 177-178, 180
Powers, Bruce R. 140, 220
printing, 4-5, 18, 25, 30, 34, 37, 39, 47, 68, 83, 91, 93-98, 107, 118-119, 121, 125-127, 129, 131, 133, 139, 141, 143-145, 148-154, 159-160, 166, 168, 172, 175-176, 179, 185, 189, 191, 193, 197. *See also* typography, engraving
Prometheus, 197
propaganda, 31, 47, 119, 141-142, 153
Prusak, Laurence, 136, 212
pseudo-events, 172, 178
psychiatry, 64, 71, 202
psychoanalysis, 43-44, 71, 169, 171
psychology, x, 30, 32-33, 36-37, 43-44, 54, 57, 62, 64, 69, 71-72, 80, 118, 142, 160-161, 163-166, 168-169, 171, 175-176, 181, 198, 202
public address, public speaking, 6, 16, 76, 77, 84, 87, 97, 137, 140-142, 154, 158, 185, 196
public discourse, 86, 107, 189
public relations, 126, 131, 141, 153, 173, 178

www.ingramcontent.com/pod-product-compliance
Lightning Source LLC
Chambersburg PA
CBHW021048090426
42738CB00006B/244